Black
Political
Parties

AN HISTORICAL AND POLITICAL ANALYSIS

BY **Hanes Walton, Jr.**

THE FREE PRESS  NEW YORK

COLLIER-MACMILLAN LIMITED · LONDON

To my mother, Estelle Walton

and

my father, Thomas Hanes Walton

whose

visions and toils
shall not have been in vain

Copyright © 1972 by The Free Press
A Division of The Macmillan Company

Printed in the United States of America

The Free Press
A Division of The Macmillan Company
866 Third Avenue, New York, New York 10022

Collier-Macmillan Canada Ltd., Toronto, Ontario

Library of Congress Catalog Card Number: 76–143514

printing number

1   2   3   4   5   6   7   8   9   10

Contents

3

4

5

6

Epilogue

Notes

Appendix

Tables

Maps

Figures

Documents

Preface

Gunnar Myrdal, in his monumental study of American Negroes published in 1944, predicted that *"there is not going to be a Negro Party in American Politics."* [1] As late as 1965 political scientist Austin Ranney stated that a Negro civil rights party could not hope for success because it would be isolated from the main channels of political power.[2] True, these are the comments of white men, but blacks have also remarked negatively on the prospects for potential black political organizations.[3]

Despite these negative forecasts some blacks not only saw the need but also envisioned the possibility of success for such organizations. In 1916, R. R. Wright, Jr., called for a nationwide black party to coordinate the votes of blacks migrating to the north and elect blacks to Congress.[4] Before and after Wright, blacks have not only made the call but also sought vigorously to organize such political organizations on the local, state, and national level.

Although no black political party existed during the period in which Myrdal was writing, such organizations had existed and the possibility remained that one would arise again. The circumstances that had inspired their creation in the past were still present. The Republican and Democratic parties, as well as the minor parties, had neglected to take effective steps to end racial discrimination and segre-

[1] Gunnar Myrdal, *An American Dilemma* (New York: Harper & Row, 1966), p. 505. The emphasis is his.

[2] Austin Ranney, *The Governing of Men* (New York: Holt, Rinehart and Winston, 1966) pp. 365–366.

[3] See "The Negro Party," *The Crisis* (October, 1916), 268. See also R. H. Brisbane, "The Negro Vote as a Balance of Power in National Politics," *Quarterly Review of Higher Education Among Negroes* (July, 1952), 100, and "Editorial," *New York Age* (October 23, 1907), 1.

[4] R. R. Wright, Jr., "A Negro Party," *Christian Recorder* (September 28, 1916), 4.

gation and the economic exploitation and disenfranchisement of blacks.[5] Having no major or minor political organization to rely on, blacks therefore developed their own from time to time.

The specific purpose of this book is to describe, analyze, and discuss the nature, role, and significance of black political parties, past and present. Furthermore some indication is given of the future possibilities and prospects of success for such organizations.

Since black political parties have been small, numerous, and short-lived, a typology of these parties has been advanced in order to include most of them and to avoid a mere exploratory study in the past. Recent black parties have been relatively more successful, much larger, and somewhat longer-lived than those of the past. Because of the impact of these contemporary parties, this study tries to concentrate on *present* parties in light of *past* parties.

Black political parties fall generally into two groups, the separate or independent parties (i.e., those not affiliated with any major or minor party) and the "satellite" or "parallel" parties (those that revolve in the orbit of one of the major national parties). A detailed analysis is given of an example of each of these two types of black parties in contemporary politics. The struggles of these parties, against the fear and apathy of both blacks and sympathetic whites as well as against hostile forces working constantly to suppress them, are explored at length. Finally, these black parties are studies in the light of the American political process, and a rationale of the "why's" and "wherefore's" of their creation is set forth.

In the literature on black politics, scant attention has been paid to black political organizations in general and almost none to black political parties in particular. While black political organizations have been primarily black middle-class voter leagues, concentrating on registering middle-class blacks to vote and endorsing the "lesser of the two evils," black political parties go at least one step further: they not only seek to increase the number of registered blacks of all classes, but they also concentrate on nominating and endorsing black candidates.

Thus black parties hold their own nominating conventions, draw

[5] Harold Gosnell, *Negro Politicians* (Chicago: University of Chicago Press, 1966), p. 319.

up their own platforms, and support their candidates in various other ways. In examining such activities, this study is in a sense the first to deal with the organization, tactics, and nature of black parties per se.

The professor at any small college who possesses the urge to contribute to his field of specialization is often confronted with a series of obstacles: excessive teaching loads, insufficient research funds, inadequate library facilities, numerous committee assignments, and so forth. And though this is generally the situation at any small college, it is particularly acute in the small black college. The author consequently wishes to acknowledge his debt to several individuals who rendered invaluable assistance to him in the writing of this book. Special thanks go to Miss Luella Hawkins, the Reference Librarian at Savannah State College, without whose knowledge of, and skill in, utilizing the interlibrary loan services this book would have been severely handicapped. Professor Leslie McLemore, whose field research into and first-hand knowledge of the Mississippi Freedom Democratic Party is unexcelled, lent his generous assistance and constantly supplied otherwise inaccessible data on the party which makes Chapter 3 particularly illuminating. Three former professors of the author, Drs. Emmett Dorsey, Harold Gosnell, and Samuel D. Cook, provided insights into black politics which are unparalleled and which proved to be quite helpful in writing this study. Further special thanks are due to Dr. Cook for taking time out from his busy schedule to write the introduction and for providing the author with a constant source of inspiration. Professor Thomas Byers made several helpful criticisms and comments on the manuscript. Numerous others, such as Mrs. Louise Smith and my parents, aided in matters large and small.

For typing the manuscript, thanks are given here to Miss Gwen Thomas, Miss Lillie Mae Key, Miss Barbara J. Mobley, and Miss Brenda D. Mobley. In addition, Miss Brenda D. Mobley was especially helpful in developing the maps and tables. Moreover, special thanks is given to my editor, Mr. Wilbur Mangas, who made the mussy data readable and coherent. Finally, the author alone assumes responsibility for any shortcoming of the work.

H. WALTON, JR.

Introduction

THE POLITICS OF THE SUCCESS

OF FAILURE

Ambiguity, ambivalence, tension, paradox, irony, contradiction, and schizophrenia have always governed the status of the Negro in the American political system and process—as indeed they have presided over his position in the total institutional firmament and public life of the country. Politics is, after all, a function of culture; inevitably, political life has reflected the subjugation and oppression of blacks within the total framework of American culture. At home but a stranger, free but bound, citizen but alien, agent but subject, involved but tyrannized, participant but victim, a "Thou" but an "It," a person but a thing, in the company of the blessed but cursed—that has been the substance, if not always the form and intent, of the black man's experience and journey in the celebrated New World experiment in freedom, equality, and self-government.

On the profound level, the black man has been excluded not only from the benefits but, more deeply, the *promise* of the American political system. Indeed, the promise and achievements of that system— and they have been many and great—in large part, proceeded from, and were informed and inspired by, an idealized and institutionalized negation of the Negro's meaning, value, and aspiration. Enslavement

All footnotes appear at the end of the book, pp. 205–218. All citations given as *NYT* refer to *The New York Times*.

1

of blacks, for example, was viewed by many as a necessary condition of the freedom of whites. The categories of perception, conception, and evaluation were selective and concealing as well as justifying and reinforcing. Obscuring the realities of power and social control, they were used to deny the incompatability between democracy and the oppressed position of blacks. Oppression was rationalized and made to square with democratic precepts and practices. Hence, self-government was proclaimed even as blacks were excluded from the most elementary participation in, and rewards of, the political process.

"The citizen, unlike the subject," say Almond and Verba, "is an active participant in the political input process—the process by which political decisions are made." [1] In the American political system, however, Negroes have been, fundamentally, subjects rather than citizens. Essentially excluded from input, they, of course, have not been beneficiaries of the output process. The political system has reflected, nurtured, and institutionalized the basically racist character of American culture. It has been blind and unresponsive to black demands, desires, hopes, and needs. In fact, the response of the system, in terms of public policy as well as philosophy, has been negative. It has made racial oppression and injustice normative. The tensions born of racial relations were destructive and negative, rather than creative and positive. Insensitivity has bred insensitivity, exclusion more exclusion, indifference more indifference, paralysis more paralysis, and negativism more negativism. Corporate disabilities were self-feeding and self-justifying.

On the whole, the American political system has generated and sustained a culture of total power and participation for whites and a culture of total powerlessness and exclusivity for blacks. This radical duality spawned in whites a collective syndrome of insensitivity, arrogance, pride, irresponsibility, and moral conceit and pretension which corrupted their sense of justice and vision of equality of citizenship and solidarity of the human family. It produced in blacks tragic frustrations, deprivations, anger, bitterness, and alienation which corrupted their civic and political consciousness and sense of participation, self-esteem, self-identity, and vision of higher possibility and creative public life. "A democratic citizen speaks the language of demands." [2] But having virtually no power, blacks had no effective methodology either of articulating their demands or of translating them into public policy and institutional life.

There is, however, an awesome paradox. Negroes, since early colonial times, have had a profound impact on the American political system and process. They have done so unwittingly and not of their own will. Blacks have not deeply influenced the American public order as political agents, participants, citizens, or actors but as political subjects, objects, victims, and issues. Consider, for example, the politics of the slave controversy, from early colonial times to the Constitutional Convention to manumission.

The slave controversy kept the political system under constant tension and led, in the end, to its collapse and the Civil War. Consider, moreover, the Confederacy, Reconstruction, the Compromise of 1877, and its aftermath, the impact of racism on the party system, electoral laws and processes, various political movements, legislative and administrative procedures and decisions, the Presidency, courts, and state and local governments. Racism has exerted tyranny over the mind of the white South on every level and in all aspects of public and institutional life. Thus, while essentially outside and powerless, Negroes have profoundly and indelibly influenced the American political system and process as sources of issues, meaning, direction, motivation, power, tension, unity, and division.

Yet, the political life of blacks has not been exhausted in alienation from, and victimization by, the American political system. Though powerless, and excluded from effective political participation and public decision-making, many blacks have displayed a genuine zest for political activity. They knocked and knocked and tried desperately to pry open the door of the house of power and public decision-making. They searched the forest and backyard and back streets of organizational life for the key. They labored mightily in the largely barren fields of petition, memorials, resolutions, proclamations, propaganda, moral suasion, conciliation, anguished cry, and feeble organization. They tried valiantly to be creators, rather than mere creatures, of the governing process.

Black political parties and pressure groups have been the function of the racist character of the American political system and the larger community. Forced into reality by existential circumstances, they have been concerned with race advancement—the achievement of equality of citizenship and humanity. White Power created and sustained black political organizations. Thus Negro political and civic groups were produced by the necessity of seeking to come to terms with the heavy burden of racism and to lift that burden. To paraphrase Myrdal, the Negro political genius has been imprisoned in the Negro problem.[3]

Black political parties and interest groups are rooted in the ethics, psychology, and philosophy of protest against racial oppression. In the face of harsh realities of power, there are occasions when the only thing the human spirit can do is to protest, to register a "no," to assert a dimension of inner freedom, dignity, and nobility that defies and eludes the sanctions of the mighty forces of darkness. One of the deepest glories of the human spirit is its ever-present and ever-powerful capacity to say "no" to experiences and events that violate its integrity and dignity. The magnificent story of Antigone, Socrates, and others crowds the mind and provides reassurance to the human spirit, whatever the consequences.

Protest, however, entails affirmation. As black political organizations protested against injustice and oppression, they affirmed something deep, precious, and abiding. They affirmed the relevance to them of the American Dream, equality of citizenship and humanity, the shame and hypocrisy of the country, and the creative power and infinite higher possibilities of the promise of American life. Thus their protests were far more than protests. They affirmed. They prophetically advocated national cleansing, reconciliation, re-union, and redemption. They affirmed their deep solidarity with other Americans and the political system which had betrayed them. They affirmed their kinship with the land of the free. They affirmed their membership in what Kant called the "commonwealth of humanity."

Dr. Walton's book plows new ground and constitutes a genuine contribution to the literature of black political and civic consciousness, aspirations, and behavior. It deals with a neglected feature of the American political landscape—blacks as party agents, citizens, creators, and subjects rather than as victims, aliens, creatures, and objects. It is the first genuine attempt systematically and comprehensively to deal with black political parties. Combining tragedy and glory, futility and heroism, idealism and realism, the experience of black political parties is an integral part of the American story. The book is an account of

Negroes desperately trying—without sure arms, legs, and hands—not only to learn to swim in the vast sea of American political dynamics, but seeking to swim against and to reverse its mighty currents of hostility and powerful waves of cruel rejection and oppression.

When today the two major parties vie for the black vote, we are inclined to forget that, for more than three centuries—except for the fleeting day of painful Reconstruction—the parties that dominated the governing process blandly ignored the Negro, avoided him like a plague, or engaged in Negrophobia. Party exploitation of white fears, insecurities, and anxieties has never been entirely absent from the American political scene.

Blacks, therefore, almost intuitively recognizing the significance of the political process and the ways of power, were forced to create their own political institutions in hope of compelling alteration of party and public policy and process. They had no viable choice, since liberation was their goal. Social change and progress, like social stability and continuity, are always functions of power. Black political parties, not unlike others, sought power—the ability to command and to control. Perhaps the unique dimension of black political parties was the ultimate objective—how political power was to be used, the end to which it was to be put—used—liberation. They have been, in essence, issue-oriented.

According to Dr. Walton, two types of black political parties emerged: the separate or independent and the parallel or satellite. Their tactics differed, but the end was the same—complete membership and full participation in the American political system. They sought entry into the "system," not its revolutionary overthrow. With all the external channels of power and social control clogged and the doors tightly closed, blacks were compelled to look to their own community resources in pursuit of a voice in, and fruits from, the course of public affairs.

This book provides a sense of history and a framework of historical understanding. It is a study of continuity and change in the party and public life of black America. It discusses recurrent problems, controversies, and struggles that characterize the attempt to use black political power to eradicate the evils of racism. Issues like separatism and coalition politics and the role of the white liberal in the black man's struggle are ancient features of black political life. They did not start with the Black Power Movement. A sense of historical consciousness should liberate us from the narrow throes of the moment. Factionalism, too, is a recurrent phenomenon. This book helps to liberate us from the tyranny of the present.

For a variety of reasons, as Dr. Walton holds, black political parties have been very small and of brief duration. Judged by the normal standard of party success—electoral victory, the winning of public office—black political parties historically have been a total failure. There is a strong possibility, however, that in selected areas with black majorities, or at least a high percentage of black voters, they will be increasingly successful on the local level, as have been the National Democratic Party of Alabama (NDPA) and the Mississippi Freedom Democratic Party (MFDP).

In addition to the vast handicaps of third or minor parties, black political parties suffer special disabilities growing out of the oppressed status of their constituencies or electorate. And black voters, for both idealistic and prudential reasons, have maintained strong allegiance to the venerable and self-perpetuating two-party system. Black voters, like others, are too sophisticated to support a party with no chance of electoral victory. They, too, want to win and to enjoy the satisfaction and fruits of carrying the day.

It is perilous, however, to evaluate black political parties in terms of normal standards. Success has many norms and dimensions of evaluation. Black political parties are, after all, expressions of radically abnormal conditions and consequences—basic defects in the political system. They have had a special mission—correction of those fundamental deficiencies. They have been, in substance, issue-laden, which sets them apart from the major parties and which unites them with the great reformist minor party tradition. In the human economy, there are successes which fail and failures which succeed. There are ambiguities inherent in the human condition. Thus if the general standards of party evaluation are used, something significant will be obscured and missed.

Black political parties have dramatized and protested against the wretched status of blacks. Dr. Walton is correct in the assertion that "black parties are mainly protest in nature and desirous of being included in the mainstream of American life." It is, of course, impossible to quantify and measure the effectiveness of their protests, but it is reasonable to assume that, in concert with others, they were cumulative and had some consequence. In a small way, they helped to prick the conscience of the country and remind her of the unfinished and urgent agenda. Along with other political and civic organizations, they have reminded the nation not only of the systematic exclusion of blacks from equality of citizenship and humanity but the meaning, consequences, and perils of that exclusion. A steady flow of protest, from many and varied perspectives, is essential for oppressed groups. The *status quo* must always be subjected to prophetic criticism and constructive imagination. It must not be allowed the deadening peril of silence and a complacent and easy conscience.

Black political parties have been agents and vehicles of creative dissent and social change. They have challenged the established political order, noted its hypocrisy, insensitivity, and neglect, and proclaimed a higher, richer, and more inclusive public good—the American Dream and Creed. They articulated, on the lonely and desolate desert of electoral powerlessness, the frustrations, dissatisfaction, disillusionment, and anguish of black folks. Although the light of political hope blinked and twinkled, black political parties helped to keep it dimly burning.

Besides, black political parties fostered the notion and ideal of self-help, self-propulsion, group consciousness and solidarity, and political sensitivity, awareness, and appreciation. They provided a frail and constructive outlet for the pent-up emotions of an oppressed and broken people. Such energies and aspirations could have been turned into collective acts of violence and other forms of destruction. Black political parties provided a challenge to blacks to develop political consciousness and know-how and an opportunity for them to gain a modicum of political experience, confidence, and sense of participation and higher possibility. They offered hope of reforming and redeeming the political system. They provided a method of adjustment and accommodation to the brutal realities of political and governmental life.

In the total scheme of things, therefore, black political parties have been no complete failure. They blend successes and failures. In their protest, they affirmed something precious; in their giant electoral failures, they succeeded in the goal of race advancement—their ultimate objective. Immediacy is seldom the best angle of vision from which to judge human institutions and organizations; the long view, the large perspective, and the total reality of being and becoming are crucial. Electoral defeats and successes are not the final standard by virtue of which political parties must be judged. There is a realm of meaning, value, continuity, public responsibility, and community service lurking beyond the election returns. Election victory for what?

SAMUEL DUBOIS COOK
*Department of Political Science
Duke University*

1

THE RATIONALE FOR BLACK

POLITICAL PARTIES

Before this country was an independent nation, politics was based on class and position. With the advent of democracy, this political pattern began to disintegrate. Political power now rested upon quantity rather than quality and upon the direct backing of numbers rather than inherited status. Under this new system, politics in its old forms was meaningless. Political democracy had isolated the individual citizen, blocked the old roads to unity, and concentrated great political power in groups and in individual politicians. But immediately the search began for a new device to mold public opinion, unify diverse interests, and mobilize mass consent, and it concluded with the emergence of modern political parties.[1]

Generally speaking, we can define a political party as a group of people who seek by legal means to gain control of the government and to advance specific interests.[2] Clearly, no organizations that fit this definition existed in early America. But the possibilities and future emergence of such organizations did not escape the prophetic insight of the founding fathers.

James Madison saw the basis for parties (which he called factions) in the diverse human interests, outlooks, and needs which he felt would inevitably develop in a democratic society. A faction or party is, in Madison's words, "a number of citizens whether amounting to a majority or a minority of the whole who are united by some common impulse of passion or of interest adverse to the right of other citizens or to the permanent and aggregate interest of the community." The most common and durable cause of factions, he argued, is therefore not only differences of religion and of economic and social interest, but the unequal distribution of property in society. Madison wrote:

> Those who hold and those who are without property have ever formed distinct interests in society. Those who are creditors and those who are debtors fall under a like discrimination. A landed interest, a manufacturing interest, a money interest, with many lesser interests grow up a necessity in civilized nations and divide them into different classes accentuated by different sentiments and views. The regulation of these various and intervening interests forms the principal task of modern legislation and involves the spirit of party and faction in the necessary and ordinary operations of government.[3]

Madison clearly saw the feasibility of parties in a society dedicated to fundamental liberties, but he feared that if any one party exercised majority control of the government it could destroy these very same liberties. If a party became a majority, the popular form of government would, in his opinion, be impaired and "the public good and the rights of other citizens would be sacrificed to the ruling passions or interests of a special few." Parties were, therefore, in Madison's view, detrimental to liberty if not checked and frustrated by a separation of powers, embodied in a federal system. The larger the republic, he argued, the less a party would have to exert its inherently oppressive nature, simply because the interest of the whole community could easily dilute a single tyrannical interest.

Following Madison's thinking in this respect, George Washington, too, foresaw the possible emergence of political parties in America. Like Madison, he argued that insofar as parties are rooted in human passion they are harmful to a truly democratic society. In his farewell address Washington spoke of "the baneful effects of the spirit of parties" in the American nation and emphatically discouraged both the spirit and the tendency. The party, in his opinion, was only "a small but artful and enterprising minority of the community." In addition, these (parties) become, in Washington's words, "potent engines by which cunning, ambitious, and unprincipled men will be enabled to usurp for themselves the reins of government."

Some time before Washington's warning, the Constitutional Convention produced a document reflecting a dual attitude toward parties.[4] On one hand, the Constitution supported the idea of parties, but it was anti-party in another respect. This duality is reflected in Madison's position that, while parties are inherently dangerous, their complete suppression would destroy the fundamental liberties that make them possible in the first place. Recognizing this, the authors of the Constitution accepted amendments and provisions establishing certain fundamental rights and liberties, such as the rights to assemble peaceably and to petition the government for redress of grievances, which are inherent in the First Amendment. These fundamental rights and liberties represented the pro-party spirit.

In essence, then, the pro-party spirit flourished because it coincided with the desire to protect those liberties which ideally exist in a democratic society. It is doubtful that the pro-party attitude would have existed had it not depended on the same civil rights that the individual colonies sought. On the other hand, the anti-party spirit expressed itself vigorously at the Constitutional Convention. It was thought that the elaborate and intricate governmental structure—including a separation of powers, which Madison advocated in *The Federalist*—would diminish the "baneful effects" of parties. This distribution of power in the federal government, the founding fathers hoped, would destroy the majoritarian tendencies of any political party that had visions of controlling the American government.

Thus the attitude expressed by Madison and Washington and by the Constitutional Convention was that parties were intrinsically evil and even dangerous to the American form of government. Yet the document—and the form of government it helped to create—led to the very type of organizations it was intended to avoid. Indeed, the controversy surrounding the drafting and ratification of the new Constitution and the acceptance of a federal form of government laid the groundwork for political parties in America.[5]

On September 17, 1787, after four months of deliberation, the Constitutional Convention completed its great task. Only 42 of the original 55 members were still present; of these, 39 signed the Constitution.[6] Although the signatures of the various state representatives had no binding force upon the states, they did attest to the shared convictions of the delegates. Washington, the president of the convention, transmitted the document to the Congress of the Confederation with a recommendation that the question of its adoption be submitted to conventions of delegates chosen by the people in each state. Thus the Constitutional Convention, after submitting the document along with its recommendation, adjourned and left the great question of ratification for the people to decide.

The conflict over ratification began immediately upon publication of the new Constitution. In the ranks of the opposition were some of the greatest names of the Revoluntionary era. In Virginia Patrick Henry led the fight against ratification, convinced that the new Constitution would subordinate the states to a meaningless role in the Union and destroy the liberties of the people. He was supported by George Mason, James Monroe, and Richard Henry Lee. In New York, Governor George Clinton bitterly opposed the new document. All these men were later to help form a political group, led by Thomas Jefferson, under the banner of antifederalism.[7]

The supporters of the new Constitution—the Federalists—included the great majority of merchants, conservatives, members of the professional class, and propertyholders, all of whom welcomed the proposal for a strong national government. In New York, Alexander Hamilton was the foremost Federalist. He was allied in Virginia with John Jay, James Madison, Edmund Randolph, and John Marshall. George Washington also exerted potent influence in their behalf.

Newspapers, other publications, and speech-makers sought to sway public opinion one way or the other regarding the new document. *The Federalist,* the most noteworthy of the sundry publications to influence public opinion, was a collection of essays that sought to win supporters for the new Constitution in the pivotal state of New York. Of the 85 essays written by Madison, Hamilton, and Jay, 77 were originally published in New York newspapers under the common signature, "Publius." Although there was considerable opposition to the publication of these essays as well as to the Constitution, the counter propaganda of the Antifederalists proved unavailing. By June 21, 1788, the ninth state had finally given reluctant assent; Washington was inaugurated on April 30, 1789, and the new government was established.[8]

However, the mere ratification of the Constitution by nine states (the number required for adoption) did not signal the automatic acceptance of Federalist principles. Quite the contrary. The supporters of the concept of a federal government had to write their ideas into meaningful legislation in both houses of Congress. In other words, ratification of the Constitution was not enough to guarantee a workable federal system. Public opinion had to be continually mobilized so that appropriate public policy would be enacted into law and thus make the ideas of the Federalists a reality. It was in response to this felt need that the Federalist grouping became a political party. This did not come about automatically or suddenly, but grew out of conscious leadership, societal conditions, and the emergence of a common interest. These forces meshed, coalesced, and created a viable political vehicle which assumed the responsibility of administering a new government.

Preeminent among the Federalist leaders were two dominant political figures in American history: Washington and Hamilton. Washington, the newly elected President, backer of the Constitution, and strong Federalist, appointed Hamilton as his Secretary of the Treasury. Once in office, Hamilton proceeded vigorously to implement the Federalist ideology. His actions and policies in this position shaped the party's basic philosophy. Moreover, his bold proposals found strong support among groups that had once resorted to revolt to express their discontent with weak governmental economic policies, as witness Shays' Rebellion of 1786.[9] In addition, enterprising entrepreneurs and speculators, seeking to improve or secure their positions, rallied behind Hamilton's financial program. Because of the Federalist party's abolitionist stance, Free Negro voters in the North, especially in New York, gratefully supported the emerging party.[10]

Although the Federalists opposed legitimacy of political parties they were compelled to establish the rudiments of an oligarchical party hierarchy to carry out their policies, and this then determined the character of numerous state legislatures. Even so, all their organizations, including the Federalist National Convention of 1808, were operated in secret so as to deny such an organization to their opponents.

But despite their successes, their vigorous leadership, and considerable public support, organized opposition soon arose. These groups, dubbed "Antifederalists," found support among many elements and in many sectors of society that had been alienated by the Federalists' relentless pursuit of certain policies which favored the large business and banking interests over the interests of the poor, the farmers, the backwoodsmen, and the ever increasing inland settlers.

At first, the Antifederalists comprised loose associations of groups, which grew under the political leadership of Patrick Henry. Later, Thomas Jefferson, the dynamic philosopher of agrarianism, captured and rejuvenated Henry's followers. Under his leadership, the Antifederalists, who subsequently became known as the Jeffersonian Republicans, developed a consistent ideology which helped them increase their ranks through artful propaganda and agitation. Arguing that the farmers were the sole possessors of virtue and morality, and that Federalist policies created an elite society which disregarded the masses, the early Republican party overcame the handicap of the early Antifederalists, whose sole function was to oppose the Constitution.[11]

Thus Jefferson, armed with personal magnetism and astute insight and wielding the dogma of states' rights, succeeded in establishing a national political organization as powerful as the Federalists. He was aided in part by weak Federalist legislation which tended to support Federalist elitism and by increasing factional strife within the party. These factors resulted in Jefferson's election to the presidency in 1800.[12] Once in office, the Jeffersonians sought to remake the government in their own image, thus helping to thwart the move toward greater federalism and permitting the doctrine of states' rights to gain ascendancy.

After revising governmental policies, the Jeffersonians moved to eliminate their opposition—not simply by beating the Federalists into submission, but by co-opting them out of existence. The Republicans soon possessed every advantage over their former rivals. With an effective party organization, presidential leadership, federal patronage, and remarkable internal cohesion, the party rose from a mere opposition status to a dominant one. The War of 1812 and the Federalists' negative attitude toward parties also aided the Republicans in their rise to supremacy. Hence what had been a growing two-party system in 1800 was rapidly becoming a one-party system by 1816. Although the disappearance of political opposition affected the party discipline and internal cohesion of the Jeffersonian Republicans, the one-party rule lasted in America through the "era of good feelings" (roughly, 1817–1828). During this interlude, party feelings and associations declined and a "cult of personality" appeared, in which people identified more with nationally prominent political figures such as Andrew Jackson, John Quincy Adams, John C. Calhoun, and Henry Clay than with political groupings.

The era of good feelings came to an end in 1828 with the election of Andrew Jackson, whose policies gave rise to the second American two-party era. New parties emerged, partly because of Jackson's policies and program and partly because of the needs of society. These parties were the National Republicans (rudiments of the old Federalists), which later evolved into the Whigs, and the Democratic Republicans (rudiments of the old Antifederalists and Jeffersonian Republicans), which later evolved into the Democrats. Finally, out of the morass of sectional politics and impending national crises, the modern Democratic and Republican parties—the third two-party system—appeared as full-fledged contestants in the 1856 election.[13]

Political parties have always played an important role in American democratic society, for the party serves as the chief instrument of popular control over government. The general effect of a democracy is to atomize the body politic and isolate the individual. But a nation must have mass consent and a semblance of unity if it is to survive. This is the factor that gave rise to political parties in the first place, and it has been a persistent factor in American politics ever since.

Political parties have in many instances become the representatives of social, economic, and political interest groups. More specifically, they have helped to translate public pressures into public policies. Through them individual groups can bridge the distance between the isolated individual and the greater community.[14] Lord Bryce, an astute observer of the American political scene, said something similar when he wrote that parties "bring order out of the chaos of a multitude of voters"; Disraeli likewise characterized political parties as "organized opinion" insofar as parties are brokers of ideas, constantly clarifying and systematizing public opinion which they hope will coalesce to form specific policies expressive of the public will.[15] But it is precisely when the political party attempts to perform certain critical functions such as electioneering and the orderly transfer of power for the particular political culture in which it exists that it encounters difficulties in advancing public policies expressive of the public will.

As Eldersveld asserts, "parties are merely a particular structural response to the needs of a social and political system in a particular milieu." In short, parties arise out of pressing needs and derive their characteristics and structure from the attempt to fulfill these needs. A party's organizational structure affects its doctrine, its leaders, and its role perception. And it is in the creation of this hierarchical relationship that the party becomes a micropolitical subsystem, involved in self-conflict, self-examination, and—at times—self-seeking endeavors. These internal problems to some extent impair the party's ability to realize optimum objectives for its clientele in terms of meaningful public policy.[16]

The pluralistic character of American society—the very thing that gave rise to political parties—has magnified the problems created by the need for such organizations. The various political, social, and economic groupings in a pluralistic society make it difficult for a party to stabilize its principles or to adopt a clearly delineated position on all public policies. Although the party is basically a clientele-oriented structure, its primary function and *raison d'être* (to win elections) forces each party in a two-party system into a directly competitive role, seeking to adapt itself to the ideas of as many voters as possible. Thus the party that aspires to achieve a majority must form coalitions. It must coalesce, however, while the coalition process is underway. Each coalescing group possesses its own set of demands, goals, and principles, and each must bargain with the others. In addition, members of the party organization will join or merge with a competing (coalescing) group, using their influence in the organization to gain more for the group with which they identify. In turn, they may gain greater power or responsibility as a result of their identification with a dominant group. In sum, the members of the party organization enter into and try to influence the bargaining processes. Once the bargaining is completed, the specific goals and policies are welded and merged in an ambiguous manner so that the political process will not be stifled— that is, so that one group does not seem to receive more than another. In other words, the party attempts to use the voters to win elections, and the voters attempt to use the party to satisfy their own self-interests.

It is in compromising that the political party faces its second dilemma. The party that tries to referee or stabilize the bargaining process becomes a part of the very same process, resulting in a new set of priorities that involve expediency, moderation, and pragmatism. The politics of expediency and compromise pursued by our political parties have caused many observers to question their reliability and responsibility.[17] Some have become disillusioned and distrustful of our two "natural" parties as adequate vehicles to affect public policy. Many of these observers, however, fail to see that a pluralistic democratic society requires a bargaining process. A compromise struggle for power in our society involves the "game of politics"—the marketplace. It is in this vein of moderation and compromise that political parties obtain popular consent for their policies, be they ambiguous or not. Party government in a democracy rests on a broad base of consent rather than on the dictates of a special group or special interests. Therefore, it is increasingly difficult in a heterogeneous society for special interest groups to secure specific policy goals and objectives.[18]

In addition, political parties are primarily electoral devices to which matters of policy are secondary, as it is generally left to the legislators to formulate policies that they consider to be in the public interest. Public policy determined by parties will reflect this coalition and compromise, which results in some ambiguity in the apportionment of rights and privileges by law.

The translation of social pressure into public policies is not left solely to political parties, however. Such pressure groups as labor, agriculture, and business are constantly concerned with how power will be exercised. The politics of pressure groups differ from that of political parties because of the avenues of access in our governmental structure available to pressure groups.[19] Instead of political compromise, the politics of pressure groups stresses self-interest. Although these groups too must bargain with policy-making agencies, they seek to promote only their own self-interests. Coalitions and alliances are limited if they are formed at all. Pressure group politics is policy politics, while party politics is personal and electoral politics.[20] But pressure groups cannot and do not displace political parties. Our political culture provides a role and function for each. They complement each other rather than canceling one another out. Since political parties are primarily—though not exclusively—concerned with who will exercise power, it is difficult to replace them. The administration and functioning of a democratic state depend on the consent of more than one societal group. That is why pressure groups are needed to complete the picture. In short, some things can be achieved by means of party politics and other things by means of pressure group politics.

What happens to the groups that are dissatisfied with both party and pressure-group achievements? What happens to the groups that cannot be compromised? What happens to the individuals in the party organization who are dissatisfied with their inability to win the party's complete commitment to their views? What happens to the groups that see the need for parties but are not offered adequate alternatives by a two-party system and pressure groups? What happens to the odds and ends of the citizenry who are left over after the major parties are assembled into a coalition system?

These social and political groups find common cause in what is called minor or third party movements.[21] Many third parties are doctrinaire in nature; others derive their existence from the fact that major parties fail to recognize certain important issues; still others develop because of the cumbersome methods of election as well as the compromising nature and general ineptness of our two-party system.[22] Third parties have appeared throughout American history and have at times competed vigorously for the presidency. In fact, the activities of some minor parties—such as the Populist, Progressive, and Free-Soil parties—have reached such intensity that they have forced one of the major parties to readjust and harmonize its policies to certain economic and social forces.

In addition to serving as a safety valve in our political system, minor parties have helped educate the public on many key issues.[23] But third parties, like pressure groups, serve only to complement our major political parties and make them more effective. Third parties, Lubell argues, expose "the inner torments" of the major parties. Third parties generally espouse lofty principles or doctrines, but when they enter the arena of national politics they are forced to face up to reality in their fight for power. This struggle for power—this political game—compels them to bargain and readjust their specific programs. As Professor Herring put it, "if they refrain, they are thrown back upon theorizing rather than seeking to create through legislation appropriate administrative devices for achieving their ends."[24] Furthermore, in their attempts to win converts from the major parties, they must broaden their specific appeals. This brings them face to face with the same traditional irrational allegiances and factors that plague the major parties, further weakening their effectiveness as political organizations.

Thus third parties, while more representative than the major parties, are not always viable alternatives.

Minor parties in the United States currently seem somewhat on the decline. The reasons are both institutional (single-member districts and plurality voting devices), and noninstitutional (the naturalness of our two-party system). The institutional reasons seem much easier to prove and measure than the noninstitutional, which, like the dualistic basis of Western or American civilization, is open to question.[25]

Notwithstanding these factors, third parties continue to exist. Perhaps they lack their former influence, but they exist nonetheless. In the 1960 election, some ten or more appeared; in 1964, six competed.[26] In 1968, George Wallace's American Independent party received more than 10 million votes and got on the ballot of all fifty states, thus proving to be a major third party effort. However, in 1972, Wallace dropped the AIP and entered the primaries as a Democratic contender, which may be indicative of the fact that his third party was not as viable as one of the major parties.

An overriding question at this point is: What happens to a particular societal group which cannot use existing mechanisms to translate its social and economic aspirations into effective political pressure? What happens to the older forms (the mechanisms for translation), when major *and* minor political parties as well as pressure groups exclude them from the bargaining process? What happens to those individuals or groups that cannot influence public policy so as to improve or change their situation? When politics is the most viable means, it is obvious that these excluded individuals or groups, like the creators of third parties throughout our history, have had to create new mechanisms and organizations in order to protest or to point up a political dysfunction of our American political system. It is from these dysfunctions that American black political parties have emerged.

Merton has argued in convincing detail that certain categories of individuals are so placed in the social structure that they are barred from legitimate access to the ladder of achievement.[27] Moreover, Cloward and Ohlin have shown that certain social categories find themselves in positions which prevent them from utilizing not only legitimate channels of opportunity but illegitimate and criminal channels as well.[28] If members of the excluded groups are to achieve success or accomplish meaningful ends, they need a new and viable mechanism, a new device for translating group needs into a politics which has some chance of securing redress of their grievances. But does this theory of excluded groups apply to the Negro American? Have the existing devices failed to help the Negro in meeting his needs? For a much more conclusive answer, let us look briefly at Negro activities and use of the chief devices for accomplishing political, social, and economic objectives in a pluralistic society—major and minor political parties and pressure groups.

Although Negroes arrived in America as slaves, many had obtained freedom through manumission during the Revolutionary War and resided in the northern states as quasi-citizens. These Free Negroes, as they were called, enjoyed the right to vote in Massachusetts, Rhode Island, Vermont, Maine, New Hampshire, New York, and Pennsylvania.[29] However, although the Negro vote was sanctioned by law in all of New England except Connecticut, it was greatly inhibited through various stratagems, social mores, and folkways. For instance, an Englishman traveling in the New England states observed: "The black may have rights and privileges [here]—but it is as much as his life is worth to exercise them—if he attempted to vote in an election, he would be hooted and pelted from that pure emblem of uncontrolled liberty—the ballot box." But the large Free Negro population in New York and Pennsylvania did make itself felt as a potent political factor. Moreover, the adverse conditions of these Negroes and the discrimination they faced in everyday life increased their sensitivity to the usefulness of political action. Therefore, especially in New York, Free Negroes supported the Federalist party until its demise.[30]

The political loyalty of Free Negroes to the Federalist party was in part due to its leaders' attitude toward slavery. The Federalists, who controlled the New York legislature and governorship from 1790 to 1811, passed a law in 1799 calling for the gradual abolition of slavery and in general expressed greater concern for Negro rights and privileges than did the Antifederalists.[31] In addition, the attachment of southern slavocrats to the Antifederalist group further alienated the Free Negro vote.

Late in 1811, when the Jeffersonian Republicans gained control of the New York Legislature, Negro suffrage rights came under attack. The Republicans, acting swifty to curtail any remaining opposition, recognized the necessity of ending the old and still powerful Negro–Federalist alliance. Their move to disfranchise the Free Negro met with little success in 1811, but was partially successful by 1821.[32] At the state constitutional convention of that year, the Jeffersonian Republicans offered an amendment which would increase the property qualifications and residence requirement of Negroes. This amendment, later approved by the voters of the state, limited the Free Negro's vote and thus increased his allegiance to the rising political group known as the National Republicans, a coalition of former Federalists.

From 1817 to 1828 party allegiances relaxed somewhat but Negro voters in New York continued to be significant in local, municipal, and gubernatorial contests. It has been reported that in one local election during these years the Negro vote defeated Tammany-supported politicians in the fifth and eighth wards of New York City because Tammany Hall had led a movement to disfranchise blacks completely. And the continual success of Whig candidates in predominantly Negro wards led one observer to say that most Negroes were "anti-Jackson" men.[33]

With the re-emergence of national political parties, Negro voters of New York, Pennsylvania, and Rhode Island moved into the Whig camp. In 1838, Negro voters proved the deciding factor in electing William H. Seward, the Whig senatorial candidate from New York, over his Democratic opponent in response to Seward's somewhat liberal views on the retention of suffrage rights for all. Although the Whig stand was ambiguous, it called for unrestricted suffrage for all the disfranchised and created enough ruckus to alarm party members as well as opposing Democrats. The successful opposition to this proposal stifled further moves to enlarge suffrage rights for anyone.

In Pennsylvania, where a few Negroes still voted in some counties despite social "extralegalism," the Whigs and probably the anti-Masonic candidates received their votes.[34] The acquistion of the Negro votes by those political groups and the continual losses of Democratic candidates led to eventual disfranchisement and repression of Free Negroes in that state.[35] By 1838, the Democrats had completely eliminated Negroes as a factor in Pennsylvania politics.

In the South, Free Negroes in some counties of North Carolina and Tennessee continued to vote until 1835; and in one parish in Louisiana, although Free Negroes had been disfranchised by 1812, they went to the polls from 1838 to 1860. Negro party allegiance in the South, however, was not so discernible as northern Negro allegiances, basically because of the lack of a strong party throughout the South during this period.[36] In North Carolina, there were 300 Free Negro voters in Halifax County and 150 in Hartford County. According to Professor Shuggs, in these counties Free Negroes held the balance of power in certain local elections, and in bitterly fought contests the Free Negro voter could be bought by one of the rival candidates. On the other hand, Franklin implies that the Free Negro cast his ballot for the candidate most amenable to his desires. During the movement to disfranchise Free Negroes in North Carolina in 1834 and 1835, the Democrats accused Whig candidates of harboring favorable attitudes toward Free Negro voting, yet Free Negroes do not seem to have reciprocated with any sort of Whig party allegiance.[37] Therefore, although it is difficult to judge, it seems reasonable to suggest that Free Negroes in the South sometimes voted for amenable candidates and sometimes sold their votes.

A similar situation prevailed in Tennessee: twenty counties had more than 100 Free Negroes—Davidson County had 500—and the political influence of the Free Negro voters was significant. But here again, evidence of strong party allegiance is missing. It appears, however, that the Free Negro voters of Tennessee, like some of those in North Carolina, voted for the most favorable or friendliest candidate.[38]

When despite a restricted franchise, Louisiana's Free Negroes continued to vote for local candidates in Rapides parish—called the "ten-mile precinct"—the American Nativist party, a local Know-Nothing party, brought this "scandalous" activity to the public's attention. When the American Nativist party lost the state treasurer's position in the 1857 election it accused the Democrats of fraudulent procedures because the Democrats had mustered some 68 Negro voters to the polls. The Democrats denied the charges and replied with similar charges against the Whigs—now "Native Americans"—for using Negro voters in the election of 1838. This, a Louisiana newspaper editorial explained, prompted the Democrats to seek, acquire, and to make use of those voters. Therefore, after 1841 the Democrats "never failed . . . to collect all the Free Negro votes in Rapides Parish," where Free Negroes, according to Shuggs, held the balance of power at the polls. This caused a traveling correspondent for the *New Orleans Crescent* to report, as late as 1860, that "about eighty colored men are voted at Ten Mile by the terrified Democrats whenever an emergency demands their loyal aid in carrying an election."[39]

Obviously, the Free Negro voters of Tennessee, South Carolina, North Carolina, and especially Louisiana were at best the tools of self-seeking politicians who were "responsible to a lawful electorate that excluded [Negroes]." Moreover, the growth of Free Negro political influence in the South was largely the cause for their disfranchisement after 1835. This attempt by Negroes to improve their lot by voting led to bitter competition between the dominant white political groupings, and this competition in turn led to the Negro's total disfranchisement.

The political affiliations of northern Free Negroes led them to virtually the same situation that confronted their unaligned southern counterparts. Both groups were disfranchised. Northern political groups that did not receive the votes of Free Negroes fought vigorously for disfranchisement, using every method from anti-Negro riots to bullying, ridicule, and voluminous propaganda based on specious political, social, and economic arguments. Such tactics were successful by and large, and the political power of Free Negroes in the North rapidly declined to the level of southern Negroes after 1838.[40]

Northern Free Negroes did not readily accept their station. They organized and petitioned for the restoration of their lost suffrage rights as well as for equal suffrage rights, but little was achieved.[41] With the avenues to both parties closed, Negro voters turned to third party activity.[42]

The emergence of the moderately antislavery Liberty party in 1840 found many ready, willing, and available Negro supporters. Even on the local level, wherever possible Negroes supported such newly organized minor parties as the Working Men's party, the Locofoco party, and the Equal Rights party. Although the Liberty party participated in the national election of 1848, some Negroes supported the emergent Free-Soil party in that year.[43] However, the anti-Negro prejudices of some leaders of these parties precluded substantial Negro support, and the expression of these prejudices combined with prior political allegiances to split the Negro vote.[44] For example, although 600 to 700 Negroes in New Bedford and the majority of Negroes throughout the Commonwealth of Massachusetts reportedly voted for the Free-Soilers, the Negro voters of Providence, Rhode Island, overwhelmingly supported the Whig party because Whigs there had opposed disfranchisement of Free Negroes.

Generally speaking, the third party activities of Free Negro voters in the 1840s did accomplish some ends; on the local level, for instance, several Negro candidates representing third parties were elected.[45] But on the whole the maneuver was detrimental. These new parties with their Negro supporters incurred the wrath of both Whigs and Democrats. And both major parties continued their efforts to destroy whatever remaining political effectiveness the Negro possessed. In addition, the increasing prejudice of the third parties—notably the Free-Soilers—soon disillusioned Negro voters, forcing them to abandon strong party attachments and to pin all their hopes on individual candidates. By the mid-1850s it made little difference whether Negroes cared to ally themselves with parties, for by then independent Negro voting no longer existed.[46] For Negroes, politics was no longer a means to an end. The major parties shunned them, the minor parties exploited their votes, and their efforts at political agitation through other groups met with little success.

With the outbreak of the Civil War and the enactment of the Fifteenth Amendment, strong Negro party allegiance re-emerged. Negro sentimental attachment to the Republican party began as early as 1865.[47] But real political attachment was not possible until after the passage of the Fifteenth Amendment, which granted suffrage rights to all blacks. By granting suffrage to some for the first time and restoring it to others, the amendment, paved the way for "Black Reconstruction"; many Negroes became state legislators and members of Congress, and a little improvement was made in the Negroes' social and economic plight.[48] But Black Reconstruction was short-lived, owing to the resurgence of the doctrine of white supremacy.

The Compromise of 1877 ended Black Reconstruction and sounded the death knell for black Republicanism; subsequently, such developments as Rutherford B. Hayes's hands-off policy ushered in a new period of lily-white Republicanism in the South.

The hands-off policy signaled the federal government's withdrawal from the race issue. Thereafter each southern state would approach its race problems in its own way, free of federal intervention. During this period, the South instituted a one-party, preeminently white political system.[49] Negroes in the South, as Henry Grady, a white journalist in Georgia, pointed out, "dropped out of serious political consideration."

The disfranchisement of southern Negroes resulting from resurgent white supremacy brought about a corresponding decline in the Negroes' already precarious economic and social situation. Since northern Negro Republicans could do little to effectuate a meaningful change in the South, southern Negroes turned chiefly to migration as a solution.[50]

As before, significant Negro third party activity began in the South with the emergence, in the late 1880s, of the Populist party,[51] characterized by the alliance of labor and farmer groups. With the southern Democratic party closed to them, lily-white Republicans shunning them, and northern Negro Republicans ineffective in national politics, southern Negroes turned to Populism in the hope that it would offer at least a temporary solution. But here again, the race prejudice of many Populists and the vigorous opposition of white-supremacist southern Democrats rendered the Populist party almost useless as a medium for rectifying the Negro's plight. Although Populism did aid the Negro somewhat by establishing a number of Negro educational institutions and by maintaining continual Negro representation in Congress, the Populists eventually lent impetus to the continuing movement toward disfranchisement.[52]

During his second term (1905–1909), Theodore Roosevelt alienated many of the remaining northern Negro Republican voters.[53] For example, while on a southern tour he urged Negroes to accept political white supremacy. This was reason enough for many of them to abandon the Republican party. William Howard Taft's continuation of the hands-off policy drove still more of them away. A final slap in the face came when lily-whitism moved into the Progressive party of 1912. Roosevelt, in his effort to build the Progressive ("Bull Moose") party, sought to win back Negro support, both northern and southern. But his capitulation to southern lily-whitism at the Progressive party's national convention speeded Negro withdrawal from Republicanism.[54] In short, Negro support for the Republican party declined rapidly after Roosevelt and Taft, and Negro Democratic activities increased.

Although the policies of Roosevelt and Taft gave impetus to this movement, they certainly did not mark its beginning: the earliest Negro inroads into the Democratic party were made in the North during Reconstruction. After the restoration of southern home rule, many Negroes were cajoled into voting for the Democratic party; others did so for opportunistic reasons. This phenomenon, however, was greatly limited in the South and occurred only on an individual basis. The fusion of the Populists with the Democrats in some southern states had sharply reduced the number of elected Negro state officers and congressmen; with the increasing dominance of southern white supremacy and the declining Negro vote, black officeholders disappeared from the scene and southern Negro support for the Democrats was in abeyance for a long period.

Eventually, Negro migration to the North lent the needed momentum to Negro Democratic party activity. The political machines, bosses, and clubhouses of northern cities welcomed Negroes as well as immigrants from abroad and acquired their votes in exchange for certain welfare considerations, jobs, housing, and help in adjusting their rural outlooks to big-city life.[55] In such northern cities as Chicago and New York, the heavy concentration of Negroes in certain wards and districts sometimes enabled them to receive help other than welfare. Many Negro local councilmen, state officials, and assemblymen were elected, the majority of them affirming allegiance to the local and state Democratic party. Substantial Negro support for the Democratic party on the national level, although limited, began with the election of 1912. Woodrow Wilson tried to play down—but did not disavow—Negro electoral support. For all that, his campaign and later presidential policies regarding Negroes were not encouraging. As W. E. B. DuBois put it, "the first attempt by the Negro to enter the Democratic party ranks on the national level, although not stymied, was grudgingly accepted." This action, along with Wilson's strong segregationist tendencies and the terrible race riots during his tenure of office, set off a new rash of Negro third party activity.

Many independent Negro voters, shunned by the northern Democrats and Republicans, entered third parties. Such activity was limited because a majority of Negro votes were controlled by state and local political machines. This did not appreciably affect their position on national issues, but voting in national elections was only marginally beneficial for Negroes and brought no meaningful alteration in their position in society. Therefore, Negro allegiance—especially in the North, and to the Democratic party more than to the Republican— was most significant on the state and local levels.

Republicanism re-emerged with the election of Warren G. Harding in 1920 and continued dominant until Herbert Hoover's defeat in 1932. Republican presidential coolness in general and party coolness in particular during this period did not significantly change independent Negro votes for third parties in national elections or the machine control of votes in northern state and local elections, though such third parties as the Communists, Socialists, and Progressives did pick up some support.[56]

Franklin D. Roosevelt's second election in 1936 won for the Democratic party the almost total allegiance of black voters on the national level. Roosevelt's social policies were an attractive lure for politically rootless black voters searching for a viable party: his welfare programs, his appointment of a "Black Cabinet," and his creation of the Fair Employment Practices Commission captured the imagination of the majority of blacks and set the stage for their strong swing to the Democratic party. Truman and civil rights legislation continued this trend. Eisenhower's election for a second term in 1956 brought a temporary shift in Negro allegiance back to the Republicans, but the election promises of Kennedy and Johnson turned the tide again to the Democrats. President Nixon's election in 1968 and his subsequent conservative policies on busing, education, and civil rights, as well as his judicial appointments, have not moved blacks out of the Democratic fold on the national level. Yet, there is evidence on the state and local levels that blacks are strongly supporting liberal Republican candidates.

In each of these cases, the voting behavior of Negroes reflected the trend, mood, and aspirations of the group. This may seem a truism, yet many political analysts hold that Negro allegiance to the Democratic party since F.D.R. has been blindly unswerving.[57] This interpretation fails to consider the attitude of the race toward the goals achieved through their strong party attachment. The protest activity of the Negro throughout his attachment to the Democratic party seems to point to a growing dissatisfaction with the slow pace of the group's advancement and a certain urgent awareness of the Negroes' situation, as well as its explosive nature.

In short, solid Negro attachment to the Democratic party as such in the past decades could be illusory. First of all, regardless of its policies and platforms, the party receiving Negro support appeared to be assured of victory in 1936, 1956, and 1964. It is noteworthy that the Negro shift came not in 1932 but in 1936 (Roosevelt's second term), not in 1952 but in 1956 (Eisenhower's second term), and not in 1960 when Kennedy won but in 1964 when Johnson ran against Goldwater. Second, the Democratic party, which includes hard-core southern segregationists, blocked civil rights legislation and sought to promote legislation inimical to civil rights. Finally, liberal Democrats in many cases have reneged on their promises. For instance, during his term as president, John F. Kennedy shelved civil rights legislation in order to get his other programs through Congress.[58]

Further evidence of cracks in the theoretically solid Negro Democratic vote came in the 1960 election. The Afro-American party in Alabama ran two Negroes for president and received 1,485 votes. This action on the part of Negro voters in Alabama at first glance appears futile. But a second glance seems to suggest something else. Why would this many Negroes, in a state where the Negro vote is vigorously suppressed, throw their votes away? Why not vote for a professed liberal Democratic candidate like Kennedy? It seems as if this would have been the better choice, particularly since Kennedy's chances of being elected were relatively favorable.

Afro-American party leaders suggested that no meaningful alternative existed. The time, they felt, had arrived for the creation of a black political party, *an organization of black individuals and groups operating through constitutional procedures, seeking to gain control of the political process as well as to place Negro politicians in office— not necessarily on the national level, but at least on the local, regional, and state levels.*

The Afro-American party appealed to a narrow electorate, but it represented the majority of Negro interests, hopes, and needs. It hoped to fill leadership positions at all levels of government where the Negro was in the majority. Its major aim was to improve Negro life and to achieve the goals that had always been denied him in America. The party felt that white political agencies and individuals had failed, because of inbred prejudice and discrimination, to achieve for Negroes their just position in society. Therefore, it was reasoned, Negroes had to fall back on their own resources to achieve social justice. In fact, such contemporary Negro political parties as the Afro-American party, the Mississippi Freedom Democratic party, and the Black Panther party (not to be confused with the Black Panther organization founded in California) are simply expressions of a phenomenon that began very early in American Negro history. However, before we look at these political organizations in detail, let us backtrack briefly to see how Negroes have used pressure groups to obtain their objectives.

Negro Pressure Groups

Pressure groups are rooted in a complex heterogeneous society. They are only one of the several types of political groups in a democratic society, differing from political parties primarily in the realm of tactics. Pressure groups do not nominate candidates for public office; rather, they hope to influence public policy by gaining access to governmental agencies. Pressure groups are organized interest groups that exist because their members share certain attitudes and seek to promote their common interests or values by influencing governmental policies. By employing a variety of methods and tactics, some pressure groups have been very successful in obtaining their objectives, others less successful. Many such factors as size, social status, and cohesion can affect the success of a given pressure group. But despite the limited success of many groups—and there are endless varieties—they persist in our society.[59]

One of the many types is the *ethnic pressure group—a minority group which, because of certain societal limitations upon its members, seeks to promote governmental policies protecting them against hostile attack and to establish full economic, social, and political equality with all other ethnic groups.* Outstanding examples of ethnic pressure groups representing Negroes are the National Association for the Advancement of colored People (NAACP), Southern Christian Leadership Conference (SCLC), Congress of Racial Equality (CORE), and Student Coordinating Committee (SCC), formerly the Student Nonviolent Coordinating Committee (SNCC).

Negro pressure groups have a long history. Like Negro political activity, the earliest Negro petitions for freedom began on an individual basis.[60] Later, to the standard pressure tactic of issuing petitions was added that of violence. The numerous slave rebellions attest to this fact; but here again, these protests were mainly on an individual basis. Significant group activity had to await the emergence of a shared interest group, a compelling force which would weld together those who shared common characteristics and common interests. It had to wait for the awareness that group activity is much more fruitful than individual activity.

The discrimination, prejudice, and harshness that Free Negroes and slaves alike faced in seventeenth and eighteenth century America soon provided the impetus for such a movement. The rise of such independent Negro institutions as churches and educational facilities furthered the movement. But until the appearance of the concept of nationalism—a strong group feeling about one's nature and destiny—the movement inched along at a snail's pace. For all practical purposes, the clarion call for Negro nationalism was issued in 1829 by David Walker. Walker was a Free Black who went north to escape terrorism and oppression. His appeal was a privately printed pamphlet in which he called upon slaves and Free Blacks to help one another in eradicating racism from American society.[61]

The theme of Negro nationalism was taken up by the national Negro conventions in the 1830s and 1840s. Although the pioneer convention of 1830 declared that "we shall cheerfully vindicate the cause of our oppressed people," it considered emigration the only solution. However, subsequent national conventions concerned themselves with many facets of Negro life; for example, they resolved to "boycott slave-made products and to petition state and national legislation against slavery and discrimination." This action continued with rising intensity until the Civil War. It was in these years that the desire for partisan political action began to be expressed.

Part of the statement issued by the national Negro convention in 1853 reveals a great deal about the pressure tactics and methods of these conventions. The convention delegates argued that they were "honest men honestly appealing for righteous judgment." They im-

plored the American people, "in the name of all that is just and mag-
nanimous among men, to be freed from all the unnatural hindrances
and impediments with which American customs and American legislation have hindered our progress and improvements." Thus the methods
of most Negro pressure groups in the pre-Civil War period relied
heavily upon moral suasion and mass propaganda. (The religious and
ethical premises of the various petitions reproduced in Aptheker's
Documentary History lend credence to this thesis.) Working within
political parties offered little hope because of the diminishing suffrage
rights of the Free Negro. Lobbying, electioneering, and strikes also
proved useless. And the issuance of petitions, especially to Congress,
was stymied because of the "gag rule" that enabled tabling of abolitionist petitions and memorials in the House of Representatives before they
had been read.[62]

The deliberate destruction of abolitionist mail in the South likewise hampered the circulation of antislavery ideas. But the Negro
national conventions found allies in the abolitionist movement. And it
was partly abolitionist efforts that focused the country's attention on
the slavery issue, which ultimately led to the intersectional strife that
southerners call the War Between the States and northerners call the
Civil War. The various Negro interest groups could not have achieved
those ends alone because of their limited resources and restricted freedom. But the inclusion of an all-Negro group in the abolitionist movement lent it authenticity and disproved the argument that only white
liberals participated in the antislavery crusade. Moreover, the need
for alliances among pressure groups to attain their objectives is well
known.[63] Independent action by certain Negro pressure groups failed
to achieve even the restoration of suffrage for Free Negroes or the
removal of legal disabilities placed upon them, to say nothing about
the slaves. In other words, moral suasion, petitions, and propaganda
failed to achieve anything significant for unaligned Negro pressure
groups. Yet these same tactics did achieve certain desired ends when
they were used by a number of groups acting together. However, the
ineffectiveness of the tactics says less about their inadequacy than
about the immaturity of these groups and their search for meaning and
direction in an evolving society. A parallel can be drawn with other
pressure groups in American society at that time. As a case in point,
the women's suffrage societies and the temperance movements met

with little success acting independently during this period; they did achieve some of their goals later when alliances had been formed with other pressure groups.[64]

The Niagara Movement

After the Civil War, Negro pressure groups such as the Equal Rights League, about which more will be said later, undertook third party activity. In other instances group activity, such as occurred in labor unions, evolved in a separate manner, but the need for concerted widespread action was lessened because of strong Negro loyalty to the Republican party. Major pressure group activity did not appear until the restoration of white supremacy and the decline of Negro allegiance to the Republican party. The first major organization to evolve from this situation was the Niagara Movement.

The Niagara Movement was convened by a group of radical Negro intellectuals in 1905 at Fort Erie, New York, not far from Niagara Falls. They had high hopes of forming a national protest organization with branches in the several states to do battle against all forms of segregation and discrimination—and, incidentally, against Booker T. Washington's gradualist and conciliatory policies. These policies, they believed, undercut Negroes' rights for a pittance and even subverted their courage to protest. The Niagara Movement held two additional meetings but did no more than issue proclamations. The organization was stymied by Booker T. Washington. It was not deemed wise for ambitious young Negroes to join this organization because Washington was *the* spokesman for the race and any opposition to his stance would jeopardize their future. Thus by 1910 the Niagara Movement had virtually ceased to exist.

The National Association for the Advancement of Colored People

There were significant rumblings elsewhere. After a bloody race riot in Springfield, Illinois, in August 1908, several white liberals called for a conference of Negroes and whites on the hundredth anniversary of

Lincoln's birth to realize the dream of democracy for all Americans. Of course, the Negro intellectuals who had inspired the Niagara Movement were invited. Out of this conference in 1910 emerged the National Association for the Advancement of Colored People (NAACP).[65] This organization, a combination of Negroes and whites, possessed the ingredients of a successful protest movement—articulateness, intellectual foresight, and general awareness. This grouping is also reminiscent of some of the strategy that existed during the pre-Civil War period when a number of Free Negro and white abolitionist groups joined forces to strengthen their protest. The coalition seemed to have sprung from the need for meaningful, concrete programs and action. Although the major traditional tactic of the NAACP has been to work through legal channels, it has resorted to sit-ins, boycotts, and protest demonstrations on occasion. Like the pre-Civil War organizations, however, it has relied mainly on moral suasion to gain its objectives by exerting pressure on the public, or legislators, or the Administration, and through the courts.

Pressure on the public became the prime NAACP tactic because court decisions, legislation, and Administration proclamations would be useless without the sanction of favorable public opinion. Thus the organization has used educational propaganda to develop a favorable public attitude toward the Negro race. Every channel of the mass media is used. The public relations department makes elaborate efforts to detail newsworthy items of Negro achievers. In addition, the program seeks to improve Negro self-concepts.[66]

These methods have at times proved successful in a limited way. Generally speaking, public opinion and attitudes are subject to rapid change. Specifically, some liberals have an ingrained respect for the law and are able to recognize and acknowledge the discrepancy between the theory and practice of the American creed. On the local level, southerners especially have been convinced little, if at all. Moreover, in its efforts to increase its effectiveness through propaganda, the NAACP has projected an image and developed a strategy that have brought it increased opposition. In the final analysis, NAACP's policy of bringing pressure to bear on the public has depended too much on the mood of the public and the temper of the times.

Pressure on legislators also is not without its weaknesses. Since effective lobbying at times depends on money and voters, NAACP accomplishments in this area have not always been encouraging. The financial needs of the organization have often exceeded its resources. And the reliance of Negro voters in the North on political machines made many legislators, even those from Negro districts, unresponsive. Why worry about the wishes of an electorate whose vote had been bought and paid for prior to elections? This situation was further complicated by the early pattern of one-party Negro voting and the dwindling Negro vote in the South.[67]

Pressure on the Administration has been much more fruitful. Memoranda, petitions, private meetings, and voter support through the years led to the establishment of the Fair Employment Practices Commission (FEPC) on equality of treatment and opportunity; federal Negro appointments such as William H. Hastings' designation as governor of the Virgin Islands; and presidential initiative in the area of civil rights. But the major weakness here is one of administrative orientation. Some presidents and governments have been liberal-minded or publicly sensitive to liberal attitudes while others have not. More important, although some gains have been made, these have been insignificant as compared to what was needed.

In the case of the courts, the NAACP pressure tactic of test legislation has met with overwhelming success. Its record prior to 1958 is remarkable: 26 victories out of 28 cases before the Supreme Court. This record includes the landmark *Brown* v. *Board of Education* case (1954) that resulted in the repudiation of the separate-but-equal doctrine in education. Since 1958, many additional victories have been won, including the landmark decision in *Heart of Atlanta Motel* v. *United States* (1964), which gave blacks free access to public accommodations throughout the country on an equal basis with whites. The organization's victory in *South Carolina* v. *Katzenbach,* which held the 1965 Voting Rights Act constitutional, launched an era of emerging black politics.

But legalism, like the other NAACP tactics, is not flawless. It is time-consuming. It is very costly, involves only a few people, and depends on the attitude of the Supreme Court at the time. The alternatives of pressure on public opinion and legalism have been the most successful tactics of the association, but they too are not without their limitations. Besides these weaknesses in methods and techniques, certain organizational and operational weaknesses exist. The association lacks a strong financial base, mass support, and a fundamental socio-economic program.[68] In addition, the interracial composition of the organization and its dependence on interracial good will, sentimental liberalism, personal aggrandizement, overcentralization, and ideological infiltration have further curtailed its effectiveness. These organizational, operational, tactical, and strategic weaknesses left a void that was filled in the 1950s and 1960s by a rash of new pressure groups with new and revolutionary tactics.

Therefore, the NAACP, the major Negro pressure group, made only intermittent and largely superfiicial and inconsequential progress in advancing the cause of the Negro in America. The group concentrated on publicity and civil rights issues, treating symptoms rather than causes—inequality and the folkways and mores of the South. The results indicated the need for new directions, new organizations, and new ways of working. The old ways were at times inadequate and at times useless.

Negro Third Party Activity

Since working through the major political parties and relying on pressure group activity have been unsuccessful more often than not, what have been the results of minor or third party activities?

Negro activity in third parties has met the same obstacles that were encountered in the major parties and in pressure group activity. The prejudices of some of the Liberty party members and Free-Soilers before the Civil War were widespread. These attitudes either alienated the Negro or so affected party policies as to render them ineffective insofar as the Negro cause was concerned.[69] After the Civil War, such third parties as the Prohibitionists, Liberal Republicans, and Union Labor sought the black vote only to win elections and paid scant attention to Negro needs or desires. In fact, if the minor party lost, as was generally the case, Negro suffrage was vigorously denounced; the Negro was accused of being a corrupting element and an obstacle to progressive reforms.[70]

The last of these criticisms was much used by the demagogues of the Populist party when it started to decline. Although the party vigorously sought the Negro vote in some localities with promises of equality, it had little to show for these promises. The Populist party did in some states stabilize black politicians in office and helped to secure the establishment of black state and local public educational facilities —which were of course segregated. On the negative side, the Populists' clamor for black votes lent impetus to the movement to remove Negroes from the political arena altogether. By the beginning of the twentieth century, third parties such as those linked with progressive movements in the South had capitulated to lily-whitism.

Other third parties such as the Socialists and Communists offered blacks an ideology, but nothing practical in terms of erasing prejudice or improving their condition. Those Negroes who came in close contact with such groups usually ended up alienated and disillusioned.

The Union party and the Dixiecrat movement, both conservative in nature, made limited overtures to Negroes but to no avail. The Progressive party of 1948, however, made a strong effort to attract Negro supporters, especially in the South. The party's policies for the Negro and the appeals of its leader, former Vice-President Henry Wallace, made significant inroads into the black community before Truman's civil rights program appropriated its appeal. When Truman, the Democratic party's presidential nominee, established a civil rights committee and endorsed the committee's recommendations, he sounded the death knell for black support of Wallace's Progressivism.

Negro third party activity has been more in the nature of a protest movement than anything else.[71] Generally speaking, major Negro third party activities have been hampered because of the minor parties' inability to win. With no chance of winning, a vote cast is a vote thrown away.

All in all, the achievements of Negroes through third party activities are not easy to pinpoint. It has been alleged that their participation in the antislavery parties increased internal dissension and led to the Civil War, that their activity in the Populist party spurred the rise of Negro public education in the South, that their involvement with the Progressive party in 1948 produced a favorable Democratic stand on civil rights. Although it is possible that these allegations are true, it is likewise true that these accomplishments were due at least in part to other factors.

* * *

Summarizing, then, the totality of Negro progress achieved through normal channels of political activity seems to be somewhat mixed. There *has* been progress, yet it seems slight when compared with the goals and objectives which Negroes sought politically. In the South, Negroes accomplished little through major or minor parties and pressure groups, especially for the black masses. Here prejudice and discrimination have been at their worst and most adverse. What is more, the overt political expressions of this discrimination have made it almost impossible for Negroes to use the normal political channels in the South—or anywhere in the country, for that matter—for meaningful change. In the North, prejudice, discrimination, and racism also have limited Negro achievements, but the situation has not been as bad in the North as in the South.

Fed by frustration and desperation, the belief soon grew that only all-black organizations could make a meaningful change in Negro life. This belief did not emerge all at once and was not a twentieth century phenomenon. It began almost with the inception of our political party system and has continued to grow along with the failure and the inability of interracial political organizations to achieve the objectives of the black community. Negroes thus have been forced to rely more and more upon their own resources, and this reliance has led to the creation of black political organizations and parties both in the North and in the South.

This separatist trend began early in black American history. We shall examine in detail in the following chapter the emergence of organizations such as the national Negro convention movement, Equal Rights League, National Afro-American League, and Black and Tan Republican parties. The first of these was an all-black movement. Although not completely political, it attempted to act as both a national and a state political unit, and at times attempted collective bargaining with other political parties and pressure groups. When this strategy failed, it tried to act as a black pressure group—as we shall see.

2

BLACK POLITICAL ORGANIZATIONS

AND PARTIES: 1830–1972

Separate Black Political Organizations

The history of Negro political organization in the United States spans nearly a century and a half of indignation and frustration. It would be stretching the truth to call the very first associations parties; they were hardly parties or even factions in the true sense of those words. Neither were they pressure groups in the modern sense. However, the national Negro convention movement initiated in the 1830s was—along with the convention for women's rights, the convention for colonization, and various church conventions, temperance conventions, liquor conventions, and peace conventions—part of the overall reform movement that pervaded nineteenth century America. These movements, which were the forerunners of present-day pressure groups, regularly used tactics similar to, if not identical with, the tactics of these contemporary groups. In one sense, the reform conventions represented an America in ferment. They all clamored for change, and what each group sought to promote it considered not only its own particular interest but also a statement of an interest that was for the greater good of society.

Whereas these reform conventions, including the Negro ones, succeeded in accomplishing at least some of their objectives, the Negro convention movement at times faced greater odds than its counterparts. Before the Civil War, even the Free Negro living north of the slave states was subject to considerable oppression. His right to vote was nearly everywhere suppressed, his opportunities for equal education were virtually nonexistent, other of his legal rights were easily violated and he was left with no meaningful way to win redress, his economic situation was extremely precarious, and in his daily life he encountered many forms of discrimination and was the butt of endless insults from whites. In truth, his life was far from free.

When Free Negro citizens began openly objecting to the outrages and injustices they suffered, the first protests occurred as individual acts in isolated instances. Philadelphia Negro James Forten's bitter condemnation of discriminatory statutes that were being considered by the Pennsylvania Legislature in 1813 is typical:

> What have the people of color been guilty of that they, more than others, should be compelled to register their houses, land, servants, and children? . . . The dog is protected and pampered at the board of his master, while the poor African and his descendants, whether a saint or felon, is branded at infancy. . . . Thus, it is to be hoped, that in our legislature there is patriotism, humanity, and mercy sufficient to crush this attempt upon the civil liberties of free men.[1]

This petition found support, and the discriminatory proposals failed to pass the legislature. However, the failure of large numbers of appeals was proof of the need for collective action, especially as discrimination became more overt.

The first American Negro newspaper, *Freedom's Journal,* was founded March 16, 1827. It presaged future attitudes in its very first issue by stating boldly that Free Negroes wished to plead their own cause:

> Too long have others spoken for us. Too long has the public been deceived by misrepresentations in things which concerned us dearly . . . thus with the civil rights of a people being of the greatest value, it shall ever be our duty to vindicate our brethren, when oppressed, and to lay the case before the public.[2]

The National Negro Convention Movement

By the 1830s, the emergence of the Negro press and the threat of forced repatriation posed by the rising American Colonization Society spurred Negro leaders to launch a series of great conventions in order to organize protest. The leadership of these national conventions was drawn from the ministry and from among businessmen, newspaper editors, and former slaves who had gained their freedom. These men, some forty representatives from seven states, first met in Philadelphia in 1830 and groped for a method of solving the problems facing them as a unique minority.[3] A proposal to buy land in Canada for the establishment of a Negro colony and a recommendation for the formation of a permanent national Negro convention—with local and state auxiliaries—were both adopted.

The first annual Negro convention in Philadelphia in 1830 was attended by fifteen delegates from five states. This first convention and six others, held annually from 1831 to 1836, adopted programs aimed at improving the status and security of the Free Negro population. To broaden their base and implement a variety of programs, the conventions eventually created "Phoenix societies" in northern urban centers. While the Phoenix societies were attending to local improvement, moral uplift, and educational advancement, state conventions continually petitioned for the restoration of Negro suffrage and for equality before the law. The national conventions meanwhile not only reflected these activities but adopted tactics for the ultimate uplifting of Free Blacks in the North.

However, convention leaders split over both means and ends. This dissension impaired the effectiveness of the annual conventions and led to their demise after 1836. To begin with, Negro delegates disagreed over whether they should remain in the United States and attempt to change American society or should move to Canada. Those who wanted to remain were further divided over tactics. Some, influenced by white abolitionist William Lloyd Garrison, considered moral suasion the ultimate weapon; others urged more direct political action. In addition, the prejudices of many white abolitionists prompted some Negro leaders to call for excluding them from the movement and limiting membership to Negroes. Many northern abolitionists confined their protests and efforts to the slavery issue alone and were unconcerned about improving conditions in general for Negroes. The feeling persisted in white abolitionist circles that Negroes were inferior to whites. The same group of Negro leaders who called for an all-black movement were convinced of the impossibility of achieving racial equality and therefore urged the establishment of separate black institutions. They were opposed by many wealthy Negroes such as Robert Puris and James Forten, who felt that such institutions would perpetuate inequality and discrimination.

After the 1836 national convention, several constituent state organizations withdrew from the national association and declared their independence. Meeting annually from 1836 through the 1840s, these state organizations sought in vain to relieve the plight of Free Negroes. For instance, when the 1837 Pennsylvania Constitutional Convention moved to disfranchise the Free Negro population, Negroes organized and petitioned vigorously. They held a mass meeting the following year and issued a strong protest, addressed to the people of the state, demanding the restoration of their rights. They complained, "When you have taken from an individual his right to vote, you have made the government in regard to him, a mere despotism, and you have taken steps towards making it a despotism to all." Therefore, their petition continued, "we lay our claim before you, with the warning that no amendments . . . can compensate for the loss of . . . equal rights, nor for the conversion into enemies of 40,000 friends." [4]

A similar situation occurred earlier in New York State, where the Reform Convention of 1821 effectively disfranchised the majority of Free Negroes by tightening residence and property qualifications. Negroes continually protested these stricter requirements, blaming their gradually worsening plight and degradation on disfranchisement. Numerous state conventions were held in New York to devise measures for gaining relief from such political disabilities. In other states similar conventions were held to protest political inequities or the denial of equal educational facilities. The barrage of petitions, memorials, and other forms of moral plea was partially successful; it led to some concessions in the area of educational facilities.

Despite divisive factionalism within the national movement, the national Negro convention managed to reconvene, after seven years, in 1843 in Buffalo, New York. The revival of the movement was due less to increasing unity than to the influence of the new Liberty party, which called for the abolition of slavery and sought to accomplish this end by political means. But the split in the abolitionist ranks over means—political action versus moral suasion—deeply affected the national Negro convention movement.[5]

The moral suasionists, under the influence of Garrison and led by the foremost Negro abolitionist, Frederick Douglass, mounted formidable opposition to the political activists. But the activists represented the wave of the future. In the 1843 convention they called for total support for the Liberty party and strengthened their position by securing approval of a resolution, with only seven dissenting votes, sanctioning the party's activities. But the resolution was limited in its impact by the Douglass forces, who had at least forced the activists to argue their cause and to reject Henry Highland Garnet's address to the convention urging slaves to engage in violent insurrection. Thus at the adjournment of the session, although the political activists had dominated, their victory was not complete.

After 1843 many state conventions leaned toward political action, but Douglass's prominence and stature made him an overriding influence. In the 1847 national convention he was appointed vice-president, and in 1848 he was elected president. Yet even Douglass soon recognized the seriousness of the rift in the movement between militants and moderates. To override petty jealousies, bridge fundamental differences, and secure support for objectives, in 1848 Douglass proposed a National League of Colored People, which he hoped would create harmony between factions and result in a well-coordinated program that would increase the effectiveness of Negro protest.[6] But because of continuing strife in the Negro movement, which was moving away from his position in support of moral suasion and toward activism, Douglass failed to gain significant backing for this proposal.

After the 1848 convention the national Negro convention movement remained dormant for five years. An external influence—the passage of the Fugitive Slave Law in 1850—revitalized concerted action in the 1850s. In the interim there had been a breach between Douglass, one of the stalwarts of the abolitionist movement, and Garrison. By the time of the resumption of national Negro conventions in 1853, Douglass had shifted his viewpoint from moral suasion to political action.

In July 1853, 114 delegates from nine states met in Rochester, New York, to consider an appropriate plan of political action. Once again discussion centered around education and propaganda. A national Negro press was proposed but never approved, and a petition addressed to the people of the United States, which was read to the delegates, demanded among other things that Negroes be given "the complete and unrestricted right of suffrage." In addition, the petition demanded that all colleges and schools be open to Negroes, that whites and blacks receive equal justice before the law, and that all existing discriminatory laws be repealed immediately. The convention reconvened on October 16, 1855, and reaffirmed these positions; the movement on the national level was dissipated over the following years.

Despite its ultimate dissolution, the national Negro convention movement succeeded in encouraging Negro independence and self-reliance. Through numerous state and local auxiliaries, the national organizations attempted to create among Negroes a new, positive self-image, emphasizing self-respect, confidence, and dignity. In terms of politics, the conventions applied significant pressure on the public by issuing an unceasing stream of petitions, addresses, and memorials and by establishing Negro newspapers to counteract anti-Negro propaganda.

Reliance on moral suasion as a major tactic met with opposition as soon as the Liberty party and other antislavery parties began gaining support. Many members of the convention movement came to appreciate the usefulness of political action in a democratic context. The establishment of a new political party was encouraging inasmuch as the old parties had sought Negro support without fulfilling Negro expectations. Negro leaders had initially rejected political activity because the number of Negro voters was limited, because the position of the Negro people was precarious from a political standpoint, and because a strong feeling of Negro nationalism was lacking. But increasingly with every convention and with the growth of antislavery parties, the political activists gained adherents.

Thus the quasi-political tactics of the early Negro conventions gave way to the politically conscious support of antislavery parties in this later phase. But major Negro political activity by the national conventions was ultimately hampered by the limited number of Negro voters and their allegiance to unscrupulous political groupings. Perhaps, had Negroes been able to retain their suffrage rights, unified political action might have been more effective. In other words, the limited pressure of the national conventions could have been significantly translated into bloc voting if disfranchisement had not curtailed the Negro vote. Lacking this, the national conventions' attempts at meaningful political action were clearly limited.

The Politics of the Equal Rights League

The next major all-Negro movement was the National Equal Rights League, an outgrowth of the national Negro conventions which had resumed activity during the Civil War. Prior to the 1864 presidential election, a National Convention of Colored Citizens convened in October at Syracuse, New York. A total of 140 delegates, including 7 from southern states, established the National Equal Rights League (NERL) and elected Frederick Douglass president.[7]

Although Negro equality in general was its goal, the particular target of NERL was *political* equality—specifically, the right to vote. The delegates to the founding convention proclaimed that Negroes had earned the franchise and that, furthermore, the American people had virtually contracted an obligation to grant it. "Why," asked the delegates, "are we so urgent for possession of this particular right over others?" Simply because, their petition continued, "in a republican country where general suffrage is the rule, personal liberty, the right to testify in courts of law, the right to hold, buy, and sell property, and all other rights become mere privileges held at the option of others where we are excepted from general liberty." The vote, they believed, would enable them to establish means of controlling violent anti-Negro mobs, of curbing corrupt politicians, and of gaining a measure of material security. "The possession of that right is the keystone to the arch of human liberty," they asserted.[8] Moreover, they maintained an additional basic reason for granting the right to vote to "colored men" was that, when the Civil War came to an end, Negro suffrage would keep former slaveholders from restoring themselves to power.

The League decided to pursue this chief objective of securing Negro suffrage by using arguments, protests, memorials, and petitions to appeal to the conscience of the American people and by taking advantage of legal processes where possible. To help secure these goals, the NERL executive board urged the immediate establishment of state and local League auxiliaries, which were also intended to deal with discriminatory problems of a local nature. In addition, agents were hired to agitate where auxiliaries could not be established.

This appeal was greeted with enthusiasm. State organizations were formed in most of the major cities, both North and South. And in less than a year most state governments had received petitions, delegations, or memorials requesting suffrage for Negroes. One notably active auxiliary was the Ohio Equal Rights League, which not only demanded the removal of all restrictions on the rights of Negroes in that state, on January 10, 11, 12, 1965, but endorsed Abraham Lincoln for President and called for the installation of abolitionist Salmon P. Chase as Chief Justice of the Supreme Court.[9] Such states as New York and Pennsylvania also had strong and active League organizations which fought unremittingly for full Negro equality.

On the national level, after the parent organization's first regular annual meeting in Cleveland in October 1865 it submitted a petition to Congress demanding adoption of a constitutional amendment guaranteeing a "republican form of government" in every state by voiding all previous discriminatory legislation. The following year Frederick Douglass, who was still one of the League's leaders, sought to inform the general public of the Negroes' right to the ballot by making speeches throughout the country.[10] His argument for enfranchisement grew more insistent as President Andrew Johnson's Reconstruction policy appeared to grow somewhat less positive with each passing day. On February 7, 1866, a NERL delegation led by Douglass called on President Johnson to express their hope that Negroes would soon obtain full enfranchisement. But the President rejected the idea, insisting that the states, not Congress or the President, should decide who could vote. He went on to say that granting the vote to Negroes would spark a race war in the South between Negroes and their natural antagonists, poor whites. And finally, Johnson argued, the solution to the Negroes' problems lay not in the ballot but in the emigration of Negroes from the South.

Following this exchange, the Douglass delegation left the White House and met with a group of Radical Republican congressmen, who gave the idea of Negro enfranchisement a sympathetic hearing. Immediately after this interview, Congress passed a law enlarging the scope of the Freedmen's Bureau, which had been set up in 1865 to care for refugee Negroes in the South. In fact, the congressional Radicals launched an offensive against President Johnson's Reconstruction policies even as Douglass was resuming his speaking tour. When public backing for Negro suffrage then increased, the President reacted by mounting a vigorous attack on the Radicals, which ultimately served to cut further into his already waning public support. The NERL leadership, mainly in the person of Douglass, gained outspoken allies from among sympathetic groups, and the Radicals intensified their efforts to override the President's policies.

The Equal Rights League and the Women's Suffrage Movement

Among the groups sympathetic to the idea of Negro suffrage were women's suffrage organizations. Although inactive during the Civil War, they afterward revived their campaign for equality and merged with NERL in May 1866 to form the American Equal Rights Association, whose chief objective was extension of suffrage to Negroes and to all women.[11] Shortly thereafter Douglass, who was chosen one of the vice-presidents, clashed with the female leaders on the issue of the Association's proper emphasis. Each accused the other of selfish motives—of seeking enfranchisement of only his (or her) sex. Despite these difficulties, some joint action did result from the union—for instance, joint petitioning of the New York Legislature to permit colored men and women to vote for delegates to the state constitutional convention. But soon renewed internal dissension put an end to even such limited cooperation.

Meanwhile, pressure from NERL and the congressional Radical effort resulted in Johnson's near-impeachment, Grant's election, Radical congressional control of Reconstruction policies, and adoption of the Fifteenth Amendment. By the time of the amendment's ratification on March 30, 1870, anti-Negro feeling and petty internal jealousies had undermined the American Equal Rights Association. At a convention in Albany one year earlier, the suffragettes had broken with the Douglass forces, dissolved the Association, and completely divorced themselves from the issue of Negro suffrage with the formation of a new organization, the National Woman Suffrage Association.[12]

The adoption of the Fifteenth Amendment represented NERL's greatest victory and vindicated its political strategy of combining moral suasion with public pressure. The help of allies, particularly such Radical congressmen as Senators Thaddeus Stevens and Charles Sumner, also proved to be of great significance. NERL suffered from a lack of coordination at either the state or the national level—the same organizational weakness that combined with internal differences of opinion on many levels to spell the League's ultimate downfall. But its strong national leadership and help from its allies enabled it at least momentarily to overcome this handicap.

Although several state NERL affiliates remained active after the adoption of the Fifteenth Amendment, the majority of them—and the parent organization—all but disbanded. With the acquisition of the vote, many Negroes moved immediately into the political arena, some even gaining elective office on the local, state, or national level. On the other hand, many splinter organizations were formed throughout the country to petition Congress and state legislatures for civil rights legislation and for laws prohibiting discriminatory practices.[13] This sort of activity was limited in scope, however, and at times was overshadowed by other events, such as political contests, labor activities, and the Freedmen's Bank fiasco. In Reconstruction, the major political contests which attracted so much interest were those in which blacks running on the Republican ticket sought nearly every state, local and municipal office. The campaigns of these black politicians in all of the states of the old confederacy were political firsts and a significant step for those who had just dropped the chains of slavery. For whites it was an inkling of things to come—a new day in which the bottom rail would be on top. Not only did blacks make political gains during Reconstruction, they ventured into the economic sphere. In December, 1869, black laborers formed their own union, the Negro National Labor Union, which sought not only to advance the interest of the black worker, but also to organize him nationwide so that his demands could bring pressure to bear upon the government and industry.

Prior to the formation of a National Labor Union, the federal government helped blacks to establish in April, 1865, the Freedmen's Saving and Trust Company whose business was confined to blacks. However, the bank failed in June 1874 in the midst of a general depression because of poor loans, mismanagement, etc., after thousands of blacks had deposited almost $3,300,000 in the bank's forty or more branches.

In other words, in both the political and economic sphere blacks were attempting to make advances but ran into difficulty in each area as white public opinion and assistance looked elsewhere. White labor unions fought the black ones and white politicians removed black ones. And whatever advancement blacks had made ended almost with Reconstruction. Blacks were additionally hampered by an apathetic public, which felt that Negroes would easily gain their civil and economic rights now that they had the right to vote. Despite these obstacles, Congress was prodded into passing a Civil Rights Act on March 1, 1875, having earlier passed the Enforcement Acts—dubbed the "Force Bills"—making it a criminal offense to prevent Negroes from voting or otherwise exercising their voting rights.

But soon the forces opposing black rights gained momentum. In the Compromise of 1877, President Rutherford B. Hayes agreed to withdraw all but a token force of federal troops from the South, which signaled the collapse of protection for Negroes. Then in 1883 the Supreme Court declared the Civil Rights Act of 1875 unconstitutional, while the restoration of home rule in the South was an almost total, and often violent, success. The tremendous loss of life and property and the infringement of voting rights experienced by southern Negroes made apparent the immediate need for a new national Negro political organization.

The Politics of the National Afro-American League

The first attempts to solve the problems created by the restoration of home rule—several mass migrations of Negroes from the South—were not completely successful, and thus the incentive for some form of national organization remained.

T. Thomas Fortune was a black journalist who became editor of the *New York Age* and the *New York World*. Fortune advocated black independence in politics. He also supported the unionization of Negro labor and industrial education for blacks. In 1900, he joined forces with Booker T. Washington and helped establish the National Negro Business League. He died in 1928. Earlier, thanks largely to Fortune's persistent efforts, the National Afro-American League (NAAL) was formed in Chicago in January 1890. A total of 141 delegates from 23 states and the District of Columbia met and discussed possible methods of improving the Negro's condition. Fortune and W. A. Pleger (a black Republican in Georgia and editor of the newspaper, the *Athens' Blade*), in their keynote addresses, justified formation of the League by pointing out, and decrying, the increasing incidence of disfranchisement of Negro voters, mob violence and lynchings, and discriminatory practices directed at Negroes in every public place throughout the South.

After some debate, the convention delegates drew up a constitution clearly stating their objectives and the means for securing them. The prime stated objective of NAAL was to secure for Negroes the full privileges of citizenship in "every avocation of life." This inclusive objective could be achieved, the delegates hoped, by using the mass media to create sympathetic public opinion and by appealing to the courts for redress in every instance of denial of rights, constitutional or otherwise. NAAL, like the earlier NERL, sought to achieve its ends through legal and otherwise peaceful methods of a quasi-political nature. But NAAL differed by adopting a nonpolitical posture. In addition to describing its objectives and the means by which to achieve them, NAAL provided for the establishment and creation of local and state leagues, similar to the auxiliaries of NERL.[14]

Like NERL, NAAL was never a strong organization. Plagued by personal jealousies and internal dissension, it lapsed into dormancy after a couple of meetings. But like the national conventions of the 1830s and 1840s, it was later revived—on September 15, 1898—as the National Afro-American Council. The following year, this organization merged with the National Association of Colored Women and issued four strongly worded resolutions—two condemning the prevalence of anti-Negro mob violence and the lynching of Negroes, the third asserting that it was the duty of the federal government to protect Negroes from such harsh treatment, and the last indicating the convention's willingness to pursue its objectives through peaceful means.

In May of the same year, the National Afro-American Council issued a proclamation urging the Negro people to protest the indignities they suffered by fasting all day on June 2 and calling for Negro churches to hold prayer vigils on June 4 to further protest their oppression. Following this nationwide activity, some state groups—notably the Massachusetts branch—sent an open letter to President William McKinley condemning his lax attitude toward the problems of Negroes as well as his imperialist policies regarding Cuba.[15]

Although the League–Council and its local branches were active for about a decade, their achievements were not particularly impressive. Internal disagreements discouraged progress. Some members advocated direct reprisals for lynchings and other acts of violence committed against Negroes; others still sought to work within the successive Republican administrations or favored the old methods of gradualism, or sought self-advancement, or hoped to improve the national organization. Ultimately, the decline of public opinion favorable to Negroes, the ascendancy of the doctrine of Social Darwinism, and the partial capitulation of Negro leadership to the passive ideology of Booker T. Washington spelled its doom. Under such circumstances, the League accomplished little as compared with some of its forerunners.

Early Black Third Party Politics

During the waning years of the National Afro-American Council, Negro participation in third party activities increased markedly. Because neither the Democratic nor the Republican party at the time encouraged Negro membership and participation, Negroes sought allies elsewhere and found them within the rising Populist movement.[16] In fact, because of such alliances, in several states a few Negro public officials managed to secure re-election after the Compromise of 1877 —at least until Populist demogogues began clamoring for even further Negro disfranchisement.

Spurned by both major parties and disillusioned with the declining third party movement, Negroes virtually abandoned protest and political organizations. The attempt to "put the Negro in his place" was further abetted by the influence of Booker T. Washington, who almost single-handedly silenced agitation for rights and rendered ineffective the national Negro protest organizations. Nevertheless, some minor state and local action continued. The Negro Protective party in Ohio, for instance, ran a gubernatorial candidate, S. J. Lewis, who polled about 5,000 votes in a futile effort to capture the 1897 state election.[17] Similar attempts within the Union Labor party in other states met with no success.

Attempts to organize Negroes politically on a national level resumed with the creation of the Negro National Democratic League in 1900 and continued with the emergence of an all-Negro national political organization, the National Liberty party, in March 1904. The National Liberty party nominated George Edwin Taylor, formerly president of the Negro National Democratic League, at a national convention in St. Louis. Some 36 states sent delegates to the July convention, where they formulated a platform demanding complete Negro enfranchisement and restoration of Negroes' civil rights that had been gained during Reconstruction and lost after 1877. But this party, as well as the Negro National Democratic League and the National Negro American Political League, did little beyond indicting the policies and activities of both major parties, and all three soon disappeared from the political arena. The accomplishments of these parties were mainly educational in nature. Although they kept the protest spirit alive, the range of their success was extremely limited.

The Rise of National Black Protest Organizations

The next major national mobilization of Negro protest sentiment was the Niagara Movement, which ultimately led to the creation of the NAACP in 1910. But the NAACP made slow headway, and it was not long before an increase in the violence committed against Negroes resulted in new attempts at forming an effective national organization.

In the wake of Booker T. Washington's death in 1915, Negro social and political thought began expressing itself in a variety of forms: in the gradualism of the NAACP legal program, in the radical appeals of Socialists and Communists, in Marcus Garvey's evocation of race-consciousness, in the religious overtures of Father Divine and Daddy Grace, and in a spate of new organizations that promised to lead the Negro to salvation. But the multiplicity of solutions simply compounded the problem. As one Negro observer saw it, Negroes were "now divided into a hundred separate camps . . . [with] untold waste and friction, rivalry, and jealous antagonism." According to the same observer, even after every effort had been made within these separate alignments, "the problem [persisted] in all of its perplexing forms and phases."

Attempting to cut through this organizational confusion and tactical chaos, black intellectual leader Dean Kelly Miller of Howard University proposed a "Great Sanhedrin"—an elite council modeled after the high tribunal that settled all important civil, criminal, and religious matters in ancient Jerusalem—"to formulate a program and achieve unity of efforts." This Sanhedrin, Miller felt, should avoid politics because airing fundamental political differences would only divide the delegates and doom the organization from the start. The organization, Miller maintained, should instead focus its efforts on arousing a sense of unity and race-consciousness among Negroes.

Negroes responded positively to Miller's clarion call: In February 1924, 500 representatives of 50 Negro organizations assembled in Chicago. Among the delegates were James Weldon Johnson of the NAACP, Dr. Channing Tobias of the "colored YMCA," Dr. George E. Hayes of the Federal Council of Churches, and the future president of Howard University, Mordecai Johnson. During the convention, delegates offered an assortment of social, economic, and educational proposals for improving the conditions of Negro urban life and the state of Negro health, for providing financial assistance to Negro farmers and students, and for encouraging participation of Negro women in civil affairs. Every area was discussed except politics, yet there was no unanimity of opinion, no unity of purpose. After Miller was elected President the Sanhedrin adjourned, with little more to show for its efforts than a poorly worded resolution and a weak organizational structure.

Almost immediately, the programs and positions of Miller's organization came under attack. While the failure of the delegates to take a stand on political issues was bound to be controversial, their critics further lambasted them for failing to speak out on "lynching, segregation, and industrial discrimination." In *The Crisis,* official NAACP organ, W. E. B. DuBois later that year attacked the Sanhedrin for failing to address itself to such vital issues as the Ku Klux Klan, housing conditions, and discrimination in general.

Increasing criticism of the Sanhedrin and its nonpolitical character, coupled with old jealousies, internal dissension, and Miller's inability to serve as president full time, sealed its doom. It collapsed the year that it was founded. The Sanhedrin's avoidance of politics, a stance considered necessary in order to ensure its perpetuation, was the very thing that destroyed it.[18]

Although the Sanhedrin failed, the idea was not discarded. A similar pan-national organization was initiated and fostered by Communists in an effort to influence Negro organizations from within. The best way to proceed, the Communists reasoned—especially in a milieu of a multiplicity of Negro organizations—was through an organization similar to the Sanhedrin. Their call for a labor congress brought together representatives of Negro labor unions, farmer's organizations, fraternal societies, and benevolent associations. This convention established the American Negro Labor Congress in Chicago in October 1925. Its purpose was "to unify the efforts—of all organizations of Negro workers and farmers—for the abolition of discrimination, persecution, and exploitation of the Negro race and working people. . . ." To achieve these objectives, the Congress was to function through local councils composed of Negro labor unions, Negro agricultural organizations, and Negro factory workers' groups. But these local units were never formed because the Congress was generally mistrusted as a nucleus of Communist agitation for a Negro Communist state and for revolutionary action against imperialist forces. Once the role of the Communists became evident—after two conventions—disillusioned Negro delegates, who had a different concept of how a functional organization should go about solving their pressing problems, allowed the Congress to fade into oblivion.[19]

Even after the demise of the Sanhedrin and the American Negro Labor Congress, the need for a coordinating organization kept the idea alive well into the 1930s—if only because of the increasing hardships brought on by the Depression and because of the indifference of white liberals and leaders.

The Politics of the National Negro Congress

The search for unity among Negro leaders after World War I had been particularly urgent. No single organization seemed sufficiently concerned with the general welfare of the race: the NAACP emphasized legal progress, the National Urban League stressed adjustment to the city, DuBois promoted his Pan-African Congress, Garvey campaigned for his Back-to-Africa movement, Father Divine emphasized spiritual values, A. Phillip Randolph and Chandler Owen sought economic and political power for the Negro labor force.[20] This specialization of focus left gaps in the program for Negro advancement, with the result that progress continued to be uneven.

The effects of this uneven development were explored at a conference on "Economic Conditions of the Negro" held in Washington in 1935 and sponsored by the Joint Committee on National Recovery and Howard University's Department of Political Economy. The conference issued a report indicating that the trend of the Depression and of recovery was forcing Negroes into an even lower economic and social position than they had formerly occupied. The report implied that the existing Negro organizations had been largely ineffective in stemming this tide and urged immediate action to rectify this condition. A small meeting held after the conference gave birth to the idea of a National Negro Congress.[21] It was to be an educational organization dedicated to the dissemination of group action techniques available to Negroes. Moreover, it was to assume the leadership in action programs dealing with the problem of Negroes' economic recovery.

John P. Davis, organizer of the Congress, advanced the idea of including all types of Negro organizations within the Congress and devised a platform for uniting them behind a program dealing with fundamental economic, social, and civil issues. In short, the Congress was deliberately designed to cut across political, ideological, philosophical, and ethnic lines in order to tackle bread-and-butter issues affecting Negroes.

The first meeting of the National Negro Congress was held in Chicago in February 1936 and lasted three days. Included among the more than 800 delegates representing over 500 organizations were trade-unionists, curious onlookers, New Dealers, old-line Republicans, ambitious young Democrats, Communists, forty-ninth-staters, Garveyites, Bahaists, publicity-seekers—in short, citizens, white and black, of every stripe. The delegates, representing in effect a conglomeration of individual organizations, debated, cajoled, argued, and proffered suggestions day and night throughout the session. Besides electing A. Phillip Randolph (president of the Brotherhood of Sleeping Car Porters) as its president and John P. Davis as executive secretary, the Congress achieved little of a substantive nature. Perhaps the chief resolution was the first one approved, which adopted a nonpartisan political posture for the organization and asserted a policy of strictly avoiding affiliation with or domination by any political grouping. After hearing endless proposals, resolutions, and protest statements, the Congress adjourned and began the tedious task of building its organizational structure. Local councils were established in many cities; the national office in Washington sent representatives to various places not staffed. A number of publications and reports of activities intended to enhance the coordinating program of the Congress were issued.

A second Congress held in October 1937 was attended by more than 1,100 delegates. This increase of more than 300 delegates over the first Congress reflected an increase in the number of Negro organizations as well as the active program of the Congress during the preceding 20 months. The second convention focused on problems of organization, growth, and—the major difficulty—finances; in fact, more time was spent on these internal issues than on the problems of Negroes or the indifference of the white public. When financial difficulties persisted after this second Congress had adjourned, the national leadership began to act on its own initiative—often without consulting either the Congress's National Executive Committee or the member organizations involved. For example, the national leaders decided to endorse the Steel Workers' Organizing Committee but failed to inform the A.F. of L. of its intentions; and it backed an anti-lynching bill without seeking NAACP counsel in advance. Such actions soon brought on internal dissension. These member organizations and others increasingly came to regard the Congress as an interloper, a nuisance, and a rival for public support in particular spheres of activity. When, as a result, member organizations started cutting back on their financial contributions, the Congress's financial difficulties rapidly worsened. To make up budget deficits and to avoid alienating member groups any further, the Congress leadership began relying on secret gifts and donations, a practice which proved fatal for the organization.

The catalyst in the process which led to the downfall of the National Negro Congress was the signing of the 1939 mutual non-aggression pact between Germany and the Soviet Union. American Communists, forced because of this cynical diplomatic maneuver to discourage American participation in the war by any and all means, sought to infiltrate the Congress, whose ties with other Negro organizations made it an ideal target for establishing a propaganda base. And so, aided by the fact that the Congress had fallen into debt, the Communists succeeded in gaining control of the third and final meeting of the Congress in April 1940. Sensing the intentions of the Communists, Randolph, the president, delivered a speech denouncing both the totalitarianism of the Soviet Union and the American Communists' reliance on Stalin's directions concerning policy. Randolph urged the Congress to remain nonpartisan and to retain its primary role as a national Negro pressure group, based largely on all-Negro organizations and reflecting the hopes and aspirations of Negroes. As he spoke, the Communists staged a demonstration and succeeded in persuading two-thirds of the audience to walk out. Subsequently, Randolph resigned as president, his position was eliminated, and the Congress capitulated to the Communist party line and faded from the scene.[22]

Although several organizations championing Negroes' civil and human rights—CORE, SNCC, and SCLC, to name just three—have emerged in recent years, no new pan-national coordinating organizations appeared until 1972.

The National Black Political Convention—1972

In the 1968 elections, three major events occurred which had a dramatic impact upon black political leaders and strategists: (1) the election of a "Law and Order" Republican (Richard Nixon), who later developed a white southern strategy in the White House; (2) the tremendous showing of a newly created third party—the American Independent Party—that captured more than 10 million votes while causing the Democrats to lose the election; and finally (3) the election of the largest number of black public officials in America's history (13 Congressmen and more than 1,600 state and local officials). The three events were not unrelated.

Wallace's third party movement in 1968 caused each party to modify its platform and its respective candidate to become concerned with racial issues. In fact, the inordinate amount of influence generated by the Wallace movement stirred and shocked the imagination in the black community, which had just begun to flex its newly acquired political muscles. And as Wallace presented his platform in detail, black politicians saw that their hoped-for political influence with the two major parties had evaporated and that the two parties were moving toward Wallace's side of the street. The basic reason that black political influence had evaporated, most observers claim, was the lack of organization and structured goals on the part of the black electorate. Hence, black political leaders and community organizers began to develop for 1972. They planned to make sure that their newly emerged political strength be felt in the major political party council and all subsequent Presidential conventions. For, from this political influence, blacks had hoped to use politics as a means to improve the life style of all black Americans.

Earlier in 1969, the 13 black Congressmen took the lead by organizing themselves into a Congressional Black Caucus and discussing strategies for action. After the Caucus had resolved its internal problems, it moved to help the black community.

In November 1971, a Conference of Black Elected Officials met in Washington, D. C., at the behest of Congressman Charles C. Diggs, Jr. (D. Mich), who also headed the Black Congressional Caucus. The Caucus was a prime mover of the Conference and had played a major role in calling it. At the Conference several matters were discussed, but the chief concern was a strategy for 1972. And the Conference urged regional meetings of black people to take place throughout the country as well as a planning session to be held on Sunday, January 30, 1972.

Earlier in 1971, however, several black politicians like Julian Bond and John Cashin began discussing types of political strategies. One strategy called for a favorite son candidate to go to the Democratic convention, while another strategy called for a bloc of black delegates to unite and swing their votes to the best candidate. Still another strategy called for promoting a black as a Presidential candidate. Black Nationalists and militants like the popular and well-known black poet and political organizer, Imamu Amiri Baraka, cried for a national black party.[22a] But politicians like Bond wrote and spoke in public that "a national Black political party, while desirable, cannot be our national strategy for 1972." Other black leaders called for creating independent black parties in each state. As the debate raged on, the first planning sessions for the National Conventions took place the last of January.

Black representatives from more than 30 states participated in the planning session that (1) created a pre-convention organization and a state convener in each state; (2) decided how the delegates to the convention were to be selected; (3) set up committees for rules, a platform, credentials, finance, arrangements, a regional coordinator, press relations, and national support; (4) named Congressman Charles Diggs, Jr., Mayor Richard Hatcher, and Imamu Baraka as Temporary Co-Chairmen of the National Black Political Convention; and finally (5) set the dates of the convention to be March 10, 11, and 12, and the place as Gary, Indiana. But before the Convention could meet, Congresswoman Shirley Chisholm announced her candidacy for the Presidency, and by doing so she outmaneuvered both the Congressional Caucus and the planned convention. The Caucus ignored her candidacy as did the National Black Political Convention to which she was a principal speaker when it convened in March.

For the first time in the history of the United States, 3,500 black delegates and 5,800 black observers assembled in a nonpartisan convention to develop a unified political strategy as well as a national black political agenda for 1972. At the convention, numerous resolutions were passed and a declaration issued. The "Gary Declaration," as it was called, urged blacks to unite and drop their "political dependence on white men and their systems." "From the Liberty Party in the decades before the Civil War, to the Republican Party of Abraham Lincoln, we trusted in white men and white politics as our deliverers. . . . Let there be no more of that." The declaration asked blacks to move independently. When the meeting adjourned, the agenda for 1972 was still to be thrashed out and presented later to the conventions of both national parties. In addition, workers in each state were to try to create permanent political units for future years. Therefore, the National Black Convention's strategy was to see if it could get either party to accept its list of goals and priorities, with the implied notion that, whichever party did accept them, that party could expect the black vote in November.

The realities of this strategy and the impact of black political influence in 1972 depended upon George Wallace's candidacy, Shirley Chisholm's actions, and the capabilities of the National Black Convention to deliver the black vote nationally. However, there is one major additional problem: the majority of the black elected officials and the Black Congressional Caucus are Democrats. This fact limits the black influence in the Republican Party councils and partly jeopardizes the struggling independent nature of the Convention.

In fact, the future of the National Black Political Convention as a pan-national political coordinating organization depends upon its achieving truly an independent status and being a political clout. If not, it will fade like the other national black coordinating organizations. However, the National Black Political Convention is unlike the Sanhedrin, the National Negro Congress, and the American Negro Labor Congress, which all avoided politics and were destroyed by shunning things political. It would be ironic if a new black national organization like the Convention would fail because of its politicalness. The possibilities are still probable. If it does fade, then as history has indicated, a new black national organization can be expected in the future.

Problems of Black Pan-National Organizations

The problems that plagued the National Negro Congress were similar to those which doomed earlier organizations. Money, for example, was a chronic problem. In any national Negro coordinating organization, the member organizations eventually discovered that the parent body, itself in a precarious situation, was unable to fund the members properly. Even the most viable Negro organizations encounter economic difficulties from time to time. The meager economic resources of the Negro community have been hard-pressed to support such a variety of organizations. Thus a new national coordinating agency of black organizations will almost from the start be under financial strain. Although this problem is not peculiar to organizations handicapped to the extent indicated here, it is much more severe in these groups.

In addition, the black community has not always been liberal in its financial support of black organizations; black leaders throughout American history have deplored this conservative streak in the black community. The larger coordinating agencies find it particularly difficult to operate on limited budgets.

Aside from inadequate financing, the problem of internal factional disputes has weighed heavily on the fortunes of black organizations. Black thought has never been monolithic, and the search for means to achieve social justice and equality for Negroes had led down many avenues simultaneously. Every spokesman—whether truly representative or self-styled—advances his solution and asserts the soundness of his policy at the expense of another's. The history of the national Negro convention movement provides an excellent case in point: disagreements concerning goals and the techniques for achieving them kept this movement in a perpetual twilight zone. The major accomplishments it promised were never realized. This destructive factionalism itself stemmed partly from the diverse character of segregationist and discriminatory practices in various localities: Jim Crow does not look or act exactly the same everywhere, and so reactions to him necessarily differ.

Another internal problem which has periodically undermined one or another of the national Negro organizations is the tendency for some leaders to surrender to the intoxicating appeal of power and prestige. Sincere, dedicated men of principle may be perverted by ambitious drives that force them to agree to unnecessary, destructive compromises. In striving to improve his own position, a leader may erroneously equate the aims of the organization with his personal idea and beliefs, thus allowing the organization to stray from its proper program—perhaps with fatal results.

Yet another internal problem is that the strong urge for organizational permanence can lead to the creation of a bureaucratic monster that demands more attention than the problems the organization was created to overcome.

In addition to these internal difficulties, which are always linked to external success and achievements, there loom those ever present external foes who seek to capitalize on an organization's internal problems so as to subvert it for their own purposes. Being absorbed by a political party or movement is a danger for a Negro organization in proportion to the organization's internal difficulties. The Communist infiltration of the third National Negro Congress is a classic case in point. After 1940, the Congress lost all value as either a black coordinating agency or a rallying point for counsel and exchange of opinion on problems facing blacks. Instead, it served as a debating stage and propaganda ploy for justifying the Soviet invasion of Poland.[23] But—and this is important to recognize—the National Negro Congress would have been rendered just as ineffective had it been absorbed into either of the major political parties. The Republicans or the New Dealers could have gained control of the organization as easily as did the Communists—simply by filling its coffers.

Beyond the problem of such external threats lie the problems of alliances and of the peculiar character of the American political culture. The near-fatal merger of the NERL with the women's suffrage organizations is an excellent example of the difficulties that can arise out of an alliance with an outside group. The anti-Negro prejudices of some allegedly sympathetic whites did work to limit the goals and achievements of the organization and can work in the same fashion in the future. Some of these allies, whether individuals or groups, may seek to exploit the strength of the Negro group in order to further their own particular cause. In other words, in an ostensibly balanced partnership, they place their interests above those of the Negroes.[24] White liberals have proved to be a persistent problem for Negro protest organizations. Negro organizations have traditionally required white liberal financial support, influence, and political insights. On the other hand, their understanding of conditions directly affecting Negroes—an understanding necessarily limited—hampers their effectiveness and thus represents an ever present problem.

Related to this last problem is the character and nature of the American political scene. American politics, like politics elsewhere, is fundamentally a struggle for power and is concerned with who gets what, when, and how. In practice, compromises and expedient solutions count more than principles and staunch commitments. The major aim is to win.[25] But no victory is a total victory. The existence of opposing groups or potential opposing groups tends to curtail—and may even prevent—achievement for any particular group. A basic assumption of the political game is that no one group can ever attain all its objectives, as this would entail stifling the political system by repressing every other group for its own advantage. These circumstances would remove the built-in safety valve and bring the system close to disaster. Hence political achievement in a majoritarian society is of necessity partial, limited in scope. No group or organization can be entirely successful all at once; the struggle must be continuous.

But herein lies the root of a perplexing problem. Can all the members of every group struggling to attain certain ends be reasonably expected to wait patiently? Will they continue to act within the limits of our political game? Or will they give up? And what can an all but powerless group hope to achieve in a bargaining situation? What can it accomplish in a give-and-take when it is asking for more than it can give?

Even if this problem, as Myrdal asserts, is essentially a moral one,[26] can moral objectives be completely achieved in a system of competitive self-interest? In short, can politics, as we have defined it, solve an essentially moral problem? Or will the legal system, backed by state and federal constitutions, remove these deep-rooted injustices? Or will the laws simply suppress attempts to correct them, forcing injustices to a new level and new forms of expression? These questions have not yet been answered; explanations have been offered, to be sure, but to the extent that they fail to provoke action they simply add to the general frustration.

The national Negro political movement has grappled with all these problems in one degree or another. And these problems have in one way or another overwhelmed the various movements. No major national black movement has been able to overcome these obstacles with any measurable degree of success. In addition, with each passing year, new and more difficult problems arise from those which have remained unsolved for years; the rash of northern ghetto riots in the 1960s is a typical result of this situation.

But to think that the black political movements failed to accomplish any of their objectives for these reasons and because of these problems is to misunderstand or misread the past. Indeed, some of their successes may have fallen short of expectations, but they have nevertheless succeeded. The national Negro convention movement was largely responsible for awakening Negroes to the dimensions of their own problems. It brought forth the idea of self-help as a continuing means to the desired end. To some extent many black organizations have failed to state their goals explicitly, and yet they *have* achieved tangible results. Moreover, despite limited success, the drive for social justice *has* continued.[27] The adaptive ability of blacks has made them start afresh, seek new objectives and new ways to achieve old objectives. Their innovations, like the sit-ins of the 1960s, have brought some success; the new innovation of local, state, and national political parties promises even better things in the future.

Satellite Black Political Organizations

A new black political phenomenon appeared shortly after the demise of Black Reconstruction in the South. Restoration of white rule had once more reordered the balance of political power. For all intents and purposes, the Democratic party became the white man's party, whereas the Republican party was looked upon as a Negro party throughout Reconstruction and for some time thereafter. During the restoration era, the Democratic party sought to impose its hegemony in the South. Before all remnants of Republican rule could be destroyed, however, some whites made a few last-ditch efforts to salvage what remained of the southern Republican party, mainly by giving the party a face-lifting. In other words, these white Republicans tried to remove the stigma of being pro-Negro by forming a separate organization, dubbed the "lily-white Republicans," thereby ushering in more than three decades of lily-white Republicanism in the South.[28] Although the move was at best a stalling tactic, the Democrats reacted by arguing that there was no need for two parties representing the white man in the South, that the existence of the lily-white Republicans created a competitive situation in which the Negro could only too easily seize the balance of power. This then meant, argued the Democrats, that the Negro could control or at least influence lily-whitism, which was of course unacceptable to southern whites. The Democrats thus made every effort to link Republicanism with Negro domination.

On the other hand the lily-white Republicans, hungry for patronage, prestige, and political gain, sought valiantly to keep their party alive. But their attempts to remove the stigma of favoring Negroes proved futile. The Democrats ultimately won out, and one-party politics has been a way of life in the South since the turn of the century.

When the Republican party in the South began its move toward lily-whitism, the few Negroes remaining in the party formed a *parallel* political party, the Black and Tan Republicans. Although neither a separate party nor a new one, but a number of separate factions operating in many southern states and united only in name, this party sought to use the existing political structure and organization to achieve its goals rather than to create an entirely new one, as past organizers had done. In a way, the Black and Tan Republican party more closely resembled the more recent Mississippi Freedom Democratic party (MFDP—discussed in Chapter 3) or the South Carolina Progressive Democratic party (SCPDP—discussed later in this chapter) than a separate entity and new political organization like the recent Alabama Black Panther party (discussed in Chapter 4). In any case, all these Negro organizations, whether they found it convenient to use existing party organizations or to establish totally different ones, arose in reaction to the well-entrenched prejudice, discrimination, and racism in American politics.

Following the collapse of Reconstruction, several minor Black and Tan factions emerged in every southern state except Kentucky and West Virginia. Most of them—the Arkansas faction is a good example [29]—never exerted significant influence in state politics. On the other hand, the activities of the Black and Tan parties in Texas and Louisiana are worthy of mention.

The Black and Tan Factions in Texas   The roots of the Black and Tan Republican party in Texas reached back to the late 1880s, when Negro and white Republicans controlled the Negro vote in the black-belt—that is, the predominantly Negro counties—and thus controlled the counties. In one county, Fort Bend, army hostilities actually broke out between the lily-white Democratic organization and the Republican organization. This conflict, known as the Jaybird-Woodpecker War, took place between 1889 and 1890. The Jaybirds, or lily-white Democrats, resented the fact that the Woodpeckers (black Republicans and their white colleagues) had run the county politically since the end of the Civil War. After the Jaybirds had lost several hotly contested county elections, they resorted to force in order to oust the Woodpeckers from political power. This feud reached a climax on August 16, 1889, when a fight erupted in the county courthouse between the two groups. The Jaybirds won and the few white members of the Republican party in the county shifted to the Democrats. Other white Republicans in the state formed a lily-white faction within the party, and the struggle between them and the Black and Tan faction continued from the early 1880s until the late 1920s.

At state Republican party conventions throughout this period, black delegates sought to gain control; and when arguments became too heated, the blacks were thrown out or walked out, reconvening by themselves. At their own conventions, the blacks generally concentrated on nominating candidates for local office and ignored positions at the state level. In addition, they sought to influence national Republican party platforms and to win the national party's sympathy, in the hope that a party victory would bring with it a more equitable position for the Black and Tans and more patronage than their white counterparts received. In fact, however, several presidents—Theodore Roosevelt and Harding, for example—received and welcomed the support of Black and Tan factions from Texas and elsewhere in securing nominations, then proceeded to ignore the Black and Tans completely after according them passing recognition. Finally recognizing this predictable pattern of exploitation, the Texas organization chose its own electors for the presidency and vice-presidency in 1920. These electors, 15 in number, received approximately 27,000 votes in the presidential election. But this move, like the MFDP freedom elections, had little significant effect. Moreover, for years thereafter the state Republican conventions were disrupted by wrangling, with both factions haggling endlessly over the right to represent the state at the national convention and no one reaching any meaningful conclusions on other matters. Almost routinely, the Black and Tans moved to a separate convention hall, where they voted to support white candidates for governor and lieutenant-governor as well as for other major state offices.

Regarding national issues, the Texas Black and Tan party upheld the League of Nations concept, endorsed the open shop, demanded repeal of the poll tax, and strongly supported national prohibition. Public recognition of the Black and Tan Republican party in Texas, however—beyond that attributable to the outstanding leadership of such men as Norris Wright Cuney and "Gooseneck" Bill McDonald— was limited to the 27,000 statewide votes mustered in the 1920 presidential election. During the period from late 1929 to late 1932 the Black and Tan parallel political party in Texas gradually faded out of existence.[30]

For that matter, the lily-white Republicans almost died out at about the same time. Both factions were doomed from the start to limited existence or growth because of external and internal pressures, the Negro faction more so than the white. The external pressures placed upon them stemmed from the growing dominance of the one-party system in the South. Not only did they lose continually at the polls but they lacked patronage and similar benefits which political parties historically require in order to gain additional supporters. On the other hand, after the advent of Populism in the late 1880s, the Black and Tans lost members every year to the Populist movement,[31] as well as to the Progressive movement. Moreover, the number of Negro voters in Texas decreased rapidly each year after the demise of Populism and the era of disfranchisement. So for two important reasons—limited numbers of Negro voters and outside competition— the Black and Tan party was caught in a squeeze. The final blow came in 1928 when the Republican nominee for President, Herbert Hoover, endorsed lily-white Republicanism in the South. Four years later the promise of Roosevelt's New Deal led the few remaining Black and Tans to renounce the Republican party altogether. Thus in 1932 the Black and Tan Republican party in Texas, after being active for a half-century and accomplishing only minor objectives, faded from the scene.

The Black and Tan Factions in Louisiana   The Black and Tan Republican party surfaced in Louisiana as it did in Texas, out of the black-belt counties. But unlike the Texas faction, the organization in

Louisiana actually succeeded in dominating the state Republican party during the period roughly spanning the years 1920 through 1928, although it had been founded some 10 years before the onset of this period and lasted another 16 years beyond it. While it dominated the Republican party, the Black and Tan faction controlled all state patronage and even engineered the political appointment of a few Negroes to some minor federal posts in the South. The fortunes and success of the faction, however, depended more on patronage in Louisiana than it did in Texas. When patronage was extended to it, it experienced years of prosperity and growth. But from the late 1920s through 1936 the faction grew stagnant and finally withered away, for much the same reasons that killed its counterpart in Texas.

The major accomplishments of the Black and Tan party in Louisiana were the few federal appointments it obtained for Negroes. Otherwise, its achievements appear to have been meager.[32]

Black and Tans in Other States

While the Black and Tan Republicans were only strong enough to compete with regularity in Louisiana and Texas state elections, they became active in national politics in the other nine southern states. In other words, in states where the Black and Tan and lily-white Republicans didn't have enough electoral support to compete in state elections, both groups merely emerged every four years and sent a delegation to the national convention claiming to be the regular Republican party from that state. Hence, nearly every four years the credentials committee of the Republican National Convention had to decide a seating challenge arising from the South between a lily-white Republican group and a Black and Tan Republican group. Whichever group got seated and recognized received the patronage for that state for the next four years, thereby enriching whomever headed up the particular faction. A case in point is the Mississippi and South Carolina factions.

In South Carolina a white man, Joseph W. Tolbert (nicknamed Tieless Joe or Fighting Joe because he was a delegate or a contestant for a seat at every Republican National Convention from 1900 to 1944) built the Republican party in the state by organizing it into a unit which "consisted of himself, a few other whites and several hand-picked Negroes over the State." [33] The purpose of the Tolbert Black and Tan organization was to choose delegates to the National Convention and to distribute patronage to its members. Tolbert's group never made any attempt to enter state or local politics, emerging only every four years to go to the national convention.

In 1930, the lily-whites were organized and challenged the Tolbert led Black and Tans at each convention until in 1938 a wealthy lumberman, J. Bates Gerald, formed a new Black and Tan group and challenged Tolbert's old group at the 1940 convention. In 1940, the Bates-led Black and Tans were seated through 1956 when the remnants of the Tolbert faction quit their seating challenges.

The Tolbert group, in an effort to get seated in 1948, put up a slate of Presidential electors in 1944 (see Figure 1 in Appendix), but this didn't have any effect for in 1948 the Bates' group was seated over Tolbert's opposition.

In Mississippi in 1915 the Republican party split into two groups, the Black and Tans and the lily-whites. A black attorney, Perry Howard, and a black dentist, S. D. Redmond, headed up the black faction and a white man, M. J. Muldihill of Vicksburg, headed up the lily-white group.

Both groups sent contesting delegations to the national convention in 1920. And both groups were seated with a half vote each. At the convention, the lily-whites supported the wrong nominee for president and this was held against them by the forces they opposed. Therefore, at the 1924 national convention in Cleveland, Ohio, the Howard-Redmond-led Black and Tans were seated over the lily-whites. Moreover, Howard was elected National Committeeman for the state of Mississippi and Mrs. Mary Booze (a resident of the all-black community of Mound Bayou) was elected National Committeewoman. Dr. Redmond was elected state chairman. In short, the Black and Tan Republicans were given full control over state party matters in 1924 and kept it through 1956. Although their seating at the national convention as the Republican party from Mississippi was contested strongly by the lily-whites, the Howard-led Black and Tans were seated each year through 1956. In 1928, the Howard-led group came close to being defeated.

In 1928, President Herbert Hoover used several Black and Tan delegations to secure his nomination. Then, after his inauguration, Hoover praised the existing lily-white Republican organizations in the South, announced his full support for them, and proceeded to destroy the Black and Tan groups. In Mississippi he had an investigation launched into the activities of Perry Howard as head of the Republican party in the state.

Late in 1928, "Howard, together with several other active Black Republicans of Jackson, Mississippi, was indicted . . . for the sale of federal offices and for levying political contributions on federal employees in violation of the civil service code." [34] The major driving force behind President Hoover's action and support of the lily-whites was a desire to successfully invade the South against the Democratic candidate Al Smith. The strategy didn't work, for Howard, despite the massive evidence against him, was acquitted.

White Democrats in Mississippi came to Howard's aid and testified in his behalf. The chief justice, associate justice and the clerk of the State Supreme Court, some of the state's major newspapers, and numerous Democratic politicians wrote glowing letters and editorials as well as made speeches in his behalf. The basic reason for this was that federal jobs in the South gotten by Howard as patronage (or any other Black and Tan leader) were sold to white Democrats. Positions like third and fourth class postmasterships were denied to blacks in the South, and other federal jobs which could be held only by whites were sold to them by Howard. Moreover, since there were never enough Republicans to go around for all the available federal jobs in the South, the Democrats naturally received them and were grateful.[35]

Secondly, the new lily-white Republican movement that threatened to supplant Howard's Black and Tans refused to deal with the Democrats. This action threatened to upset the apple cart and motivated white Democrats to speak out in Howard's defense.

Thus, Howard was acquitted and his Black and Tan delegation was seated at the Republican National Convention in 1932 through 1956, despite lily-white challenges. *Most ironic is the fact that after the 1928 incident Howard moved to Washington, D.C., where he set up a law practice and continued to direct the Black and Tans. Then he left Washington to head the Mississippi delegation to the convention every four years. He died in 1961 and his group collapsed upon his death.*

The South Carolina Progressive Democratic Party   Another satellite or parallel black political party, forerunner of the Mississippi Freedom Democratic Party, was organized in Columbia, South Carolina, on May 24, 1944. To the party's first convention came 172 delegates from 39 of the state's 46 counties as well as observers from North Carolina, Georgia, Alabama, Mississippi, Virginia, and other southern states.[36]

The idea for this new party evolved out of two desires of blacks in South Carolina: to vote for Franklin Delano Roosevelt for a fourth term and to abolish the state's white primary, which barred blacks from participating in the primary elections. Barring blacks from the primaries in a one-party state was tantamount to denying them the right to vote. In the general elections, blacks had no choice but to vote for candidates who had already been chosen by whites in the primary elections, because only one party's candidates appeared on the ballot then.

Although the two reasons for forming the new party in South Carolina were different, they shade into each other and in the final analysis are meaningfully interconnected.

The desire of blacks to vote for Roosevelt grew out of the appeal of his New Deal programs, which provided jobs for poverty-stricken blacks in the state at the same rate of pay that whites were receiving, thus reversing an age-old custom.[37] Most of the state's demagogues and racists—men like Senator "Cotton Ed" Smith, Jimmy Byrnes, ex-Senator Cole Blease—shared the sentiments of other regular white Democrats and of Republicans as well. They opposed Roosevelt because he recognized blacks and included them in his governmental programs and administration.

Thus before the general election in November 1944 white public officials talked seriously of leaving Roosevelt's name off the ballot or at least making it difficult to vote for him by some type of election scheme as yet undecided. If these plans could be carried through, blacks in the state would be effectively excluded from the polls—at least for that election. They would be unable to vote for a president whom they supported.

Thus blacks were faced with two alternatives if the whites carried out their threats. They could forget about voting in 1944 or they could put up a slate of their own electors and in this way support

Roosevelt's bid for a fourth term. The latter alternative meant forming an organization that could hold its own primaries.

In the mid-1930s blacks in the state had formed the Negro Citizens Committee, a statewide organization with numerous local affiliates created to help blacks register as well as to raise funds in order to challenge in court the state's white primary law. Beginning in 1940 and for three years thereafter, the Negro Citizens Committee had enrolled more than a hundred blacks at the courthouse in Columbia, so that they could vote in the state Democratic primary elections. The tactic failed each time. Courthouse officials let the blacks register, then later notified them that their names had been purged from the party's books because state laws banned blacks from voting in such elections.

The problem of forming a political organization that could hold its own primary was not the forbidding task it appeared to be; blacks had already formed one political organization and had learned much from the experience. The need for a new organization was now even more acute not only because of the importance of voting for Roosevelt but also because the old Negro Citizens Committee had left much yet to be accomplished.

The Negro Citizens Committee members, in search of a new political organization, began during the first months of 1944 to study South Carolina election laws to see whether a legal basis, or barrier, for their plans existed. Their investigation revealed that the state of South Carolina had no laws governing the formation of political parties and "that the only election returns certified by the state were those of the general election." [38]

On March 18, 1944, John H. McCray, member of the Negro Citizens Committee and publisher of the *Lighthouse and Informer,* announced editorially in his newspaper: "We have formed a plan by which every Negro so inclined in the State of South Carolina may be a Democrat and vote for his Democratic President (Roosevelt). . . ." The plan called for "the formation of 'Fourth-Term-for-Roosevelt Clubs' throughout the state incorporated under the 'South Carolina Colored Democratic Party.'" In addition, the editorial declared, the proposed party would hold its own convention, choose its own presidential electors, and be completely controlled by blacks.[39]

Brim Rykard, city editor of the white *Columbia Record,* requested and received permission to reprint the editorial in his newspaper, and the Associated Press wire service picked it up and distributed in nationally. Immediately, the *Lighthouse* office was besieged by calls, letters, and requests, and visitors came from several adjoining states. The response took everyone by surprise, and McCray now found himself being pressured to spearhead the proposed new political organization —the South Carolina Colored Democratic Party.

On March 26, eight days after the publication of the editorial, members of the Negro Citizens Committee and interested friends met at McCray's office to discuss the reactions to the editorial—mainly, that the proposed party be launched with McCray as its head. McCray agreed to accept the challenge and was elected acting chairman; Osceola E. McKaine, McCray's associate editor on the *Lighthouse* staff, was elected acting secretary; and J. C. Artemius was elected acting treasurer. In addition, a rudimentary organization with temporary committees was set up.

After the first meeting, visitors continued to show up at McCray's office to offer support and inquire about the new organization. One of the visitors was an elderly white woman who came to express an interest in the party and say she was against limiting it to blacks. She suggested to McCray that the new party should be "progressive" and donated her five-dollar old-age pension check to the organization, taking special delight in putting it to use against a government that expected her to live on this pittance. Following her suggestion, the word "colored" was removed from the party's name and a new title, the South Carolina Progressive Democratic Party (SCPDP), was adopted at the next meeting.

On April 3, 1944, eight days after the first SCPDP meeting, the Supreme Court ruled in a Texas case (*Smith* v. *Allwright*) that "white primaries" were unconstitutional. But before the new party could move to have the Court's ruling implemented in South Carolina, Governor Olin D. Johnston called a special session of the legislature to circumvent the decision. This special session repealed all state laws relating to primary elections and left the task of conducting state elections to interested citizens.

Until this special session South Carolina had no laws governing the formation of political parties, but it is quite possible that the state would have sought to curtail the activities of SCPDP had it really become a serious threat to the regular Democratic party. But when the legislature repudiated all responsibility for the conduct of elections, the way was open for SCPDP. The threat of state intervention had been obviated. SCPDP could now do what it had intended from the outset: conduct its own elections.

On May 13 McCray sent a letter to the secretary of state, W. P. Blackwell, who was also ex-officio Chairman of the State House and Grounds Commission, asking for permission to hold the SCPDP convention in the hall of the House of Representatives. Four days later McCray wrote to the 35 county organizations that the temporary party organization had been established, calling on them to elect delegates to the first convention on May 24, 1944. Since he expected a rejection from Blackwell, McCray asked the delegates to convene in the old Masonic Hall in Columbia. Blackwell never answered McCray's letter, but he did say in an interview with the Associated Press that he had no jurisdiction over the requested facility.

In addition to the letter and call, the SCPDP chairman sent two requests to the regular Democratic party before it held its convention. These requests were (1) that blacks be admitted to regular party membership and (2) that blacks be allotted 8 of the 18 delegate positions to the national convention. On May 17, when the regular Democrats held their convention, they turned down McCray's requests. Added to the refusal was a declaration that the convention members would resist any demands that blacks and whites be admitted to the same public schools.

On May 24th the SCPDP held its first convention. In attendance were 172 delegates along with observers from Florida, Arkansas, Mississippi, Alabama, Georgia, Virginia, and North Carolina.

The SCPDP convention elected permanent officers, a state delegation, and a national delegation, adopted a constitution and temporary rules, and established three levels of committees. The committees formed the base for the party organizational structure. A state executive committee (elected every two years at state conventions) was to coordinate the activities of the congressional district committees. The congressional district committees were to coordinate the activities of all counties within each district. And the county committees were to direct the respective wards in each county.

Keynote speaker Osceola McKaine told the convention delegates:

"It is to correct these unfair conditions, to give the disinherited men and women of both races in South Carolina some voice in their government, some control over their destinies, and some hope for reasonable security and happiness in the future that the Progressive Democratic Party has been founded." [40] An organizational song—"Climbing Jacob's Ladder"—was adopted for use at all party meetings and at the close of each party function.

Following the convention an SCPDP delegation was sent to Washington to confer with national Democratic party leaders over the exclusion of blacks from the regular delegation to the national convention and the right of blacks to at least 8 of the 18 delegate spots. In Washington, John McCray, A. J. Clement, Jr., and Dr. Roscoe Wilson, who made up the delegation, met with Democratic National Committee Chairman Robert Hanagan, Federal Security Administrator Oscar Ewing, and freshman Congressman William L. Dawson of Chicago. The discussion between the two groups resulted in a pledge to eliminate discriminatory practices such as those that confronted South Carolina blacks. In reply to a direct question from Mr. Clement—"How do we know you'll keep your word?"—Mr. Dawson answered, "A politician who breaks his word is a dead politician."

Having received no assurance that blacks would be included in the state delegation, SCPDP sent 21 people to the national Democratic convention in Chicago to contest the seating of the regular Democrats from South Carolina. As the SCPDP delegation got off the train in Chicago it was met by Edgar Brown of the National Negro Congress, which by 1944 had become a Communist front organization. Brown offered financial assistance and better hotel accommodations than the delegation had been able to find. But the group turned down Brown's offer and proceeded to the convention site in the Stevens Hotel. At the convention, the SCPDP delegates were quietly turned away and the Credentials Committee never heard their challenge. Following the Chicago convention, SCPDP reassembled and nominated Osceola McKaine as its candidate for the U.S. Senate to oppose Governor Olin D. Johnston. McKaine received 4,500 votes in the race.[41]

The party then shifted its attention to voter registration drives in the black community. Professor Luther Jackson credits the party's registration efforts with having raised the number of black voters in South Carolina from approximately 3,500 in 1944 to 50,000 by

1947.[42] In addition, SCPDP expanded its organization to 43 of the 46 counties in the state and began to mobilize the black electorate in several local and statewide contests to support white candidates who were friendly or partial to the black community.

However, at the suggestion of NAACP attorney Thurgood Marshall (now a Supreme Court Justice), U.S. District Judge J. Waties Waring, and Rev. James Hinton (head of the statewide conference of NAACP branches), SCPDP dissolved as an official party at the annual convention in August 1946 and continued as a caucus group concerned with the issues and problems peculiar to black Democrats in the state. The argument for dissolution was that the existence of the party would bring down the wrath of the state Democrats on the heads of the budding black electorate, as well as on the party itself, and thus disrupt national Democratic unity. In addition, the feeling was widespread that SCPDP could not replace the regular party because it lacked the resources to involve itself in the campaigning and electioneering that would be necessary for an effective challenge to the regular Democrats at the polls. SCPDP did not have enough black voters registered in the state to support it and consequently could not hope to win at the polls. Nor could it expect federal help in 1946. However, even as a political action caucus group the Progressive Democrats continued their electioneering and voter registration efforts. And in 1948 the Progressive Democrats contested the seating of the all-white regular delegation from the state at the Democratic national convention in Philadelphia.

At the Philadelphia convention a group of white democrats headed by Rev. Maxie Collins and attorney David Baker also were challenging the regular delegation. Both groups based their challenge on the fact that the regular delegation was not loyal to the national Democratic party because it was pledged to J. Strom Thurmond, who was heading the Dixiecrat revolt. (The Dixiecrat party of 1948 was a third party movement led by southern segregationists because President Truman and the national Democratic convention endorsed a strong civil rights plank for the party's platform. See Chapter 6.) Although the Credentials Committee agreed to seat the regular delegation, a minority report from the committee expressing some sympathy for the claims of the Progressive Democrats led the South Carolina regulars to walk out of the convention.

The Progressive Democrats sent yet another contesting delegation to the 1956 national convention and received a pledge that the national Democratic party would finally revise its rules so as to prevent the future seating of all-white delegations from states practicing any form of discrimination against black representation in the delegations. The Progressive Democrats were further told that blacks need do no more than indicate discrimination for future conventions to take action. However, as the 1964 convention proved, convention rules and pledges are not necessarily put into practice.

Following the 1956 national convention some of the Progressive Democrats were slowly absorbed by the regular South Carolina Democratic party in some areas. State chairman John McCray was elected vice-chairman of ward 18 in Columbia, which at the time of his election was about 70 percent white. Other black Progressive Democrats obtained offices in local and county organizations. Once the absorption process had started, the Progressive Democratic caucus lost most of its vitality, members, and leadership. Recently there have been indications that South Carolina blacks are not happy with the situation and are moving once again to form a new political organization.[43]

It is noteworthy that although white Democrats in the state did not welcome SCPDP at first, white Republicans did think that SCPDP might be useful to them. According to McCray, in the summer of 1944 six wealthy white Republicans visited his office and told him that the state GOP members welcomed the new SCPDP as an important step in creating a two-party system within the state. These Republicans felt that SCPDP should not seek to identify with the Republican party in any way, but should instead identify with the Democratic party as much as possible. With the influx of blacks into the Democratic party, white Democrats would gravitate naturally to the rising Republican party. According to McCray, the spokesman for the group compared the Democratic party to a cylinder crammed full, with whites spilling out at one end as blacks powered in at the other. "We Republicans will serve as a box catching the Democrats who spill out," he remarked, and with that the white Republicans left.

But despite these hoped-for consequences, SCPDP contributed less to the success of the Republicans than to black political activity in the state. Its statewide activity is just one of many efforts of blacks throughout the South to move into the political arena before the arrival of white liberal organizations, such as the Southern Regional Council's Voter Education Project.

Moreover, the three seating challenges of the party were inspired and led by South Carolina blacks themselves and in this way differ from the Mississippi Freedom Democratic party challenges, which were led in part by nonresident whites. These three SCPDP seating challenges represent the first contest of this kind that was brought before the Democratic national convention by blacks. Thus SCPDP becomes the first satellite black political organization to pose a meaningful challenge to a regular state political party. In another way the party represents the duality of purpose of all black parties—they must concern themselves with voter registration, electioneering, and campaigning at the same time that they go on fighting repression.

The United Citizens' Party   On November 22, 1969, at the annual meeting of the South Carolina Voter Education Project (an organization that coordinates black voter registration efforts in the state) in Columbia, plans were developed for a new black political party—the United Citizens' Party (UCP).[44]

The organizers of the party, led by James E. Clyburn—a social agency director in Charleston—charged that the South Carolina Democratic party had failed to reward the black electorate for supporting the Democrats. This failure, the organizers held, could be seen in the fact that South Carolina had no black state legislators and that no blacks had been able to win nomination for the state legislature in the Democratic primary.

Therefore, the organizers announced, beginning on December 1 the members of UCP, along with black college students from Benedict College, and Allen University, in Columbia, would launch a statewide drive to obtain the signatures of 10,000 registered voters which the state law required for a new party to obtain a state charter.

From November 1969 to August 1970, UCP workers and volunteers canvassed the state in an effort to obtain the required signatures to get a state charter. Late in August, the party succeeded and the Secretary of State on September 1, 1970 gave the UCP a charter which certified it as a legal political party that could participate in any and all state elections.[45]

However, certification brought additional problems. First of all, being certified as late as September 1 gave the party leadership hardly two months to nominate, select, and campaign for its candidates that would compete in the November general election. Secondly, it was too late to get the party's candidates on the state ballots because they had already been printed.

But even with these new obstacles, the political organizing strategy and tactics of party leaders, Attorney John Roy Harper II, president (a graduate of Fisk University and the University of South Carolina Law School), and Mrs. Victoria DeLee, vice-president (long time community organizer and militant civil rights advocate), had, in a UCP meeting on July 25th, decided in an effort to build the party throughout the state to run a write-in candidate for governor and lieutenant-governor. At the August 8th meeting of the party, a black attorney in Columbia, Thomas D. Broadwater, and Rev. Julius M. McTeer, were nominated by the party membership as candidates for the governor and lieutenant-governor positions.

Moreover, several of the blacks who had entered the June 1970 state primary as independents and had won (thereby automatically being placed on the November ballot) were UCP members and supported. These individuals received the party backing and endorsement in the general election. For instance, several of the black independents who were running for the state legislature, like James Clyburn from Charleston, Hyman L. Davis from Beaufort, and James L. Felder, accepted UCP endorsement. Hence, in this manner, the UCP had candidates or supported candidates for statewide offices like the governorship and the state legislature.

In local elections, the UCP backed and supported UCP members and sympathizers as well as nominated candidates for offices and in municipalities where they could still get on local election ballots.

The time for organizing, nominating, and campaigning proved in part to be too short especially statewide. The UCP gubernatorial candidates, Broadwater and lieutenant-gubernatorial candidate McTeer, lost, receiving less than 1000 write-in votes. Several UCP-backed candidates for the state legislature also lost. But three of the party-backed and -supported candidates, James L. Felder, Herbert Fielding, and I. S. Levy Johnson, won and became the first blacks to be elected to the state legislature since Reconstruction.[46] On the local level, while many of the party's candidates lost, several won positions ranging from city councilmen to seats on school boards. (See Table 15 in the Appendix on UCP.)

After the November general election, the UCP leaders announced on January 16, 1971 that they would select at a special statewide convention to be held in Charleston, South Carolina, January 30th, a candidate to run for the seat in Congress left vacant by the death of L. Mendel Rivers, chairman of the House Armed Services Committee. At the special convention the UCP nominated its vice-president, Mrs. Victoria DeLee, to run for the 1st District congressional seat against the white candidate Mendel L. Davis. (See Table 16 in Appendix for results.) Mrs. DeLee's campaign, while better financed than the general election UCP campaign and better organized, suffered a defeat. In a nine county area where blacks are the majority in only two counties, she polled 8,029 votes.

At the time of this writing, the UCP was vigorously organizing in all of the 46 South Carolina counties in an effort to be better prepared for the 1972 elections in the state.

* * *

We have observed in this chapter the rise and development of two Negro political phenomena: the Negro separate political organization and the Negro parallel or satellite organization, both of which emerged in response to certain forms of racial discrimination, either overt or implicit, in political, legal, religious, and other institutions.

Even though these black political organizations failed to accomplish much of significance, their very existence represented protest against racial discrimination and injustices in the daily life of our society. These devices were forced upon their creators. And they demonstrated both the will and the ability of blacks to rely on their own means in order to seek fulfillment of their own goals.

Now, in the following two chapters, let us narrow the focus of our investigation of black political parties in order to make a tentative assessment of two political groups, the Mississippi Freedom Democratic party and the Black Panther party of Alabama.

3

THE MISSISSIPPI POLITICAL SCENE

On April 26, 1964, between 200 and 300 delegates of the Council of Federated Organizations (COFO) met in Jackson, Mississippi, and founded the Mississippi Freedom Democratic party (MFDP), a parallel political party open to all Democrats of voting age in the state. The party was formed primarily to "give Negro citizens of Mississippi an experience in political democracy and to establish a channel through which all citizens, Negro and white, could actively support the principles and programs of the National Democratic Party. . . ." [1] Originally, the political philosophy of the party was closely tied to that of the Student Nonviolent Coordinating Committee (SNCC). However, MFDP's ultimate goal was, and still is, to help Mississippi Negroes obtain political power as well as to rekindle Negro political interest as a means for improving their lot in life.

Black political organizations differ from black political parties. The former are concerned with increasing the number of black voters and endorsing candidates. Black parties, on the other hand, not only add to the voter rolls but nominate candidates, devise platforms, and campaign and otherwise help to elect their candidates. For the most part, black political organizations seem to be middle-class organizations and have some difficulty in delivering votes. [2]

Black third parties take one of two forms: parallel parties and independent parties. A black satellite or parallel political party such as MFDP revolves in the orbit of a major political party on the national level and runs parallel with the state party to modify the practices of the regular party in light of its own goals and objectives. Moreover, the satellite party seeks to identify with the national organization because the patronage benefits that can accrue from this source can make the new party economically viable. However, the satellite party will at the same time try to keep its identity separate from the regular state party, which it seeks to displace. Thus one gets such names as the South Carolina Progressive Democratic party, the Black and Tan Republican party, and the National Democratic party of Alabama.

A new satellite party, which in effect is a new political entity, can be organized without the aid of the national party. However, after it has been launched the satellite party seeks to become part of the national party organization and to represent it in a particular locality. In short, the satellite party is a new political organization seeking voter acceptance in its locality and affiliation with the national party.

On the other hand, the separate political party is an independent organization which does not seek to affiliate with any local, state, or national group. In fact the separate party deliberately remains aloof from other political organizations in order to maintain its integrity, as expressed in its goals and objectives. Moreover, the founders hope that the victories achieved by its candidates will bring rewards enough to make reliance upon another party unnecessary and to insure that the party's principles and integrity are never compromised. In this respect, black separate parties are typical of third parties in general; that is, they search for distinctiveness and for electoral victory. The search for distinctiveness leads the black separate parties to assume such names as the Afro-American party, the Negro Protective party, and the Party of Christian Democracy.

Whatever the differences betwen satellite and separate political parties, their organizers share these problems in common: first, the task of launching the party; second, the task of keeping it going in the face of opposition from the political organizations that are already in the field. Thus either party may face repression. In addition, the satellite party has the staggering problem of gaining the acceptance of the national organization. Just how does the new satellite party get the national political organization to accept a new representative, especially when no rules cover a change of political representative? This is the core of the problem. To be accepted by the national party organization the new satellite black party must persuade, cajole, fight, prove worthy, propagandize, and if necessary plead for acceptance.

Negro Politics in Mississippi, 1871–1964

The reasons that Negroes felt compelled to form a parallel political organization in the state as late as 1964 lie in the long history of the Negro's political status in Mississippi.

From 1871 until 1876—in other words, so long as Reconstruction policies permitted—blacks actively participated in the political affairs of the state. The black man's entrance into state politics was made possible by the Mississippi Compact, an agreement between congressional Radicals and Mississippi politicians to call a state constitutional convention to draw up a new constitution granting blacks the franchise on the same basis as whites. Moreover, the state politicians agreed to maintain nondiscriminatory voting procedures once the new constitution went into effect and the state had been readmitted to the Union. The new constitution was ratified in 1869 and Congress then readmitted Mississippi to the Union in 1870. In that year almost 70 percent or approximately 100,000 of the black population of voting age was registered to vote. (See Table 1 in the Appendix.)

Internal white resistance to black suffrage began almost immediately, and in the rapidly changing national political scene the Compact became a dead issue. But before this occurred, blacks actively participated in the state government of Mississippi. In 1871, 38 Negroes were elected to the Mississippi House of Representatives, and three blacks assumed high office: A. K. Davis was elected lieutenant-governor, F. W. Cardozo became superintendent of education, and James Hill became secretary of state. In 1873, Mississippi sent two Negroes to the U.S. Senate and one to the House of Representatives.[3]

In the 1875 election, terror tactics proved effective in curtailing Negro voting.[4] As a result, control of the state legislature passed into the hands of the white-supremacist Democrats, a group of politicians bent on undoing all the accomplishments of Black Reconstruction. Although some Negro officials, including those who were not up for re-election, managed to retain their positions, the new Democratic legis-

lature forcibly removed from office most Negroes and at the same time imposed overwhelming financial and legal pressures on minor Negro officials.[5]

The restoration of white control in the South gained additional impetus from the national election of 1876. In return for southern support, Republican presidential candidate Rutherford B. Hayes promised to withdraw the remaining federal troops from the South. Southerners responded favorably, enabling Hayes to win over his Democratic rival Samuel J. Tilden, and he kept his word. The subsequent removal of all but a token force of federal troops left Negro public officials with nowhere to turn for redress of their grievances. Although some Negroes continued to hold minor public office for a while, Black Reconstruction and black politics in Mississippi had come to an end.

The illegal methods used to bar Mississippi Negroes from the political arena, which had brought the white-supremacist Democrats to power, soon received legal reinforcement. In Mississippi's 1890 constitutional convention, amendments were adopted that were to strip Negroes of their remaining political power and to remove them from the state's political life for another three-quarters of a century. Many legal techniques were employed to attain this end. The state constitution was rewritten to include an "understanding clause," requiring voter applicants to read and interpret sections of the state constitution at the request and to the satisfaction of local white county registrars. A literacy test was adopted which was particularly effective in disfranchising Negroes, for at that time the majority of them were illiterate. Finally, in addition to the poll tax, the convention instituted a "grandfather clause" stipulating that, to qualify as voters, residents had to demonstrate that their grandfathers had been voters—hardly possible for blacks whose grandfathers had been slaves.[6] Coupling the poll tax and the grandfather clause with the literacy requirement proved far more devastating than the earlier illegal techniques of restraining the black vote—murder, terrorism, and so on. Furthermore, some historians have argued that the poll tax in effect disfranchised more Negroes than the understanding clause because few Negroes earned enough money to enable them to pay the tax.[7]

Despite these legal obstacles, a limited amount of Negro political activity took place in Mississippi during the era of Populism—the 1890s. Under the "fusion" rule (when Republicans temporarily collaborated with Democrats), a black quota was established and a few blacks were allowed to return to political office.[8] This arrangement soon fell into disrepute, however, and terrorism was once again visited upon the remaining black voting population. In the ensuing years the black voting population declined drastically. Although by the twentieth century Negroes had been isolated from Mississippi politics through repressive measures, they were not ignored. As Professor Key has pointed out, "on the surface at least, the beginning and the end of Mississippi politics is the Negro." [9]

One provision of the primary election law passed by the state legislature in 1902 granted to the party holding a primary the right to exclude arbitrarily any persons or groups of persons. The very next year the Democratic state executive committee adopted a resolution limiting voting in the primary elections to white Democrats.[10] This rule, which remained in effect until the 1960s, nullified the votes of the few undaunted blacks who had surmounted every other obstacle and had actually registered. This is because primary victory in a one-party system such as Mississippi's is tantamount to victory since only the names of primary winners appear on the ballot in the general election.[11] Thus black votes in Mississippi general elections became meaningless; the candidates had been selected in the primary election. At best, black voters merely "seconded the motion" and gave their approval to decisions made by the white-supremacist Democrats.

In addition to the constitutional and legislative tactics which throttled Negro voting in Mississippi for years, the state's political leadership increasingly insisted on the exclusion of Negroes from white public schools and the maintenance of separate school systems, which made the "understanding clause" that much more effective. Moreover, the state legislature periodically enacted laws making voting requirements progressively more difficult for Negroes to meet. For example, in 1936 the state legislature passed a new primary election law which required persons seeking to vote in primary elections to pay the poll tax two years in advance.[12]

White supremacy suffered a temporary setback in 1944, when the Supreme Court ruled that the exclusion of Negroes from Democratic primary elections in Texas was unconstitutional.[13] The decision set off a great hue and cry among white Mississippians for the adoption of new measures, and once more they set about devising methods, legal and illegal, to prevent Negroes from voting. Subsequently, Negroes could often find no one to accept their registration applications.[14] Others received anonymous threats: "Last warning: if you are tired of living, vote and die." These activities were not without their effect. In many counties in which Negroes were in the majority, not a single Negro was a registered voter. In several counties, Negroes had not been permitted to vote since the end of Reconstruction.[15] In short, the Democratic party in Mississippi has systematically excluded Negroes not only from public life and politics, but from the Democratic party as well. Nevertheless, ever since the restoration of white control in Mississippi in 1875, Negroes in the state have persistently sought to return to politics and political life.

The most recent attempt by Negroes to re-enter Mississippi politics is represented by the efforts of the Mississippi Freedom Democratic party. The regular state party had had the help and backing of the national Democratic party when it began in Mississippi. Patronage, money, organizers, and so on were provided to the fledgling state organization. And continued assistance from the national organization has at least in part kept the state party in existence. But MFDP, being a new and unaffiliated political entity, could not from the outset get special help from the national organization and had to look elsewhere for help in getting started. Its primary sources of help were the federal government and liberal allies outside the state.[16]

Notable among the federal agencies which have lent help to Negroes seeking to re-establish themselves in state politics is the Justice Department—specifically, its Civil Rights Division, which investigated the wholesale denial of Negroes' right to vote in 65 of Mississippi's 82 countries during the late 1950s and early 1960s.[17] Plainly, the major problem facing Negroes seeking re-entry into Mississippi politics in the middle of the twentieth century was the same as it had been since the era of restoration: to find a suitable vehicle for cracking the monolithic political establishment. This search culminated in the creation of MFDP. Why MFDP? Why another state Democratic party? The answer is to be found in the nature of the political parties in Mississippi since the end of Reconstruction in 1877.

During Reconstruction the Republican party became completely identified with black people. On the national level the party of Lincoln was associated with the Civil War, the Emancipation Proclamation, and the Thirteenth, Fourteenth, and Fifteenth Amendments. On the state level in the South, the Republican party's power was based on the black voter, and nearly all black politicians in the southern states were Republicans.

On the other hand, on the national level the Democratic party had been associated with secession, support for the southerners' right to have slaves, and opposition to the Civil War. On the state level in the South the Democratic party was the party out of power, the party of the vanquished whites, the party that upheld the superiority of the white race not only in politics but in all matters.

It was shortly after the Democratic party recaptured control of the state government from the Republicans and their black supporters that whites began to leave the Republican party ranks. During the 1880s, as the Democratic party became the southern white man's party and the Republican party became primarily a black party, no self-respecting white man would associate himself with the Republican party lest he be tagged a "nigger lover" and ostracized. However, Republican presidents Hayes, Theodore Roosevelt, Taft, and Hoover tried to rebuild the party in the South and sponsored lily-white Republican clubs.[18] When Herbert Hoover became president, the Black and Tan Republican organizations, which had been generally recognized as the regular Republican parties in the southern states, were replaced with lily-white organizations. The effort was not successful. Over the years the Republican party faded away not only in Mississippi but throughout the South. When Eisenhower ran on the Republican ticket he won considerable support in the South for himself, but not for his party. Thus Eisenhower cracked the solid South. But it was not until 1964 when Republican presidential candidate Barry Goldwater took an unusually conservative stand (for a presidential candidate) on civil rights that the party at last made significant inroads in the South.

Since 1875, when the Democratic party initiated the era of restoration and one-party rule, the party has employed one technique or another in order to achieve what most white Mississippians considered their right—or, as one Mississippi newspaper put it in 1875, "a white man's government, by white men, for the benefit of white men." At about the same time the *Yazoo City Banner* declared that "Mississippi is a white man's country, and by the eternal God, we'll run it." Having recaptured the state government, the Democratic party now responded to such sentiment by setting out to disfranchise the Negro electorate and remove it from the ranks of the party.

On the national scene, Mississippi Democrats have been among the staunchest opponents of the party's liberal stands. For example, Governor F. Wright played a key role in the southern Democrats' revolt against the strong civil rights platform adopted by the national convention in 1948. The southerners insisted that their states knew best how to treat Negroes and that the South would brook no interference in its way of life. When the convention ratified the platform despite this, all the southern delegates walked out. Under the auspices of Governor Wright, these delegates created the Dixiecrat party, adopted a states' rights platform, and nominated Senator J. Strom Thurmond (S. Car.) and Wright as its presidential and vice-presidential candidates, respectively.[19] Although the Dixiecrats failed to sway the national party, Mississippi Democrats seeking to preserve white supremacy in the state have since persisted in their attempts to influence national politics: witness such devices as the unpledged presidential electors and the switch to the Republican camp when Goldwater ran against Johnson in 1964.[20] In short, Mississippi Democrats have actively sought to suppress Negro political aspirations nationally as well as locally.

The combination of an increasingly hostile white Democratic party and a virtually defunct Republican party left Mississippi Negroes with but a single course of action to pursue if they were to fulfill their political ambitions—the creation of their own political organization. Before this could come to pass, however, there had to be registered Negro voters who would support such a party. Thus the path was clear: an unprecedented number of Negroes had to be registered to vote.

From the disfranchising constitutional convention of 1890 to the 1960s, the vigorous exclusion of Negroes from state politics by Mississippi Democrats had produced a number of strong-willed Negro leaders who saw voter registration as the first step in bringing Negroes back into state politics.[21] But despite their vigorous efforts, often in the face of economic reprisals, violence, and intimidation, Negro voting strength in Mississippi remained below 7 percent. Handicapped by repressive measures, voting drives remained unsystematic, uncoordinated, and unsustained. Moreover, before the 1960s the few registered black voters in the state were mostly middle-class Negroes who, because their economic welfare depended on their keeping in the good graces of the white power structure, could be trusted to vote properly. Usually, they voted for the more moderate of the candidates, the one they considered the lesser of two evils (even though he was for segregation and against civil rights), but even this soon proved futile.[22]

Failure at the polls made some Negro voters apathetic or indifferent; intimidation made others fearful; and many finally refused to vote.

The Council of Federated Organizations

The combination of apathy and fear was the crux of the problem as Negro community leaders saw it in the early 1960s. Slack registration along with indifference to politics among Negroes left the black community with a poor power base and a weak bargaining position. In any event, there seemed little purpose in voting for either of two white candidates when both were indifferent or hostile to Negro interests. In short, there was no motivation for Negroes to register so long as there was no real choice among candidates. To face up to all sorts of hostility only to vote for a hostile candidate seemed pointless. Nevertheless, it was recognized that this vicious cycle had to be broken if a start was to be made; moreover, it was felt that some Negro community leaders had given up the fight too easily.

A start was made and things began to change in July 1961, when C. C. Bryant, a leader in the McComb NAACP, invited civil rights organizer Robert Moses to that city to initiate a voter registration drive among Negroes. Moses, then a field secretary for SNCC and a vigorous organizer of local programs for mobilizing political activity, began by promoting the idea of a freedom vote—a mock election in which all unregistered Negroes of voting age in the area would take part. Moses hoped that the freedom vote would at least be of psychological value by refuting Senator James O. Eastland's contention that the small percentage of registered Negro voters in the state reflected their lack of interest in politics. (Two years later, in 1963, the Justice Department sued to end voting discrimination in his home county, Sunflower, where only 144 of 13,354 Negroes of voting ages were registered.) [23] Although Senator Eastland was in part right, and although this was not in the original plan, the voter registration drive was also to prove significant in establishing the requisite voter base for the future MFDP.

Before Moses could rally effective support for the freedom vote, two Negroes jumped the gun by running for public office in the 1962 Democratic primary. One, Rev. Merrill Lindsey, ran as a candidate for the House of Representatives from the second congressional district, which contained a majority of black-belt counties. Predictably, he lost in the June 5 primary. (See Table 2 in the Appendix.) Although he challenged the primary winner in federal district court, on the ground that his district was denied equal representation as guaranteed by the Fourteenth Amendment, here too he was unsuccessful.

The other candidate, Rev. Robert L. T. Smith of Jackson, also opposed a white candidate—in this case, John Bell Williams (later elected governor of the state) in the third congressional district. Like his counterpart, Smith too was defeated. Neither man alone, it seems, was able to overcome the cumulative effects of many years of Negro exclusion from the ballot box and from politics in general.

Yet Smith and Lindsey captured the imagination not only of the state's Negroes but of the nation, and their feat set the pattern for events to come. In less than two years, additional Negro candidates were to take the field. Moreover, because the activities of Smith and Lindsey attracted the attention of northern civil rights organizations, they were partly responsible for the influx of civil rights workers the following summer for Moses' voter registration drive.

After the defeat of Smith and Lindsey in 1962, Moses realized that he would need not only additional help in his drive, but also a much broader and more systematic program than he had first envisioned. Consequently, he revived the Council of Federated Organizations for the purpose of unifying and coordinating the effort. This organization, a confederation of the state chapters of SCLC, SNCC, NAACP, and CORE, had been formed in 1961 after the jailing of the Freedom Riders—civil rights workers seeking to integrate interstate bus lines operating in the South. At the time the governor of Mississippi, Ross Barnett, had refused to talk with representatives of any civil rights organization regarding the release of the Riders. The confederated organization was created for this specific purpose, and after meeting with the governor and securing the release of the Freedom Riders it was disbanded.

Moses' revitalization of COFO in June 1962 was motivated by a need for similar concerted, coordinated action among the state's civil rights organizations, which had been planning independent voter drives. When COFO was reactivated it immediately opened voter registration training schools in seven of the state's major areas, all heavily populated with unregistered Negroes. Having been denied the right to participate in politics for so long and so harshly, many Negroes in Mississippi had lost interest in politics. To counteract this, the crash program's aim was primarily to rekindle Negro political interest and enthusiasm and secondarily to lay the groundwork for political know-how by educating the poverty-stricken Negroes and by establishing a political advisory council to aid them in decision making.

Implementing this crash program were COFO's regular staff of 95 members and, during the summer, more than 200 college student volunteers who came to the state during their three months of summer vacation to canvass and to teach.[24] Moreover, the white students sought to gain as political allies of COFO the poverty-stricken white farmers in the Mississippi Delta. Although most of this activity was directed to the freedom elections scheduled for June 1963, it also served as the prelude to the formation of MFDP. Because this activity was conspicuous and threatening to white Mississippians, they mounted stiff opposition to these programs.

COFO's mock runoff election in June of 1963 between the two Democratic gubernatorial candidates, Paul Johnson and James P. Coleman, was in anticipation of the official August runoff. Open to all unregistered voters in the state, the mock election's foremost purpose was to provide Negroes with some degree of political education and motivation. The winner of the freedom election, Coleman, was the moderate candidate; his opponent had linked him with President Kennedy's liberal civil rights stance. Though Coleman lost in the official runoff, the mock election at least awakened some Negroes in the state to the possibility of political action. In these terms, the mock election was judged a success, a workable tactic for impressing the state's Negroes with the need for registering and voting and a tactic that should be broadened and further explored. The first freedom elections proceeded on a section of Mississippi law, which said in effect that "a citizen might present himself to vote" if he did not appear on the voting rolls but could submit an affidavit that he was qualified to vote. But the results of the first freedom elections went unheeded by white Mississippians and affidavits were not needed.[25]

In a COFO meeting called by Moses after the June mock election, another freedom vote was planned to coincide with the general election in November. This time, however, COFO chose to run its own candidates: Negro Dr. Aaron Henry, an NAACP official, for governor; and Rev. Edwin King, a white chaplain at predominantly Negro Tougaloo College, for lieutenant-governor.

In the mock election held November 3 and 4 the Henry–King ticket's vote has been variously estimated at 88,000, 90,000, and 93,000.[26] A vote of this size could have been a deciding factor in the real election, especially in a close gubernatorial race. Thus during his campaign Henry said, in trying to impress the state's Negroes with the potential political power they held: "Once we withdraw our votes, and the man who loses figures that if we'd voted for him, he'd [have] won, then the next time he'll do something to get those votes of ours." [27] But despite the relative success of the two freedom votes of 1963 and the tremendous effort expended, less than 6 percent of the state's eligible Negroes were added to the voter rolls.[28] In short, the freedom elections did not generate enough votes to justify mounting a challenge to the power of Mississippi's strongly entrenched Democratic party.

The Mississippi Freedom Democratic Party

Discouraged by the small increase in Negro voters after so much work, Moses and other leaders in the voter registration drive realized that much more effective tactics were required. Apparently powerless to register Negroes in significant numbers with the techniques used so far, Moses urged consideration of new methods. First, COFO's voter registration forces obviously needed to be strengthened. Thus was conceived the freedom summer of 1964, during which more than a thousand white volunteers from the North—mostly college students —came to Mississippi at COFO's invitation. Second, in order to prod the federal government into taking direct action, techniques were needed for dramatizing nationwide the plight of Mississippi Negroes and its roots in their disfranchised condition. Third, Moses and the others acknowledged the need for some means of protecting those Negroes who had recently obtained the vote to ensure that they were not frightened off. MFDP's challenge of the regular Mississippi delegation's credentials at the 1964 Democratic national convention provided the necessary drama, for it certainly played no small part in influencing the passage of the Voting Rights Act of 1965. Finally, some instrument was needed for translating the power of the newly enfranchised Negroes into meaningful action and public policy—the very things the established parties had failed to do. This last need was met on April 26, 1964, when COFO delegates formed the Mississippi Freedom Democratic party.

At this meeting it was decided that, since voter registration was fairly well underway, major attention should be focused on party-building. To help coordinate the two activities, party leaders divided the responsibilities according to the existing congressional districts, four of them to be the responsibility of SNCC and one (the fourth district) of CORE. The third congressional district (assigned to SNCC) was the dangerous southwest district, in which virtually no registration activity had been possible. The population of the second district (also SNCC's), which is Delta country, was 66 percent Negro and predominantly rural. Greenwood, one of the Delta's three large towns (the others being Clarksdale and Greenville), was chosen as the headquarters for SNCC's operations, while CORE based its headquarters in Jackson, the state capital.

According to most accounts, this historic meeting was remarkable for the delegates' zeal and optimism. Members of the new party elected a temporary state executive committee of 12 persons, one of them white and, significantly, all Mississippians, to coordinate the party's affairs.[29] Before adjourning, the convention decided to enter MFDP candidates in the June 1964 Democratic congressional primary. An integral part of this campaign was to be the employment of "freedom registration forms," the first significant tactic in MFDP's assault on the regular Democratic party. In fact, this tactic was part of a larger plan to model the MFDP structure and formal procedures on those of the state's regular Democratic party in most respects. Thus at the Democratic national convention, as part of MFDP's challenge, the forms were submitted as evidence that substantial numbers of Mississippi Negroes possessed the motivation but were denied the means for obtaining the vote.

In the June primary, MFDP ran four candidates for office: one for the Senate and three for the House of Representatives. Among them were two Negro women—a historic first in Mississippi. One of the women, Mrs. Victoria Jackson Gray, a member of the board of directors of the Southern Christian Leadership Conference and veteran civil rights leader, schoolteacher, and businesswoman, opposed Senator John Stennis of Dekalb County for his seat. The other woman, Mrs. Fannie Lou Hamer, a former plantation timekeeper who later impressed a nationwide TV audience during the Democratic convention as a courageous and deeply inspiring civil rights leader, opposed Representative Jamie L. Whitten in the second congressional district. (A third Negro woman, Mrs. Annie Devine, sponsored by CORE but not backed by MFDP, opposed William Winstead in the fourth congressional district.)[30] As for the other two candidates, James Huston, a Negro furniture dealer, challenged Representative John Bell Williams in the third congressional district and Rev. John Cameron challenged Representative William M. Colmer in the fifth congressional district. Running on a platform which demanded full civil rights for Negroes and backed government aid to education, rural development, and numerous antipoverty programs,[31] all four candidates campaigned vigorously. Mrs. Gray, for example, took her campaign for the Senate all the way from Monroe County in the north Delta to Mississippi's Gulf Coast.

MFDP's first (and Mississippi's third) freedom vote was held on June 2. The same day, in the regular primary election, the Freedom party candidates were defeated by the candidates of the regular party. (See Table 3 in the Appendix.) Determined not to allow defeat to deter them, the MFDP representatives proceeded to several of the regular party's precinct meetings immediately following the election. Up to that time, fear of reprisals—economic as well as physical—had dissuaded Negroes from attempting to attend these meetings. Fortified now with strong party spirit, however, Freedom party members were venturing further than they ever had before, if only to obtain additional evidence of discrimination against Negro voters.

In several instances, in fact, MFDP representative got full cooperation. But in eight precincts (six counties), the MFDP members were unable to determine the location of the meeting places. In ten precincts (five counties), Negroes were allowed to attend but were given only a limited voice in the proceedings. In three precincts (3 in each of 6 counties), Negroes were excluded altogether. In one precinct, the one Negro who showed up for a meeting was the only person in attendance; he declared himself the official candidate for that precinct. In Meridian, Negroes searching for the precinct meeting approached a white school-yard where a group of whites were gathered under a tree. Upon reaching the group, they were informed that the precinct meeting had just been adjourned and that another one would not be held for four years.[32]

Despite these and similar setbacks, in some cases Negroes were actually granted the right to vote in regular Democratic party precinct meetings, and in a few precincts Negroes were even elected delegates to county conventions. One noteworthy instance was the election of J. B. Harrington, a Negro, as a delegate from an integrated precinct in Jackson.

At the county conventions of the regular Democratic party, the Negro delegates were disheartened to find matters more consistent with past practices. Negro delegates representing all-Negro precincts as well as integrated precincts were in many instances limited merely to observing the proceedings. Others were not only denied the right to take part, but were also refused admission, on the ground that their credentials were invalid. Still other Negroes were deliberately misled about the locations of convention meeting places. One group of Negro delegates in Madison County located the meeting after great effort, only to be told that the convention was over.

Professor McLemore—a charter member and organizer of MFDP and the source for much of the material in this chapter—observed that Negroes were not treated as harshly in the county meetings as they had been in many precinct meetings. The reason for this, he maintains, is that the whites at the county conventions were generally more sophisticated than their counterparts at precinct meetings. Thus, while they may have been irritated by the presence of Negro Democrats, they did not, like their counterparts, feel especially threatened. They simply ignored them.[33]

After the white precinct meetings had been held, MFDP convened its own precinct meetings in 26 counties, attended, McLemore estimates, by 3,500 persons. At MFDP's subsequent county conventions, 282 delegates met in 35 counties. Following these conventions, delegates to MFDP district meetings in each of the state's five congressional districts in turn elected delegates to the MFDP statewide convention.

The 1964 Convention Challenge

The regular Mississippi Democratic party, aware of the credentials challenge that MFDP planned for the national convention, held its state convention on July 24. No Negroes attended as delegates, none having been elected at either the precinct or the county level. When a few Negroes attempted to enter as observers, they were refused admittance on the technical ground that convention business did not permit observers. In the convention, Governor Johnson asked the state's delegates to the national convention to play "wait and see" and to exercise caution in committing themselves to any candidate or position. It was a strategy obviously intended, first, to allow the delegates maximum flexibility pending the first reaction to the MFDP challenge and, second, to give them time to consider the Republican presidential nominee's position on civil rights. In response, MFDP not only pointed to the state convention and the uncommitted regular Democratic delegation as evidence of the party's shameless political expediency, but decried the composition of the convention delegation, which included not a single politically prominent Mississippian: not Governor Johnson, nor the lieutenant-governor, nor the attorney general, nor either U.S. senator, nor any congressmen, nor even the state Democratic party chairman.[34]

Approximately 800 delegates attended the MFDP convention in Jackson two weeks later. After the keynote speech was delivered by Mrs. Eleanor Baker, coordinator of the party's office in the northern section of the state, the delegates settled down to the business of electing a national committeewoman (Mrs. Victoria Gray), a national committeeman (Rev. Edwin King), and 44 delegates, together with 22 alternates, to the Democratic national convention.[35] Among these elected delegates were four whites, whose participation in the party had been limited not by any ideological consideration but simply to avoid possible reprisals against them at the hands of their fellow-white Mississippians.

The day following the MFDP convention, delegates elected at this historic meeting were certified with the national Democratic party chairman, John Bailey. Accompanying the list of delegates was a letter requesting that the MFDP delegation be seated in place of the state's regular Democratic delegation. An earlier letter to Bailey from MFDP chairman Aaron Henry, which included a similar formal challenge, also invited Bailey to visit the MFDP statewide convention in his official capacity as national chairman. Although Bailey replied that he was unable to accept the invitation, he did say that the MFDP challenge would be duly considered by the Credentials Committee at the start of the national convention.

In addition to the two requests for exclusive recognition as Mississippi's official delegation, MFDP sought to strengthen its claim—and to embarrass the regular Democratic delegation—by announcing that each of its delegates had signed a loyalty statement pledging to support President Johnson and the vice-presidential nominee. In reaction to this move, the regular Democratic organization, anticipating MFDP-inspired convention pressure on its own delegates to sign a similar pledge, once more resorted to repression and succeeded in getting state chancery judge Stokes Robertson to place all the MFDP delegates under an injunction forbidding them to leave the state during a period spanning the time of the national convention. The move failed. Determined, the MFDP delegates left the state for Atlantic City, site of the convention, with the injunction still hanging over their heads.

Prior to the convention, MFDP also solicited support for its challenge from other states' Democratic delegations. Two MFDP workers, Frank Smith and Walter Tillow, traveled throughout the North, urging state delegations to pass resolutions supporting MFDP. In addition, letters addressed to the heads of numerous state delegations asked that they urge their members to align themselves against the Mississippi regular delegation. These appeals found some support. Nine conventions—Massachusetts, Oregon, Michigan, Minnesota, Colorado, New York, California, the District of Columbia, and Wisconsin—passed resolutions pledging to support MFDP, to at least some extent.[36] In Michigan, the convention went so far as to make its resolution of support for MFDP's challenge binding upon the state delegation. Besides these official pledges of support, various national, state, and local groups and committees declared themselves in sympathy with MFDP's challenge; for instance, the National Christian Missionary Convention, the Michigan Young Democrats, the American Federation of Teachers, and the ninth ward of the Democratic Committee of Boston. In the convention itself, however, most of the support for MFDP's challenge soon dissipated.

From the outset MFDP had a choice of alternatives in presenting its case to the Credentials Committee. The first alternative was to call witnesses and offer arguments as to why it should be seated in preference to the regular delegation, then await the Credentials Committee's recommendations to the entire convention after having heard both contending groups. If this were done, and if the committee's recommendations were approved by the majority of its members, they would probably be approved by the entire convention.

The second alternative open to MFDP was an outgrowth of the first one: to force the Credentials Committee to split on the seating issue and issue majority and minority reports. Eleven members of the committee would have had to sign a minority report calling for the seating of MFDP. Were such a report issued, only eight delegations of all those present could have called for a rollcall vote on the seating issue. And a floor vote in the convention, MFDP felt, gave the party its best chance of victory over the regular delegation. MFDP had counted on support from the nine delegations whose conventions had already responded favorably as well as from the delegations from Puerto Rico, the Virgin Islands, and Guam.

But as Holt points out the only method of getting a rollcall vote—at the request of at least eight delegations—was effectively circumvented when Georgia Governor Carl Sanders persuaded the convention's Rules Committee to institute a new ruling whereby only states—not territories, such as Guam and Puerto Rico—could be among those requesting a rollcall.

This new rule stymied MFDP's effort to win delegation support, thus eliminating one alternative. Then the MFDP supporters on the Credentials Committee dwindled from 18 to 4, making a minority report impossible. Holt's explanation of how this support was eroded is difficult to prove. Among the negative factors he considers responsible were the hurriedly called news conferences by President Johnson, pre-empting TV coverage of exposés by Mrs. Hamer and of interviews with members of MFDP; the possibility of jeopardizing the delegates' personal hopes and ambitions if they opposed his wishes; and the skillfully placed suggestions from key politicians that judgeships, district poverty programs, governmental contracts, and high official jobs could be withheld from members of the Credentials Committee and their families. In short, according to Holt, President Johnson's political maneuvering—motivated by his fear that five southern delegations would walk out of the convention if the MFDP delegates were seated—eliminated whatever support MFDP had had prior to and during the Credentials Committee hearings.[37]

With the disintegration of the second alternative, MFDP had no choice but to present its arguments and witnesses before the Credentials Committee and then await the committee's recommendations and the convention's response to them.

Thus the first stage of the battle was set in the Credentials Committee. Here, each of the two contesting groups presented legal arguments in support of its request to be seated. According to the committee's chairman, former Governor David Lawrence of Pennsylvania, the issue would be decided on the basis of the rules adopted at the 1956 and 1960 national conventions. One of these rules stipulated that every state Democratic party must use every means to assure all potential voters equal opportunity to vote for the presidential and vice-presidential nominees of the national Democratic party. The second key rule required that delegates to the national convention be bona fide Democrats with the best interests of the party at heart. Some MFDP sympathizers said this rule was being brazenly violated by several members of the regular Mississippi delegation who had placed Goldwater bumper-stickers on their cars.[38]

These two rules constituted the context in which the challenge would take place. To determine whether the challenging delegations met these criteria, the Credentials Committee put questions directly to individual delegates from each group so as to ascertain which individuals would be willing to give unequivocal support to the party's nominees. In short, a loyalty oath was invoked to determine which group was most loyal, duly and properly elected, and representative of the state's population.

The regular delegation presented its case first. State Senator E. K. Collins, the leadoff witness, maintained that the state's regular party was unswerving in its loyalty to the national party and vigorously denied that voting discrimination played any part in Mississippi politics. He further asserted that Negroes throughout the state were "absolutely free to participate" in the proceedings of the state Democratic party machinery, "including the selection of national convention delegates." [39] Collins' testimony set the tone for subsequent regular-party witnesses, each of whom, including the state's assistant attorney general, reaffirmed Collins' statements.

After this parade of denials of voter discrimination by the traditional party representatives, members of the MFDP delegation gave their testimony. The first witness was Aaron Henry, chairman of the MFDP delegation, who was followed by vice-chairwoman Fannie Lou Hamer, national committeeman Rev. Edwin King, and Mrs. Rita Schwerner, wife of Michael Schwerner, a white civil rights worker who was brutally murdered along with two co-workers—one black and one white—during Mississippi's 1964 freedom summer program. Many other witnesses followed; one after another they testified to the rampant discrimination which prevented Negroes from voting in Mississippi. They further testified to the methods by which this discrimination was enforced—not only by legal means but also by violence and fraud. Lending further strength to MFDP's case were the appeals of such outstanding civil right leaders as Roy Wilkins, James Farmer, and Dr. Martin Luther King, Jr., all of whom urged the Credentials Committee to respond favorably to the MFDP plea and seat its delegation in the convention. Also calling for MFDP's seating was Joseph Rauh, general counsel for the United Automobile Workers of America, who was responsible for organizing MFDP's brief and presenting its case before the Credentials Committee.

In support of its case, MFDP set forth three reasons why the regular delegation should not be seated. First, it argued that the regular state party was responsible for the passage of a bill in the Mississippi Legislature in 1963 containing this provision: in a primary held in the year of the national elections, two slates of electors were to be presented to the voters of Mississippi, one slate pledged to the national nominees and one slate unpledged. While this tactic appared harmless, MFDP held, the electors pledged to the national nominees had no chance of winning because public opinion in Mississippi was against the national Democratic party. Thus the unpledged electors would win outright in the primaries and be able to cast their electoral votes for anyone they chose to support.

Second, argued MFDP, the members of the regular delegation were not chosen in good faith because not one of the state's top officials was in the delegation. In addition, the argument went on, the regular delegation had failed to demonstrate its loyalty because its members had not signed an earlier pledge vowing unswerving support of the party's nominees at the state convention and therefore, strictly speaking, were not bona fide Democrats.

At this point the Credentials Committee had not yet asked the regular delegation to sign a loyalty pledge. But it was MFDP's conviction that an earlier commitment, similar to the one its delegates had made, would have shown that the regular democrats were acting in good faith and had the interests of the national party at heart. Moreover, even while being challenged, the regular delegation had not signed a loyalty pledge.

Finally, MFDP asserted that by systematically and continually excluding Negroes from the state's political machinery, the regular state party had violated the Fourteenth Amendment.

Both sides having been heard, Governor Lawrence declared that a decision on the Mississippi contest would be announced after private deliberation of the committee. Meanwhile, during the hearing President Johnson, who had kept abreast of the Mississippi dispute, felt it important enough to send Senator Hubert Humphrey (later revealed as Johnson's choice for running mate) to the convention to mediate a satisfactory solution. To accompany Humphrey, Johnson dispatched Tom Finey, who had earlier that year journeyed to Mississippi for the President to gather background material on the dispute. Exactly what the President's intentions were in sending these emissaries is debatable. At least one commentator, Len Holt, says that the President originally hoped the regular delegates would agree to sign loyalty oaths, after which they could be seated, but that growing public opinion in favor of MFDP made such a simple solution unlikely.

Arriving at the convention, the mediators presented a three-point plan to each of the contesting delegations. The points included (1) seating those party regulars who would sign a pledge of loyalty supporting the national Democratic party; (2) seating the MFDP delegates without granting them voting rights; and (3) taking measures to guarantee that the 1968 convention would be open to all Negroes. Without hesitation, MFDP chairman Henry rejected this "back of the bus" compromise. Supporting Henry's stand was Dr. King, who contended that if such a proposal were accepted, the Negroes of Mississippi would have virtually nothing to do on election day but go fishing. As for the regular delegation, its members immediately rejected the compromise and made it clear that they would reject any proposal offering recognition to MFDP and its delegates.

In an attempt to break this impasse, Congresswoman Edith Green (D. Ore.), who was a member of the Credentials Committee, offered another compromise. Under its terms the traditional party members would be required to take a loyalty oath, and subsequently the MFDP delegates and any regular delegates who also took the oath would be seated and given voting rights. Although this proposal was acceptable to MFDP, it was immediately ruled out by the President's representatives, who vetoed it on the ground that the proposal would have established a precedent for any contending faction in any state to come to future Democratic conventions and demand a seat. Were there to be many of these occurrences at any one convention, the party's entire nominating machinery could break down and the convention sessions could deteriorate into a wrangle over seating and recognition. Fearing this, Humphrey and Finey refused to accept any proposal that seemed to create a legal basis for MFDP.

The President's men then countered with yet another proposal, which had basically five points: (1) Any member of the regular Mississippi delegation who took a loyalty oath would be seated; (2) the MFDP delegates would be given the status of honored guests; (3) the chairman of the MFDP delegation and its national committeeman —that is, Aaron Henry and Rev. Edwin King—would be accorded the special status of delegates-at-large; [40] (4) for the 1968 convention the Democratic National Committee would obligate every state to select and certify delegates without regard for race, creed, or color; (5) a special committee would be established to aid the states in meeting the foregoing standards for the 1968 election. Holt contends that Senator Humphrey, in his drive to secure the vice-presidential nomination, hand-picked Henry and Rev. Edwin King without MFDP's consent and convinced them, along with Martin Luther King, Jr., to accept the proposed at-large status. In addition, according to Holt, Humphrey used his influence in the Americans for Democratic Action (ADA), which exemplifies the liberal wing of the Democratic party, to get MFDP attorney Joseph Rauh, Negro Congressmen Charles C. Diggs, Jr., and William Dawson, as well as Bayard Rustin, James Farmer, Dr. King, and a host of others, to try to persuade the majority of the MFDP delegation to accept the delegate-at-large proposal. But the move failed.

The proposal was approved by the special subcommittee assigned to resolve the dispute and then by the full Credentials Committee. On the morning of Tuesday, August 25, the entire convention approved the proposal by voice vote. A floor fight, feared by some and hoped for by others, never materialized.

Immediately upon the announcement that this proposal had been approved, almost all the Mississippi regulars walked out of the convention hall. Of the sixty-eight members of the Mississippi delegation only three (one of them a close friend of President Johnson) signed the oath and stayed at the convention.

After the walkout of the regular delegation, Mississippi Governor Paul Johnson declared from his office in Jackson that the delegation members were to be applauded for their courageous action. He said further that the delegation was an independent political group free to pursue whatever course of action it deemed correct. Subsequently, several other southerners joined in denouncing the Credentials Committee, maintaining that its final proposal was illegal.

Later that morning, an MFDP meeting was held to consider what its response should be to the Administration's plan, which had already been approved by the full convention. According to observers McLemore and Holt, in a tense and crucial gathering lasting all day MFDP delegates examined the compromise and debated its relative merits. Although some favored accepting its terms and others remained neutral, those who opposed it prevailed; the vote was to reject the proposal in its entirety and to withdraw from the convention.

The decision to reject the proposal created a furor, especially among those who had insisted that it was the best possible alternative. However, an MFDP spokeman said that in light of the discrimination prevalent in Mississippi, the group could not accept anything less than total victory. In essence, partial victory to them meant defeat. Chairman Henry, who had supported the proposal at first, argued after the vote to reject the compromise that the national party had revealed its paternalistic attitude toward Negroes by offering them this plan. Congresswoman Green said that the black people in Mississippi deserved better than mere consideration as honored guests. Civil rights leader Dr. King expressed an ambivalent attitude. While he would have voted for the compromise proposal had he been a member of the freedom delegation, insofar as it was about the best one could hope for from a national political convention, he also considered the delegation right in refusing the proposal insofar as it represented tokenism, which could not be tolerated in view of the rigid system of segregation in Mississippi.

Both James Farmer of CORE and civil rights organizer Bayard Rustin characterized the proposal as an act of tokenism. Civil rights leaders John Lewis and Robert Moses and several others supported the MFDP stand on the ground that the proposal was morally indefensible. Some convention delegates and sympathizers heralded as a significant concession the part of the proposal which established a special committee to help states meet the new nondiscriminatory standards for selecting delegates to the 1968 national convention. Those who saw in this section a new avenue for Negroes to pursue their political rights maintained that this was a revolutionary decision and no less than a turning point in the national convention in favor of MFDP.

Although lacking the victory they sought, the MFDP delegates made three resolutions before returning to Mississippi: (1) to support the Johnson–Humphrey ticket there; (2) to challenge the seats of those congressmen from Mississippi elected in the coming November election, on the ground that Section 2 of the Fourteenth Amendment had been violated; and (3) to attend the 1968 national convention and again seek to replace the state's regular delegation.

The 1964 Freedom Elections

In September of 1964 Governor Johnson urged Mississippians to support the Republican presidential nominee, Goldwater, and said that party labels were meaningless in the state.[41] And throughout the summer—particularly while the challenge was taking place—action to suppress MFDP had increased across the state and reached a climax with the murder of three civil rights workers. But the shock stemming from the murders of James Chaney, a Negro, and Andrew Goodman and Michael Schwerner, white students from the North, had ultimately intensified the pace of summer registration work and gave new meaning to the upcoming November freedom vote. Even in the face of vigorous opposition and threats against their lives, MFDP workers carried on their door-to-door campaign urging voters to support the national Democratic ticket.

During the same period, more than a thousand signatures were collected on a petition requesting state officials to place the three MFDP congressional candidates—Henry, Hamer, and Gray—on the November ballot. The strategy which MFDP had now adopted was both to participate in the regular November elections if possible and to hold its own freedom election as well. The first part of the strategy failed when, on October 6, the Mississippi State Election Commission ruled that the MFDP petition contained an insufficient number of registered voters' signatures. In fact, there were enough names on the petition, but in many counties white registrars refused to certify them as legal. This was in violation of the newly ratified Twenty-fourth Amendment, which made the poll tax illegal. Many Negroes who had signed the petition had not been certified because they refused to pay the poll tax prior to the election as the registrars demanded. Efforts to force the Election Commission to change its ruling failed, even though the petitioners had the law on their side. In fact, the state attorney general, Joe Patterson, expressed contempt for the MFDP petition by terming the entire procedure "ridiculous."

Left with only their freedom vote, MFDP leaders made immediate preparations for a mock election to be held on October 31 and November 1 and 2. Polling places were set up in 56 of the 82 Mississippi counties, and plans were made for "underground ballots" to be mailed in from the remaining 26 counties deemed too dangerous for MFDP workers to enter. On the whole, this freedom vote was considered partially successful. Despite the state's repressive measures, a total of 68,029 Negroes voted, with the five freedom candidates and the Johnson–Humphrey ticket winning by wide margins. Predictably, the

Johnson–Humphrey ticket received more votes in the freedom election than it did in the official election. (See Table 4 in the Appendix.)

The 1965 Congressional Challenge

The results of the MFDP mock election provided the party with some facts for its upcoming congressional challenge. The challenge rested on the following grounds: (1) that the congressional elections held in Mississippi violated Negroes' rights granted in the Fourteenth and Fifteenth Amendments; (2) that these elections violated Article 1, Section 2 of the Constitution, which says that members of the House shall be elected by the people of the several states; and (3) that the state had failed to comply with the provisions of the Mississippi Compact of 1870, by which it was readmitted to the Union.[42]

MFDP's challenge was filed in accordance with the procedure for contesting elections specified in the U.S. Civil Code (title 2, secs. 201–226). A notice of the challenge was served to the contested delegation in the presence of the Clerk of the House of Representatives on December 4, 1964. The challenge was answered by the white Mississippi delegation 30 days later, from which time both sides were given 40 days to gather evidence for their respective cases. This evidence was to be submitted to the Clerk of the House; then, in consultation with lawyers for both sides, he was to decide which materials would be submitted to the Subcommittee on Elections and Privileges of the House Committee on Administration. A 30-day period was then to be granted during which the contesting parties could file their briefs; then the Subcommittee on Elections was to decide whether to hold public hearings, bring the matter to a subcommittee vote, or present a resolution to the full House.

When Congress convened in January 1965, New York Representative William F. Ryan introduced a "fairness resolution" (independent of the MFDP statutory challenge) which proposed that seating of the five regular Mississippi Democrats be postponed pending an inquiry into the legality of their election.[43] Immediately, another resolution was offered by Representative Carl Albert (D. Okla.) proposing that the Mississippi congressmen be sworn in separately. After some debate on the question, Albert's motion to close the debate was carried by a vote of 276 to 178, and then his resolution to seat the regular delegation was approved by a voice vote.

During the House debate, about 600 MFDP members held a two-hour outdoor vigil in front of the House of Representatives to rally support for the fairness resolution. At the same time, in a counter demonstration, members of the American Nazi party slipped into the other side of the building dressed in blackface and demanded a meeting with the Mississippi delegation (the white one, of course). Neither tactic proved successful. The regular Mississippians had been sworn in—at least until the hearing concluded. Despite this setback, MFDP members expressed optimism about eventually unseating the congressmen and revealed plans to return to Mississippi in order to gather further evidence that Negroes were discriminated against by the state's electoral procedures. Several lawyers, most of them white and all of them interested in preserving civil liberties, volunteered their services in this regard.[44]

As of January 1965, approximately 6 percent of the eligible Negroes in Mississippi were in fact registered voters. The 94 percent who remained unregistered, despite the tremendous efforts of COFO and MFDP, included vast numbers who had been the victims of threats, harassment, and intimidations of various sorts, as well as of economic reprisals and police brutality. Nevertheless, many volunteered to give testimony on behalf of MFDP and recount how they had been denied the vote. Although their accounts varied in detail from county to county, the pattern was the same.

In Panola County, for example, where repression of potential Negro voters had been most severe, "only two Negroes had been permitted to register from 1890 to 1962," according to one account. At hearings held by MFDP in Batesville, the county seat, more than 200 Negro residents told of crosses burned in front yards, shooting incidents, floggings, false arrests, denials of federal surplus food, sudden evictions, and all manner of other tactics calculated to discourage them from attempting to register and vote. In response to their testimony, the county registrar, the sheriff, the district attorney, and numerous plantation owners vociferously denied at the hearing that there had ever been intimidation, threats, harassment, or slayings of would-be voters.[45]

But this was the story of only one county. Statewide, MFDP lawyers gathered nearly 15,000 typewritten pages of depositions alluding to the disfranchisement of Negroes through violence and intimidation. In May, the federal government's Commission on Civil Rights, which had been studying the Mississippi situation since 1960, made public additional evidence confirming the information gathered by MFDP lawyers.

Filing the depositions with the Clerk of the House constituted only one step in the official challenge, which from the outset was conceived as a two-part venture. The first part consisted of unseating the incumbent white Mississippi representatives based on Section 2 of the Fourteenth Amendment and on the constitutional provision that "each House shall be the judge of the elections, returns, and qualifications of its own members." In short, the first part of the challenge was founded on the allegation that these five white congressmen were nominated and elected in primary and general elections from which Negroes "were regularly and systematically excluded by intimidation, harrassment, economic reprisal, property damage, terrorization, violence and illegal and unconstitutional registration procedures." [46] This the MFDP depositions sought to prove conclusively.

The second part of the challenge proposed that three of the five seats held by white incumbents be awarded to the MFDP candidates elected in the 1964 freedom election.[47] This portion of the challenge was presented in the form of a two-part legal brief. The first part, a challenging brief filed by MFDP, provided lengthy arguments in support of its contention that its 1964 election was the "only fair and democratic one held in Mississippi" insofar as no exclusion was practiced, as it was in the official election. That is, the brief stated, MFDP's registration, polling, and voting procedures in electing its candidates were fair and nondiscriminatory. A seating brief constituted the second half of this two-part brief.

The entire brief angered many of MFDP's supporters and legal advisers. These people, among them a number of early supporters of the party, had urged its leaders after the Democratic national convention episode to take every legal step to get its candidates on the regular state ballot. If it had used every legal means to get on the June and November ballots and had failed, the party's role could have shifted from objecting aggrieved citizens to bona fide claimants. This status would have entitled the party to a hearing in federal court as well as in appropriate committees of Congress as a legitimate challenger of the regular party. Moreover, it could have sought a federal injunction enjoining the governor from certifying the regular party congressmen (that is, simply signing an official statement that these men were duly and properly elected according to state election laws). A powerful case for such action could have been made under existing civil rights statutes and Section 2 of the Fifteenth Amendment, which makes it illegal to deny any citizen the right to vote "on account of race, color, or previous condition of servitude." This the party's earlier legal advisers believed to be the best legal basis for challenge. But the two-part brief based its appeal on the freedom elections because MFDP had not tried to get its candidates on the November 1964 ballot. Nor had it exhausted all legal means in this effort. Instead, when the party had been rebuffed by local and state officials, it abandoned plans for further legal steps and concentrated on conducting a more successful mock election in November than it had in June. It was precisely this failure to follow through with proper legal recourse in the attempt to have the candidates certified that severely weakened this legal brief.[48]

The weakness became apparent shortly after the House began its public hearings on the matter. Joseph Rauh, the former legal counsel of MFDP, was asked to testify—but because he could not attend he sent a memorandum in which he effectively pointed out this weakness. He declared that "the contention of the freedom democrats as to the democratic character of their freedom election is without legal support [since candidates] Hamer, Devine, and Gray were not elected in any . . . constitutional state election," but, in Rauh's words, "selected in a mock election . . . and there is no plausible legal basis on which the winners of a mock election can be deemed to have been elected to Congress under the Constitution and laws of the United States." He concluded by asserting that "their illegal exclusion from the ballot is not a substitute for their election on the ballot."

Rauh's argument pointed up the dilemma facing Congress. If Congress were to accept the MFDP arguments—that is, if it were to accept the results of the mock election—it would set a precedent that might trigger a battery of mock elections throughout the country by minority groups, and the resultant round of demonstrations, investigations, and hearings could impede or hamper congressional functions. Sensing this dilemma, MFDP withdrew its original brief, revised its legal arguments, and filed a second brief with the House on June 29.

The new document, "Brief of Contestants Urging the Vacating of the Contested Seats and Holding of New Elections," abandoned MFDP's earlier position that its contestants were bona fide candidates and now identified them only as "contestants." The brief simply urged that a new and fairer election be held in which MFDP candidates be allowed to run and its supporters, registered or unregistered, be allowed to vote. By stressing the moral issue and avoiding the question of legality in this way, MFDP hoped to make a better case for its claim to the regular Democrats' seats.[49]

By mid-June, because MFDP had failed to adhere to certain procedural requirements and because of other, unaccountable reasons, the Clerk of the House had refused to have the MFDP testimony and depositions printed up for distribution to House members. His refusal brought immediate action from SNCC, by now the principal backer of MFDP, to prod him into printing the depositions. A lobbying demonstration was held, as well as a rally in Lafayette Park across from the White House—but all to no avail. Later the same day a sit-in demonstration was held in the clerk's office, a move that aroused his anger and ended with the arrest of the SNCC student sit-ins. (Prior to the 1964 convention challenge, the civil rights organizations that had worked with COFO were strong supporters of MFDP. After the rejection of the compromise, the ouster of Aaron Henry, and the dropping of attorney Rauh, the chief supporter of MFDP became SNCC. In fact, the new chairman of the party, Lawrence Guyot, was a SNCC field secretary. However, it should be borne in mind that all the major MFDP officers and members were native Mississippians. SNCC brought in volunteers and the resources of its national office only to help the party in its organizational and registration work.)

Not all the results of the SNCC demonstrations were negative.[50] Some members of the House Committee on Administration brought pressure to bear on the clerk, and on June 7, after lengthy debate, the House decreed that the testimony taken by the challengers be printed in its entirety.[51] The printed deposition filled three volumes and bore the unwieldy title, "Papers Omitted in Printing Pursuant to Provisions of the Statutes Involving the Five Congressional Districts in the State of Mississippi."

The Challenge was now in the hands of the House Subcommittee on Elections and Privileges. Having cleared some obstacles, the challenge faced still more formidable ones—in the persons of subcommittee chairman Robert Ashmore (D. S.Car.) and the three Republicans and four other southern Democrats who were members of the subcommittee. This southern-dominated committee was entrusted with passing judgment on the deposition and reporting it directly to the House floor, bypassing the House Rules Committee.[52]

To understand the feelings and attitudes involved on both sides of this challenge, one must take into account the background of events in the civil rights movement at about this time. Dr. Martin Luther King, Jr., after his success in bringing about the desegregation of buses in Birmingham, had planned to lay siege to another bastion of segregation in Alabama, the town of Selma, in order to dramatize the need for a strong voting rights law. But his nonviolent demonstrations of late 1964 and early 1965 had done little more than provoke strong police repression. This reached a climax on March 9, 1965, when about 500 Negroes set out on a march from Selma to Montgomery in defiance of Governor George Wallace's ban on such demonstrations. At Selma's Edmund Pettus Bridge, the marchers were met by an entourage of Selma Sheriff Clark's deputies and Colonel Lingo's state troopers. Before the marchers could retreat, in the words of one eyewitness,

> . . . helmeted state police, . . . on foot and . . . on horseback charged into the ranks—battered the pilgrims to the ground, tear-gassed them into misery, then whipped their heads and bodies some more. . . . [To] make the punishment stick, as the marchers . . . recovered from the gassing, the troopers, aided by a posse of able-bodied white men, whipped the marchers all the way back to the starting point—that is, to a Negro church six blocks away.[53]

Recorded on film and subsequently viewed by millions on nationwide television, this brutal, inhuman police action aroused the conscience of the nation. Within a few days President Johnson responded to public clamor by announcing that he would submit to Congress a new and stronger voting rights bill.[54]

This bill was submitted to Congress about the time that the MFDP challenge was encountering difficulties. Technically, the House Administration Subcommittee on Elections and Privileges was to report the challenge out on July 5; but under the circumstances the Voting Rights Act clearly took precedence (the law went into effect on August 6, 1965), and so the report was not forthcoming until September. Finally, the southern-dominated subcommittee reported that the majority of its members found the MFDP challenge unsupportable. In essence, the report maintained that the regular election of November 3, 1964, had been conducted in accordance with federal and state laws. Nothing about the election could be regarded as illegal, the report stated, inasmuch as it had not been set aside by the decision of any court of competent jurisdiction. In other words, the report considered the fact that inordinate numbers of Mississippi Negroes were disfranchised insufficient ground for declaring that the incumbents had been improperly elected.

In addition to the report of the Subcommittee on Elections and Privileges recommending dismissal of the MFDP challenge, a minority report was filed by a small band of House members who strongly backed most civil rights measures: Conyers of Michiagan, Edwards and Burton of California, Ryan of New York, and about a half-dozen others. The minority report, which opposed immediate dismissal of the challenge and proposed further study of the matter, failed to gather enough supporters, however. And this despite the presence of three Mississippi Negroes, who were allowed to sit in the House chamber during the debate of the subcommittee's report, and despite the efforts of the 300 who lobbied all week during the House debate, and despite the efforts of the seven MFDP members who brought the challenge.

The subcommittee's report met no further obstacles. With the matter out of committee, on September 17, 1965, a motion to accept the report and thus in effect dismiss the MFDP challenge was approved by the House, 228 to 143—although, significantly, the wording of the original motion was amended so that it would not say the regular Mississippi delegates were "entitled to their seats." [55]

A glance at the votes reveals that congressmen with significant Negro constituencies or with sympathy for the civil rights movement were largely with the minority that opposed the subcommittee report. In short, the voting was mixed, although Dr. King, in a telegram to Negro Congressman John Conyers of Michigan, deplored the adoption of the report as a "testament of shame."

Why was the voting mixed? What happened to the pro-civil rights majority that had only five weeks earlier passed the historic Voting Rights Act? Indeed, what did happen to friends and supporters of the challenge? One explanation offered is that a bloc of about a hundred House southerners were united solidly against the challenge and used their influence to defeat it. Just as President Johnson's support of the Voting Rights Bill probably was helpful in getting it passed, his failure to support the MFDP challenge probably helped to defeat it. Another reason given is that the challenge was itself "quixotic" and unrealistic. Still others maintained that the sit-ins and lobbying demonstrations that were held while the House considered the challenge alienated some congressmen. One observer hinted that many of the MFDP lawyers were members of a Communist-backed organization and sabotaged the challenge on orders, while another stated that the Speaker of the House exerted behind-the-scenes influence against the challenge. And there are more hypotheses.

One lawyer who helped gather testimony for MFDP reasoned that many congressmen who were in sympathy with the challenge, but who found it expedient to vote against it, felt they had done enough by supporting the Voting Rights Act. Yet another commentator charges that the governor of Mississippi succeeded in soft-pedaling the challenge issue by calling off a special session of the state legislature that was to enact countermeasures to the Voting Rights Act and by encouraging the regular session to revise the state constitution so as to facilitate the registration of Negro voters—that is, he allowed the shock of Selma in 1965 to blot out memories of the murder of Chaney, Goodman, and Schwerner in 1964.

Whatever the cause, the fact is that the challenge was defeated. In retrospect, the passage of the Voting Rights Act obviously played a role—whether major or minor—in the defeat of the challenge. In addition, one can readily see that part of the reason for the defeat was MFDP's failure to exhaust every legal channel in trying to obtain certification of its candidates. Basing the challenge completely on the mock election was questionable strategy, for it put the House of Representatives in an untenable position. Even if the majority of House members had been in sympathy with the challenge, which is doubtful, there remained grave reservations about setting a precedent for a rash of similar petitions from all over the country.

On the other hand, the fear of setting a dangerous precedent may have been unduly exaggerated. The House has been known to make exceptions in isolated cases, and its actions are not so bound by precedent as are the decisions of America's courts of law.

The 1966 and 1967 Elections

Following passage of the Voting Rights Act and the defeat of MFDP's congressional challenge, SNCC severed its ties with MFDP and adopted a separatist or go-it-alone political strategy. The MFDP experience was instrumental in prompting SNCC to formulate the then radical position that coalitions with white liberals had outlived their usefulness. SNCC contended that the defeat was due not to any inherent weakness in MFDP's case, but to the moral bankruptcy of the white establishment and to a sellout of the party by its white liberal members. MFDP chairman Lawrence Guyot shared this attitude: "We are returning to Mississippi having learned the bitter lesson that the very institutions and people whom we petition for relief are deeply implicated in the crimes committed against us." [56]

Despite this reduction in support, MFDP continued to operate through the efforts of indigenous leadership, and in fact secured victory for some of its black candidates in the 1967 state elections (the first blacks to be voted into office since Reconstruction). This goal, which SNCC had sought, was achieved after its withdrawal from the party ranks.

Ironically, passage of the 1965 Voting Rights Act, which focused on eliminating the administrative means used to perpetuate voter discrimination, was ineffective in localities where discrimination was enforced by other means.[57] Thus, although the act provided for federal registrars to register prospective Negro voters in the South, in Mississippi the old barriers of apathy and fear—the ever present enemies of voter drives there—remained. To surmount these barriers, MFDP again began to conduct door-to-door voter drives, urging Negroes to register at courthouses staffed by federal registrars. Where it was thought that the regular registrar was still discriminating against Negroes, the U.S. attorney general had been asked to send in federal registrars. For those counties where he was not persuaded of the need and did not send federal registrars, the task of getting Negroes registered was particularly complex.

Thus after passage of the Voting Rights Act MFDP needed even more money and personnel if it was to survive and grow as a viable political organization. Therefore, following the withdrawal of SNCC's support, MFDP created an international bureau for the party, with headquarters in Paris, in order to attract the additional funds needed to continue the tedious job of voter registration.

Conflict: NAACP Versus MFDP

Weakened by SNCC's withdrawal of support, MFDP launched its new voter registration drive in the fall of 1965, acutely aware that enlarging the state's Negro electorate was crucial to the organization's survival. Further hampered by the fact that COFO had disintegrated in the heat of the 1964 national Democratic convention challenge, this drive lacked the spirit of cooperation and the coordination that had characterized COFO efforts. In fact, in addition to financial and personnel shortages, MFDP now found itself in a competitive struggle with the only other major civil rights organization in the state, the NAACP, which was conducting its own voter registration drive.

The roots of the conflict between MFDP and the NAACP, whose independent voter drives soon overlapped in several counties, dated back to 1962–1964, when COFO made an unsuccessful attempt to achieve maximum black voter registration through the combined efforts, resources, and skills of all the major civil rights organizations in the state. According to NAACP accounts, at that time it suffered from unjust law suits, loss of funds, and embarrassing, even fraudulent, practices committed in its name by unscrupulous and uncooperative members of the other organizations which supported MFDP.[58] The resultant bad feelings later came to a head during MFDP's Democratic convention challenge and, in combination with other disputes, led to COFO's breakup. If the NAACP allegations are correct—and evidence seems to support them—the reasons for the demise of COFO are similar to the ones which plagued the National Negro Congress specifically, and national confederations in general: factional disputes, overambitious leaders, clashing ideologies, and so on. (See Chapter 2.) What particularly embittered the NAACP was MFDP's treatment of Aaron Henry, who was both president of the state NAACP and chairman of the MFDP delegation. Henry was harshly criticized by MFDP and dropped from membership because of his favorable re-action to the final seating compromise, particularly his apparent will-ingness to accept the delegate-at-large status offered to Rev. Edwin King and himself. Furthermore, the NAACP has charged that during its 1965 voting project in the state, which roughly coincided with MFDP's congressional challenge, MFDP members undermined its efforts by invading and disrupting its offices, by seeking to keep Ne-groes from joining NAACP voter efforts, and by attempting to break up a meeting during an address by NAACP national secretary Roy Wilkins.[59] Disillusioned by such experiences, the NAACP therefore broke off cooperative activities and launched a voter registration project clearly divorced from MFDP's.

Although the NAACP crash program to register voters was initi-ated in November 1964, following the demise of COFO, its major efforts did not get underway until the sumer of 1965. A central ad-ministrative office for the state was established in Jackson, and NAACP units throughout the nation recruited volunteers for their scheduled summer campaign. The NAACP summer project, according to the organization's reports, was directly instrumental in registering 20,002 Negroes and indirectly responsible for an additional 8,370 Negroes who were registered by federal registrars.[60] The latter figure should be included, the NAACP argued, because of its activity in the counties in question both before and after federal registrars were assigned. Furthermore, NAACP spokesmen pointed out, not only did the NAACP citizenship classes and systematic house-to-house convas-sing produce scores of new Negro voters, but the more than 250 com-plaints which the organization registered with the Justice Department brought additional federal registrars to several Mississippi counties.

The success of the NAACP 1965 summer voter registration project in Mississippi stemmed in part from a highly concentrated team effort, utilizing only twenty-one workers in six southwestern Mississippi counties under the energetic leadership of state field secretary Charles

Evers. (His brother Medgar had two years earlier lost his life, the victim of an assassin's bullet, as the price for daring to urge Mississippi Negroes to exercise their constitutional rights.) After the summer project, Evers and Althea Simmons kept alive voter registration activities and were responsible for registering another 5,000 Negroes in the same six-county area during November.[61]

The more successful the NAACP voter drive became, the sharper the conflict and competition with MFDP. Although the roots of the conflict date back to COFO, the areas of contention were inherent in the actions, orientations, and perceptions of the two groups.

MFDP saw the NAACP as a large and financially secure organization that was interested in helping the black middle class, not poor blacks. Moreover, in MFDP's view, the NAACP had failed to offer it any assistance although it was seeking to provide help to these poor blacks who needed help most. Depleted of resources, having no more than a skeleton organization structure, and with no major organization backing it, MFDP felt that if the NAACP were really sincere in its quest to help blacks and advance their welfare, it would maintain the party and help revise its organization structure so that it could achieve its laudable goal.

On the other hand, the NAACP had come to look upon MFDP as unconcerned with the realities of power, lacking any understanding of the realities of politics, essentially idealistic and utopian, and therefore without any real chance of affecting the political situation of black Mississippians. Moreover, the NAACP got its support from the only element in the black community that could afford to support it—the black middle class—and in turn it supported this element. What is more, it felt that by helping the middle class, it was also helping lower-class blacks. And it did lend a hand when possible, but this group did not get top priority.

In sum, the MFDP view was that the NAACP had money, skills, and a national organization but was conservative, middle-class-oriented, and unconcerned with poor blacks in the state. This is the reason for the MFDP efforts to discredit, disrupt, or counter the NAACP activities. On the other hand, the NAACP view was that the MFDP organization was visionary, immature, uncompromising, impatient, and at best doomed to fail. Thus the histories, orientations, and perceptions of the two organizations explain why they competed to become the dominant civil rights group in every area of the state where they confronted each other.

In response to NAACP activities, in August MFDP conducted an intensive five-day voter registration drive—dubbed "freedom week"— in Hinds County. The Negro population of Jackson, headquarters for the campaign, apparently responded well; according to one eyewitness, by the time the county clerk opened his doors on Monday morning, August 16, a line of more than a hundred Negroes had formed in front of his office. But the MFDP efforts were partially blunted. Despite the Mississippi electorate's overwhelming endorsement of an amendment to the state constitution liberalizing voter registration qualifications, the federal attorney general refused to send in additional federal registrars to aid in the registration process. The clerk of Hinds County consequently succeeded in undermining the MFDP efforts by slowing the registration down to a trickle, registering an average of only ten Negroes per hour in the morning and four per hour in the afternoon.

Toward the end of freedom week, an incident indirectly involving MFDP aroused even greater NAACP animosity. Amid increasing instances of anti-Negro violence and rising white hostility toward the voter drive, Rev. Edwin King of the MFDP executive committee organized a forum under MFDP auspices at Tougaloo College in Jackson. (The central administrative offices of the NAACP Mississippi branch were also in Jackson.) At the forum Charles Sims, president of the militant Deacons for Defense and Justice, exhorted Negroes to arm themselves for possible retaliation in defense of their rights.

During their stay in Jackson for the forum, several members of the Deacons journeyed to Natchez, where white violence and terrorism had developed because of increasing black voter registration attempts and had resulted in the death of two blacks and the serious injury of one other. Once in Natchez the Deacons urged blacks to "wake up" and defend themselves. These exhortations came at a time when blacks were already pelting white motorists with bricks, bottles, and tomatoes as they drove through black neighborhoods.

When Charles Evers heard of the Deacons' presence in Natchez he hurried there in the hope that he could forestall further anti-white outbreaks and the inevitable white counterviolence that would follow. Evers insisted that Mississippi Negroes neither needed nor wanted the

Deacons, and he succeeded by force of his personal prestige in temporarily easing tensions. The incident drove the two organizations further apart, heightening the competition between them for predominance within the Negro community.

Blacks in Natchez *did* take steps to counteract white terrorism by boycotting the downtown stores and merchants. In short, a don't-buy-from-white-merchants campaign was put into effect by blacks. The boycott only succeeded in lessening some of the white violence and terrorism, not all. Therefore the boycott was continued in a limited fashion.

By the end of August, a battle had developed between the two groups over the Natchez boycott, with both groups seeking to capture leadership. In order to bolster the NAACP position, Evers acted on his own, without national office approval, and called in Rev. Andrew Young, an aide of Dr. King, to offset the challenge of young MFDP militants. The NAACP appeared victorious when Evers succeeded in calling off one of the protest marches. This move deeply angered the young SNCC and MFDP militants,[62] and competition between the groups went on.

Following the House dismissal of the MFDP seating challenge in September, party chairman Guyot announced that, despite the poor results of its summer voter drive, MFDP would put forward a slate of candidates to oppose Senator Eastland and the five House members in the 1966 election. Anticipating the usual difficulties, the party sent a telegram to President Johnson and U.S. Attorney General Nicholas Katzenbach requesting the appointment of federal registrars in all Mississippi counties. Later, at the MFDP nominating convention in Jackson in October of 1965, it was announced that the six candidates would run on a common slate in the June 7 Democratic primary election and, even if defeated, would later run as independent candidates in the general election. In reaction to MFDP's newly adopted policy of running only all-black slates of candidates (which was never put into practice), the NAACP formally announced that it sought to establish an integrated political grouping in Mississippi, an alliance of Negroes, white moderates, and state labor leaders.

Following its October nominating convention, MFDP sought to enhance its chances for victory in the coming 1966 election by bringing suit in federal district court demanding that the Mississippi legislature be reapportioned and that the lines of the state's congressional districts be redrawn to comply with the Supreme Court's recent one-man-one-vote ruling. The suit, naming Governor Johnson, the state attorney general, the secretary of state, the speaker of the house, and the president of the senate as defendants, charged that "the present apportionment established irrational, invidious, discriminatory and unequal districts which deprives Negroes of their rights guaranteed by the United States and the State Constitutions." On other fronts, the party participated in food distribution in several counties and continued to relay to the Justice Department complaints of discriminatory behavior on the part of county registrars.[63]

Early in March 1966, MFDP backed several Negro candidates in an effort to integrate local school boards in Clay, Panola, and Bolivia counties. Because the Negro community did not support the candidates wholeheartedly and the white community used its ingenuity to offset black efforts, not one of the candidates was elected. In West Point, for example, 500 whites and 40 Negroes met in the school auditorium to elect a single member to the school's board of trustees. Although the white voters immediately elected a white chairman to supervise the election, Odiea Holiday, a Negro factory worker, succeeded in nominating Charles Graves, a MFDP member, to oppose the white incumbent. Then, despite protests from the 40 Negroes, the chairman appointed an all-white committee to conduct the secret balloting. It was later announced that the incumbent had won overwhelmingly.[64]

Following these local defeats, qualifying petitions for all six MFDP candidates scheduled to run in the June Democratic primary (one of them white) were filed before the April 8 deadline. In the meantime, new measures were enacted by the state legislature to curtail the party's activities. First, in order to save the House seat held by Jamie Whitten, a staunch segregationist, the legislature revised the boundaries of congressional districts, dispersing the Negro majority in his district. Then a law was passed requiring that anyone seeking to run for office in a state election sign a pledge endorsing segregation and condemning the 1964 federal Civil Rights Act before he could be certified a bona fide candidate. Both issues were of course immediately challenged in court by MFDP.[65] Regarding the new qualifications for certification of candidates, the party's court action appeared to pay off when, on May 9, the all-white State Democratic Executive Committee notified the MFDP candidates that their names would be placed on the June primary ballot despite their refusal to sign a pledge supporting segregation and condemning the Civil Rights Act.

Just before the June primary election, James Meredith began his "march against fear" to increase Negro voter registration in the state. Meredith was the first black admitted to the University of Mississippi. His first attempts to register as a student had set off a series of violent white protests and terrorist activities. However, with federal help he entered the university in 1962. After he graduated he conducted several one-man campaigns against segregation.

Neither Meredith's march and the anger of Mississippi Negroes when he was wounded by a sniper nor the tremendous MFDP efforts had sufficient immediate impact on the primaries, and all the freedom candidates were defeated. Despite many monitors from the Justice Department as well as members of the House of Representatives who were present to observe the polling, there were numerous complaints of voter discrimination. Some Negroes reported that they were "prevented from voting or were hampered while trying to cast their ballot," while still others stated that "voting officials had told them their names were not on the list of registered voters."

An MFDP official personally handed all these complaints to the House observers. Later, on June 16, the Justice Department acted on a number of such complaints and filed suit against Leflore County, accusing it of having failed to protect Negroes' voting rights in the recent primary. Moreover, the suit accused county officials of violating the 1965 Voting Rights Act and of having denied Negroes the rights guaranteed them by the Fourteenth and Fifteenth Amendments.[66]

Despite its growing influence and power, the NAACP chose not to enter any candidates in the June primary. In a show of strength, however, it turned out 95 percent (approximately 4,430) of the registered Negro voters in Jefferson and Claiborne counties; one year earlier only 32 Negroes were registered to vote in these two counties combined. Engineering the voter turnout was Charles Evers. First he subdivided each county into five districts; then he appointed a dependable chairman to supervise activities in each. On election day, ten workers canvassed each district door-to-door, reminding registered Negroes of their duty to vote. In addition, each district unit had access to five cars for transporting voters to the polls. Evers even saw to it that on the Sunday before election day, every Negro minister in both counties preached on the importance of voting, and schoolteachers conducted classes on the mechanics of voting.

Evidence of the Negroes' new voting strength, coupled with Evers' dedication and his denunciation of black power, quickly won him the respect of many white residents of the two counties. The purpose of this show of strength, Evers contended, was to make it unmistakably clear that Negroes would be elected to local and county offices in coming elections. At the same time, Evers repudiated the idea of all-black governments in predominantly Negro counties and predicted that some whites would be elected along with Negroes. Thus he backed the state's Young Democrats, a coalition of Negroes and white liberals bent on effectively tying the Mississippi Democratic party to the national party. (The Young Democrats in the state had an effective liaison with the White House; the group's leader, Douglass Wynn, had managed the 1964 Johnson–Humphrey campaign in Mississippi and was a personal friend of the President.)[67]

After the primary election, the NAACP's intensive voting efforts seemed to give it an edge in its rivalry with MFDP. On July 13, however, came the news from Jackson that the MFDP suit for reapportionment of the Mississippi legislature had been successful. A federal district court panel headed by Judge J. R. Coleman, former governor of Mississippi, ordered the state legislature to reapportion its seats in accordance with the Supreme Court's one-man-one-vote ruling.

Just as MFDP was recovering from its primary election defeat and mapping strategy for the forthcoming general election in November, its major challenger announced that there would be five NAACP candidates in local and county contests. Negro minister R. L. Whitaker, the announcement said, would run for justice of the peace in Holmes County—where Negro voters outnumbered whites 3,882 to 3,400—in a special election to be held on September 27. The other contests, which involved positions on school boards in Jefferson, Holmes, Claiborne, and Wilkinson counties, would take place in November. Immediately following the NAACP announcement, MFDP learned that it had lost another of its suits challenging the state legislature's redistricting plan because it divided the predominantly Negro Delta region into three districts instead of leaving it intact. Because MFDP had begun to concentrate its activities in the Delta region to offset the tremendous NAACP success in the southern part of the state, the court's action in this case weakened the party's bases of support.

Nevertheless, MFDP sought certification of three independent candidates in the November election—Rev. Clifton Whitley, Dock Drummond, and Mrs. Erma Sanders. The State Election Commission rejected the petitions, however, on the grounds that they lacked the required number of signatures and that Whitley and Drummond had been unsuccessful Democratic candidates in the primary elections. Subsequently the MFDP legal arm, the Lawyers' Constitutional Defense Committee, filed suit in federal district court, contending that the new state law—which had been passed only days after the June primary and had increased tenfold the number of signatures required on an independent candidate's petition to run for Congress—was in violation of section 5 of the 1965 Voting Rights Act. According to the provisions of this section, a state is required to submit proposed changes in its voting laws to the federal district court in Washington before putting them into effect. Ten days after suit had been filed, a three-judge federal district court panel ordered the state to place the MFDP-backed independent candidates on the ballot.

The court's action in favor of MFDP was of little avail, however. In the three-way senatorial race involving incumbent James Eastland, Prentiss Walker, and Negro Clifton Whitley, Eastland won handily. In fact, by drawing nearly 10 percent of the Negro vote, which otherwise could have been expected to go to Walker, Whitley probably contributed to Eastland's victory. (See Table 6 in the Appendix.)

The NAACP also had its day in court before the elections; it filed suit in the U.S. district court requesting postponement of the election until Negroes could be given proportional representation on county election commissions, which perform the critical function of determining the eligibility of independent candidates for local offices and which prepare official ballots. But a federal judge refused to oust the 246 county election commissioners or to put off the November elections, on the ground that Jefferson and Claiborne counties had not excluded NAACP candidates from the November ballot. In the meantime, the state had revoked the NAACP charter, but was subsequently ordered by a federal court to restore it.[68]

In the November general election, the two MFDP House candidates and the NAACP school board candidates were defeated.[69] But the two groups refused to give up. In January 1967, another MFDP suit was instituted in federal district court challenging the state's redistricting plan. During the proceedings, the court ordered the state legislature to present satisfactory reasons for retaining the apparent inequities cited by MFDP. When the legislature failed to do so on time, the court declared its proposed redistricting plan unconstitutional and subsequently extended an invitation to both MFDP and the legislature to submit proposals for a new plan; only MFDP accepted the invitation. The party's plan called for realigning eight counties in order to establish a population balance closer to equality, but the court rejected the proposal as tenuous and lacking factual support.

Meanwhile, Charles Evers assembled the state's Negro leaders in Jackson on March 11 for the purpose of forming a political committee to unite and enlarge the Negro electorate in anticipation of the coming elections. At the meeting a 15-member executive committee was established to spearhead efforts to increase Negro registration and to help coordinate Negro political action throughout the state. Two weeks after the meeting, the federal district court decreed that its own plan for reapportioning the state's legislative districts was effective immediately. This plan divided the state into 36 senatorial districts, each represented by one to five senators, and 32 house districts, each represented by one to ten congressmen.[70]

Immediately following implementation of the court's redistricting, MFDP, with the help of the National Committee for Free Elections, began preparations for a special May election to be held in Sunflower County. This county includes two communities, Sunflower and Moorhead, in which Negroes make up 70 percent of the population. The special election was being held by order of the U.S. Court of Appeals which, acting on MFDP's suit, had invalidated an earlier election on the ground that Negroes had been denied the right to vote.

The party prepared all-Negro slates for both Moorhead and Sunflower contests, including mayor and all the aldermen's seats in each city. Nevertheless, the Negro mayoral candidate in Sunflower, Otis Brown, said that, if elected, "we would put white people in every department and in some we would have white assistants to Negroes and in others Negro assistants to whites." Because 185 Negroes were registered to vote in Sunflower, as opposed to 153 whites, party leaders expected Brown to win. In Moorhead, on the other hand, although Negro residents outnumbered white residents, white voters outnumbered Negro voters. One of the campaign workers for the Negro mayoral candidate in Moorhead gave him a 50–50 chance of winning.

In a move that appeared to enhance the Negroes' chances, the Justice Department dispatched election observers to "help insure that local election officials are able to conform their practices fully with state and federal law." But even this move did not help; both all-Negro tickets were defeated.[71] This was to be expected in Moorhead, where white voters were in the majority. But in Sunflower Negro voters outnumbered white voters. Also suspicious was the fact that the five white incumbent aldermen in Sunflower won by wide margins: 83 to 43. In Moorhead, Negro candidates for alderman ran 103 to 131 votes behind the white incumbents. After the election the mayor of Sunflower admitted that he "got a few more votes than expected." He added that while he had not approached the radical Negro voters, he did campaign among the "good niggers." Another victorious white candidate for alderman, J. B. Romine, Jr., voiced similar thoughts, maintaining that no Negro could win with MFDP backing and that the "caliber" of candidates offered by the party had a major effect on the outcome.

Although there were no reports of violence, and although federal observers had been on hand to supervise the elections, MFDP lawyer Morton Stavis announced that the party would challenge the results in federal court. He complained that in Sunflower only white officials were allowed to aid illiterate Negro voters and that 38 ballots cast by Negroes had been unfairly declared defective and 13 others had been unfairly challenged. Moreover, as several MFDP officials pointed out, an anonymous pamphlet circulated among the townspeople before the election certainly had some effect on the outcome. It read in part: "Your house and property are at stake. You have a chance to vote for a good town or a bad town in the Election. The choice is yours. If you are smart you will not be misled by paid racial agitators who would promise you everything and give you nothing but misery. . . ."

The MFDP suit asked that new elections be held, but it was turned down because significant evidence was lacking and no irregularities had been reported by the federal election observers.

In the wake of these challenged municipal elections came the race for the governorship and an announcement by Charles Evers that the

NAACP would sponsor about 25 candidates in local races for positions ranging from sheriff to superintendent. Shortly thereafter, the MFDP plans were announced: it would back about 60 candidates.

Altogether, the Negro political organizations in the state, including NAACP and MFDP, fielded approximately 125 candidates in the August 8 primary.[72] While the NAACP campaign concentrated on local and county offices in the six southwestern counties of the state, the MFDP effort backed about 60 candidates in an attempt to capture every available local, county, and state office in the Delta region. In this election, the fading MFDP came to life, although the NAACP at first fared even better.

In the August primary, 16 Negroes won posts outright and 23 others polled enough votes to qualify for special runoff elections on August 29. Of the 16, 11 won in the six southwestern counties and 5 in the Delta region. Moreover, the NAACP proportion of successful candidates—11 out of about 25—was considerably more impressive than the MFDP record—5 out of about 60.

Both organizations made special preparations for the runoff elections. To bolster morale, Charles Evers brought in black Representative John Conyers (D. Mich.), who urged blacks to vote in the six-county area where NAACP efforts were concentrated. At the same time, MFDP renewed its numerous voter sessions (at which it explained the importance of voting and told how to register) throughout the Delta to rally support for independent candidates it backed in counties where it had no regular organization.

The extra efforts of both groups failed. White candidates won in each of the runoffs mainly because newly enfranchised Negroes failed to turn out in sufficient numbers to support local candidates and played only a limited role in the NAACP-organized counties. Afterward, although both organizations charged that white election officials had taken advantage of Negro illiterates and were guilty of other fraudulent practices, the courts rejected the MFDP and NAACP plea for an investigation because the two organizations failed to offer concrete evidence of illegal practices and because on-site federal election observers turned in no reports of irregularities.

In the November general election, therefore, the NAACP backed the eleven victorious candidates it had sponsored in the original primary, while MFDP supported three Negroes for the state legislature and five Negroes for county offices. The NAACP-backed candidates faced little or no opposition and won easily in the general election. MFDP backed more candidates in the general election than had won with its backing in the primary election, and six of its candidates won posts; all five running for office on the county level were successful, and one MFDP candidate was elected to the state legislature. The latter, Robert Clark, a part-time college instructor and former director of a local antipoverty program, was elected state representative from Holmes and Yazoo counties, defeating James P. Lowe, a 65-year-old white planter and cattleman who had held the seat for more than ten years.[73] (See Table 7 in the Appendix.)

The victories of Clark and the five candidates for country offices boosted MFDP's image and increased its importance in the state. Yet the organization hardly had time to revel in the victory before trouble came. At first only Clark and the party were involved. Lowe challenged Clark's general election victory on a technicality, alleging that Clark had qualified in only one county (Holmes) but that his district was composed of two and he should also have qualified in the other county (Yazoo). To fight the challenge, MFDP enlisted the support of Manhattan Borough President Percy Sutton, who issued a nationwide appeal for help.[74]

Before this conflict could be resolved, the remaining 16 candidates (11 backed by NAACP and 5 by MFDP) ran into another kind of trouble. Every bonding company in the state (all white-run) turned down the surety bond applications of all but two of the newly elected blacks. By Mississippi law, public officials must be bonded; those who are not face the possibility of having their election declared void. A survey bond is in effect an insurance policy covering an official in the event of a lawsuit involving him in his official capacity or in the event of cash shortages in office funds during his tenure of office. The county in question always pays the premium for county-level offices.

Confronted with the bleak possibility that their candidates' victory would be voided, the two feuding Negro political groups forged an alliance to secure the necessary surety bonds for their respective candidates.[75]

At a news conference in Jackson on December 19, 1967, Charles Evers and MFDP chairman Lawrence Guyot announced that their organizations would seek to have nationwide pressure put on the local surety bonding companies that had declined bond to their candidates. The threat of a nationwide boycott of bonding companies that had offices in Mississippi began to show results on December 23 when several other national insurance companies agreed to provide bond for three of the new officeholders. Additional legal action by the MFDP Lawyers' Committee for Civil Rights Under Law made the effort completely successful when Kermit Stanton, an MFDP candidate who required a bond of $125,000 (the largest of all these involved), received it.[76]

During the bonding struggle, newly elected Governor John Bell Williams—a moderate by Mississippi standards—persuaded Representative Lowe to withdraw his challenge to Robert Clark. Lowe did so, saying he honored the governor's request because he did not want liberals and radicals from all over the country getting involved in another Mississippi election and bringing further bad publicity to the state.[77] After Lowe's challenge was dropped, Clark became the first Negro member of the Mississippi legislature in 74 years. Negro politicians had re-emerged in the state, and the tremendous efforts of MFDP had been vindicated.

Moreover, cooperation between MFDP and the state NAACP survived the bonding drive. On January 25, 1968, Charles Evers announced his intention to run for the congressional seat left vacant when Williams became governor. This effort required the coordinated resources of both groups because Evers sought to represent the third congressional district, covering both the six-county southwestern area and part of the Delta region. Naming MFDP Chairman Guyot as his campaign manager, Evers took a leave of absence from his NAACP post in order to devote all his energies to his campaign. Although white voters in the third congressional district outnumbered Negro voters almost two to one, Evers took first place in the six-man race when the white vote was split among the five white candidates. Because he lacked a majority, however, Evers was forced into a runoff election with the runner-up, Charles Griffin, who had served as an assistant to Mississippi governors for 18 years.[78]

Although he lost the runoff election by a three-to-one margin, Evers noted with optimism that more Negroes had voted for him in the election than were even registered in the entire state five years previously. He announced, moreover, that he would run as an independent candidate against Griffin in the forthcoming general election. The announcement provoked the state house of representatives to pass a bill designed specifically to prevent Evers from winning. The bill would have moved the general election up to October and provided for an unprecedented general election runoff in the event that no one received a majority of the votes. Thus, if Evers had again won with only a plurality, he would have had to enter another runoff against the highest ranking white candidate, who as a consequence would have been assured of victory. Although the bill failed to pass, Evers withdrew his candidacy in the wake of Dr. Martin Luther King, Jr.'s assassination.

The 1968 Convention Challenge

In the June primary election, MFDP entered three candidates against white incumbents who held seats in the state house of representatives, but all lost by three to one margins. Following this defeat, the party kept alive the spirit of cooperation by joining with the Mississippi AFL–CIO, the NAACP, the Young Democrats, and other liberal groups within the state to form a biracial coalition, the Loyal Democrats of Mississippi (LDM), for the purpose of mounting another challenge of the regular delegation at the 1968 Democratic national convention. In order to stave off this challenge, the regular Democrats named three Negroes to their delegation. But the strategy faltered when two of the Negroes withdrew their names and refused to cooperate with the regular delegation. Thus the regular Democrats proceeded to the August convention with only one Negro in the delegation, while LDM was represented by an almost precisely balanced delegation, with Aaron Henry once again serving as chairman.

At the national convention, LDM argued that the regular Mississippi Democrats had failed to fulfill the 1964 convention mandate for fairer representation of Negroes in subsequent state delegations; that they had barred Negroes from participating in the selection of state delegates; that they had gerrymandered the state's legislative districts so as to prevent fair and equitable black representation; and that the appointment of three Negro delegates to their ranks had been a cynical gesture in mock recognition of Negro voting strength in the state. On its own behalf LDM maintained that its delegation constituted a much fairer representation of the state's racial mix.

The regular delegation defended itself against the charge by arguing that its sole Negro member made the delegation sufficiently representative and by insisting that the regular party had made great strides toward permitting Negroes to participate fully in state politics. In addition, the regular delegation called on its single Negro member, Dr. Gilbert Mason, to testify to the fair delegate-election processes in his district. But the Credentials Committee seemed to regard the steps taken by the Mississippi regulars as a matter of too little too late. After a close study of particulars, the committee voted to recommend seating the LDM delegation instead of the regular delegation, basing its decision in part on the guidelines established by the 1964 convention in response to MFDP's first challenge. Moreover, all three of the major contenders for the presidential nomination, perhaps motivated in part by the year's political and social upheaval and shocking assassinations, indicated that they favored the seating of the LDM delegation. The full convention overwhelmingly approved the recommendation of the Credentials Committee, a move that wrought great changes in the political makeup of the state because it removed the old Democratic machine from the seat of power and from control of patronage.

MFDP may continue to operate as a relatively independent parallel political organization, or it may continue to cooperate with LDM in supporting liberal and moderate candidates for state and national posts while retaining a separate identity in order to support local and county candidates. The choice will depend to a great extent on LDM's future success in influencing state politics. Recent events, however, especially the 1969 and 1971 municipal elections, indicate that the MFDP and NAACP organizations are going their separate ways and will tend to join forces only when the occasion demands that they cooperate.[79] The MFDP entered more than forty candidates in the 1971 state and municipal elections (see Table 16) and these MFDP-backed candidates were running for offices ranging from state representatives and sheriff to circuit clerks and justices of the peace. The campaigns are poorly financed but the speeches and slogans of the MFDP candidates reflect the need and desires of the people. In the main, the MFDP politicians are grass root people with a folksy and down home style.

Moreover, the MFDP party assisted Charles Evers, now the mayor of Fayette, Mississippi, in his campaign for governor of the state.

Thus, once again the MFDP and the NAACP are cooperating in aiding a statewide black political campaign and, at the time of this writing, were expected to coalesce for the 1972 Convention.

In Mississippi elections during 1968, five MFDP candidates were elected to county election commissions and one to a position on the Holmes County board of education. (See Table 8 in the Appendix.) In the 1969 municipal elections, MFDP candidates captured eight aldermanic positions in six Delta cities, while one NAACP candidate —Charles Evers—was elected mayor of Fayette and five others were elected to posts on the city council. (See Table 9 in the Appendix.) Whatever the ultimate effects of the competition between NAACP and MFDP, it is nevertheless clear that MFDP has dramatically changed the political status of Negroes in the state.

4

BLACK POLITICS IN ALABAMA:

1867–1965

The federal Reconstruction Bill of March 2, 1867, made black politics and politicians possible in Alabama. Lowndes County sent J. W. Jones, a Negro, to the state senate for every session from 1872 to 1876 and Mansfield Taylor, another Negro, to the state house of representatives from 1870 to 1872. As early as 1868 James Turner, another black man, was elected to the Selma city council and later became Dallas County tax collector. Elsewhere in black-belt Alabama (see Map 2 in the Appendix) nine Negroes—more, according to some sources—were elected to the state legislature between 1872 and 1876.[1] On the national level, from 1871 to 1877 three Alabama blacks were elected to the House of Representatives. Black power had come alive in Alabama, and Negro politicians had begun to flourish.[2]

By 1874, however, black power in Alabama came increasingly under attack from the white-supremacist Democrats who had been waiting in the wings. As soon as all but a token force of Union troops were withdrawn from the state in late 1874, the Democrats used force, intimidation, and suppression to take control of the state government. According to one white Alabama historian, "the Ku Klux Klan and other hooded orders helped redeem the state." Redeeming the state, the former slaveowners felt, was a noble task. First, it would put southern gentlemen in power in place of northern carpetbaggers, black Republicans, and scalawags (a term used for southern poor whites who helped northerners and blacks). Second, it would restore white supremacy and do away with the rule of ex-slaves. While power remained in the hands of carpetbaggers, blacks, and scalawags, former slaveowners and Confederate soldiers sought ways to retrieve their former power—in other words, to redeem or retake the state. Any method, including violence and terrorism, was considered valid so long as it would help to achieve the goal.

As time went on, force was resorted to less often as it became less necessary in achieving the desired ends.[3] Ingenious new methods were used to suppress Negro political activity: the theft of ballots, the exchange of ballot boxes, the removal of polls to undisclosed places, false certification, the importation of voters, the purloining of ballots, the use of fictitious names, and the system of "counting in" all votes cast for Democrats and "counting out"—or not counting—all votes cast for Republicans. When none of these practices proved completely successful, the Negro was paid for his vote. As a result of such activities, whites often won elections by incredible majorities. For instance, in the 1874 mayoralty race in Mobile between Radical Republicans and Democrats, stuffing the ballot box became the order of the day; more than 20,000 votes were "officially" cast by a voting population of fewer than 8,000.

These extralegal techniques were soon reinforced with legal methods provided by the 1875 state constitution. In order to forestall northern intervention and the return of federal troops, the constitutional convention delegates stopped short of disfranchising Alabama Negroes outright. Instead, they adopted measures drastically limiting Negroes' voting rights and political power—without arousing northern suspicion. Governor W. C. Oates, who had served as chairman of the judiciary committee of the 1875 convention and was later to call for another convention to rectify the weaknesses in the constitution, said that the latter "was far from being such a constitution as I desire the state to have but perhaps it is the best that can be ratified under the circumstances that now surround us." Another delegate to the 1875 convention, George P. Harrison, recalled in 1899 that "it was the best we could do under the circumstances with federal bayonets glittering about our Capital and the Negro then with his heel on the neck of the white man." [4]

The 1875 constitution spelled a dim future for Negro politicians and voters in Alabama. Those who survived illegal and extralegal political suppression now faced additional obstacles. The first legal method of suppression offered by the 1875 constitution was that of stacking legislative districts, or gerrymandering, which the legislature was now free to do. All the black-belt counties that had not fallen under the control of Democrats were legislatively lumped in one congressional district instead of three, thereby limiting Negro political strength. (The consensus was that these areas would go Republican anyway.) Negro Representative John T. Rapier from the old second congressional district had lost his seat in Congress to J. N. Williams, a white man, in 1874, and in 1876 he was forced to compete with several other Negroes in the newly created fourth district, established specifically to include the vast majority of Alabama's Negroes. He lost again in 1876.

In the same year, Negro State Senator J. W. Jones from Lowndes County lost his seat to W. M. Buckley, a white man; Jones was only one of countless victims of the resurgent white-supremacists. It was also in this swelling tide of white supremacy that the last Negro in Congress from Alabama, Jeremiah Haralson, lost his seat in 1877, even though he was running from the overwhelmingly Negro fourth district.[5] In the 1880s, by which time whites had regained control of all the black-belt counties and other Republican bastions, the state legislature gerrymandered the state's voting districts once again, this time in shoestring fashion with all nine congressional districts running from north to south. This move further sapped the political strength of the black-belt counties (which ran east to west) by dividing these counties among seven of the nine new congressional districts. This time, with the base of Negro political power effectively diluted, the gerrymandering succeeded in removing the last of the state's top Negro public officials.

A few local Negro officials remained unaffected by the gerrymandering, but another legal loophole granted by the 1875 constitution proved quite efficient in dealing with them. This loophole was the provision entitling the legislature to abolish local governing bodies (even when duly elected) and empowering the governor to replace them automatically with his (white) appointees. This power was first exercised in 1876, when the governor abolished the Court of County Commissioners in Dallas County and appointed a new Court of Revenues, with identical powers, in its place.[6] In 1877, the procedure was repeated in two more black-belt counties, Montgomery and Wilcox: here local Negro officials were swept from office by legislative fiat and replaced by the governor's appointees. Inasmuch as the governor's appointive powers extended even to such offices as justice of the peace and notary, Negro public officials had little or no chance of retaining their offices.

Besides these tremendously useful legal devices for rendering Negroes politically ineffective, the 1875 constitution provided still another method. Gerrymandering and the governor's power of reappointment mainly affected Negroes who held public office, so another legal method whereby Negro voters could be rendered ineffective was also adopted. This technique, in the form of Alabama's Sayre Election Law of 1893, placed tremendous discretionary powers in the hands of local voting registrars. First, it required all voters to register in May for the elections in August, on the assumption that illiterate Negroes would misplace their certificates of registration by the time these were demanded by the registrars at the polls in August. Furthermore, even if an illiterate Negro still had possession of his certificate, the white registrar was allowed to enter the voting booth with him and see that he voted "properly." [7] Thus illiterate Negro voters were at the mercy of white Democratic registrars, who could usually be counted on to make sure that Negro votes would not upset the status quo.

Thus extralegal tactics, combined with the legal methods afforded by the 1875 constitution and the Sayre Election Law of 1893, made it possible for Democrats to remove all vestige of Negroes from public office as well as to curtail Negro voting power drastically. Negro politicians in Alabama had become rare by the 1880s. But the Negro still retained the right to vote; he was not yet altogether disfranchised.

During the 1890s, the depressed state of economic affairs forced a split in the formerly monolithic white Democratic party, which had been held together after the Civil War by the whites' universal fear of "Negro domination." Now, economics took precedence over race, and poor whites sought political power in order to reverse the rapid deterioration in their economic position. The restoration of white rule had specifically placed the white plantation aristocracy (Democrats) in power and had left the upland or hill whites (Populists) out. And now that the outs were also the have-nots, they attempted to wrest control of the Democratic party and state government from the haves —the former slaveholders and white upper classes who had themselves wrested control from the carpetbaggers, scalawags, and black Republicans.

In this struggle for power, the Negro vote became a much sought-after commodity. Both Populists and Democrats pleaded for Negroes' support and both sides played up to them. But the majority of Negroes lived in the black-belt counties, that region of rich black soil and large black population, where the power-holding aristocratic whites also lived and where many ex-slaves still worked for their former masters. During the elections, the upper-class Democrats resorted to all the old tricks they had used to overcome the Negro—but this time the purpose was to defeat the poor white Populists. With Negro voters so close to having dominant power where they were in the majority, the Democrats scandalously and fraudulently used them to repress the agrarian revolt.[8] With this enormous power arrayed against them, the poor whites gave up the struggle in 1898.

With the Populists firmly suppressed, the drive for Negro disfranchisement was resumed in that same year, 1898. Both sides were eager to strip Negroes of their voting power: the Populists because they felt that black voters hindered such progressive movements as theirs and led to corruption in government, the aristocratic whites because they feared that the Negro vote might be influenced in such a way as to remove them from the seats of power in state politics. When the whites split into opposing camps, the Negro vote became a threat to white supremacy. Faced with the possibility of Negro domination— or even the possibility of Negroes' regaining political offices—whites began demanding a new constitution that would remove the threat of a Negro vote once and for all. According to McMillan, a close student of this movement, the Alabama constitution of 1901, which effectively disfranchised Negroes in the state, was the offspring of Jeffersonian Democratic attitudes and of Populism. Certainly, however, impetus for disfranchisement also came from such sister states as Mississippi and Louisiana, each of which already had disfranchised its Negro citizenry, the former as early as 1890.[9] Further encouragement came from the federal government's conservative attitude toward Negro rights at the time and, in 1896, from the Supreme Court's enunciation of the separate-but-equal doctrine in *Plessy* v. *Ferguson.* Throughout the South, segregation became a legally sanctioned way of life, and Booker T. Washington's philosophy of accommodation became the major theme of Negro leadership.

Lacking both leadership inclined to protest and a federal government disinclined to interfere in such matters, Alabama Negroes were summarily stripped of their voting rights by the 1901 constitution. Although more than a hundred prominent blacks met in Birmingham on September 25, 1901, to urge poor whites to oppose the proposed constitution—pointing out that it would also disfranchise them—the plea fell on deaf ears. Racial solidarity was the strongest consideration in the stand taken by the poor whites, and the argument by the blacks that lower-class whites were being used to effect their own political destruction carried little weight. When the constitution of 1901 was submitted to the voters for ratification, some poor whites opposed it, but their opposition was too weak and came too late. Black-belt whites carried the vote by majorities that often exceeded the white voting population.[10]

On that day, November 11, 1901, Alabama blacks boycotted the polls for the first and last time. Their hope for redress of their grievances through the federal government were not to be fulfilled until the Voting Rights Act of 1965. Between 1901 and 1965, black voting in Alabama was almost nonexistent. For more than a half-century black political life in the state was a will-o'-the-wisp. Politics soon lost all meaning not only for blacks in the state but for poor whites as well, because the 1901 constitution disfranchised as many poor whites as it did blacks.[11]

There were, however, in Alabama several attempts between 1901 and 1965 by blacks to re-enter the political arena. For instance, Mrs. Indiana Little, a black schoolteacher in Birmingham, led in January 1926 a black registration campaign. Mrs. Little "led 1000 black women and a few men before the board of registrars and demanded the right to vote as American citizens. . . ." As always, "this militant Negro political leader was arrested and charged with vagrancy. . . ." And "not a single one of the one thousand was registered." In 1937 blacks in the same city launched another "gonna register" campaign with some 4,000 individuals, but it also failed. Similar attempts elsewhere in the state also proved fruitless.

Before the passage of the 1965 Voting Rights Act, the registered Negro voters in the state constituted less than 20 percent of those eligible. To remedy this situation, several civil rights organizations made plans to enlarge the state's Negro electorate. Early in November 1966, the Southern Christian Leadership Conference (SCLC) announced plans to increase its staff in Alabama from 34 to 70 in order to carry on an intensive 45-day campaign to place Negroes on the voter rolls, particularly in 17 black-belt counties and in the cities of Birmingham, Montgomery, Tuscaloosa, and Mobile. The primary aim of the drive was, as SCLC official Hosea Williams put it, "to elect several legislative, county, and municipal officials at the next election." [12] The secondary aim of the drive, said Williams, was to encourage the federal government to send additional federal registrars to counties with large Negro populations where whites were still harassing Negroes who were trying to register.

Later, the Alabama Democratic Conference (ADC)—the strongest predominantly Negro political action group in the state—announced plans for its own voter registration drive. In addition, several members urged that the group initiate a statewide third party, the National Democratic party, a coalition of white liberals and Negroes. Such a party, argued American Civil Liberties Union (ACLU) lawyer Charles Morgan, Jr., could eventually align itself with the national Democratic party, bypassing both the regular state Democratic party controlled by Governor George Wallace and the state Republican party, which based its programs on a combination of segregationist and "anti-Washington" policies. However, ADC refused to commit itself to the establishment of a statewide third party until the regular state Democratic party's executive committee had been given a chance to align itself more closely with the national party's politics, programs, and principles at its January meeting. (There was no such realignment in January, but the regular Democrats did make several gestures toward the rising black electorate, thereby decreasing the chances that a third party would succeed.) Major action, the Negro group decided, should begin with a drive for the removal of the white supremacy clause from the state Democratic party's constitution. [13]

SNCC Forms Lowndes County Freedom Organization

In addition to the plans announced by SCLC, ADC, and white moderates, the Student Nonviolent Coordinating Committee (SNCC) also aired a political program for Alabama Negroes. SNCC's plans were shaped in part by its experiences in the MFDP 1964 convention challenge and the 1965 seating challenge, both of which ended in failure. This new effort, SNCC decided, would be a county political organization rather than a statewide organization such as MFDP. "We decided," said a SNCC field secretary, "after the Mississippi experience that it would be better for political organizations to be on the county level so they would be closer to the people." [14]

According to SNCC, this organization would function as an all-Negro third party; would operate only in Lowndes County, where Negroes outnumbered whites four to one; would be called the Lowndes County Freedom Organization (LCFO); and would have a black panther as its symbol. The party, SNCC asserted, was a pilot project in a new drive to bypass existing southern institutions and appeal directly to the "dispossessed Negro." [15] If this undertaking proved successful, SNCC was to organize similar groups in such other Alabama black-belt counties as Dallas, Wilcox, Hale, and Greene, where Negroes had a mathematical chance of gaining control of the county government. To support the legality of such organizations, SNCC's research staff found a state law that allowed for the establishment of independent county political parties, provided that they had a membership equal to 20 percent of the county's eligible voters.

SNCC's new theoretical construct, formulated at a time when its coffers were all but empty, reflected a new attitude of distrust for and disenchantment with existing white political institutions and coalitions with white liberals and moderates. [16] According to numerous observers, SNCC had now begun to travel a separatist path, moving toward a philosophy that encompassed black nationalism, isolation, and race pride. Many of SNCC's supporters and sympathizers deplored this new direction—the distinction between race pride and racism was not always clear—and the concept and its manifestations as they were later put more vividly into practice.

Before launching LCFO, some groundwork was felt to be necessary. In January 1966 a group of Negro voters—prodded by SNCC—sued in federal court for a special election that year for all Lowndes County administrative, law enforcement, and judicial offices. The suit contended that white officials were holding office illegally because they had been elected before the state's Negroes had acquired the right to vote. The suit stated that, although some county officials were up for election in 1966, the terms of others continued until 1968 and 1970.

In essence, this challenge rested on the contention that the white minority, under sanction of law and by threats, terror, and violence, had prevented Negroes from even attempting to exercise their suffrage rights, in violation not only of the Fourteenth and Fifteenth Amendments to the U.S. Constitution, but of the 1965 Voting Rights Act as well.[17]

In the face of this new Negro political activity, Governor Wallace urged the state's legislative council to take steps to prevent Negroes from being elected to local offices. At his request, Lieutenant-Governor James Allen introduced a resolution, which the legislature approved, instructing the state's legislative reference service to study ways of curtailing "mass changes in the status of governing bodies of counties in Alabama." The reference service, which researches and drafts legislation, subsequently suggested extending the terms of local offices, thus removing them from the county ballot in the upcoming election. The state legislature passed such a law in 1965 affecting only Bullock County.

After the state acted, the executive committee of the Lowndes County Democratic party increased tenfold the qualifying fee for the primary on May 3, 1966. For instance, the fee for running for the office of sheriff, tax assessor, or tax collector was raised from $50 to $500 and for the board of education from $10 to $100. Although white candidates had to pay the same amount as blacks, the greater poverty in the Negro community made it much harder for prospective Negro candidates to raise the qualifying fee. Robert S. Dickson, Jr., chairman of the county Democratic party executive committee, attempted to justify this action by stating: "We've never had a two-party system here before, but now we've got a lot of opposition and the party needs more money to combat it with." [18]

But SNCC sidestepped this obstacle and put its theory directly into practice; on March 3, 1966, at the founding meeting of LCFO, Lowndes County Negroes agreed to boycott the regular Democratic primary and to support LCFO candidates in their own primary. Thus was born the smallest political party in the country—an all-Negro political party with a black panther as its symbol.

SNCC also tried to help several other black freedom organizations in some of the other black-belt counties (see Map 2 in the Appendix). This help was limited because SNCC was short of funds and because its energies were focused in Lowndes County. But despite its financial weaknesses, SNCC helped to get blacks registered, organized and participated in mass meetings, tried to help black candidates obtain information on how to run for political office, and gave some assistance in campaigning. But in the final analysis this help was sporadic, limited, and not well coordinated.

Elsewhere in Alabama, other Negro civil rights organizations were planning to back 33 black candidates in the black-belt counties and 6 more in counties with white majorities. For instance, SCLC announced its first candidate late in February: Walter Calhoun was slated to run for sheriff in Wilcox County, where Negro registered voters numbered 3,600 and white registered voters numbered 2,600 (the Negro population totaled 14,500 and the white, 4,100). Despite this small edge, Calhoun had his troubles. After he announced his candidacy, he was ordered to vacate his grocery store. Also, his 60-year-old white opponent had held the sheriff's job for 28 years.[19]

But the situation in Wilcox County was not typical in terms of registered Negro voters; in fact, it was an exception. Negro voter registration lagged even in some predominantly Negro counties, and many legislative districts included several counties, most of them *not* predominantly Negro. Moreover, the state poll tax *at first* was not illegal. And to top it all off, some Negro leaders favored a coalition government instead of an all-Negro one. Despite these difficulties, Negroes sought positions throughout the state as sheriff, state representative, state senator, tax assessor, county commissioner, member of the board of revenue, and tax collector. LCFO specifically sought the offices of sheriff, coroner, tax assessor, tax collector, and member of the county board of education.[20]

The 1966 Primary Election

Many Negro candidates ran into difficulties throughout the state, as segregationist tactics were employed to keep them from winning. In Bullock County, Negroes attempting to run for seats on the county commission were turned down after being told that the term of office for incumbents had been extended by a 1965 state law. Other would-be candidates were disqualified after failing to pass reading and writing tests.[21] In Lowndes County, only five offices were at stake in the November election (tax assessor, tax collector, coroner, sheriff, and district attorney); and although LCFO sought to have all public offices contested in the November election, court action by a group of Negroes under SNCC sponsorship failed to achieve this objective.[22]

During the court action, SNCC tried to form all-black parties in Dallas, Wilcox, Sumter, Macon, and Perry counties, and it encouraged Negroes in these counties to boycott the May 3 Democratic primary so that segregationists would receive the nominations, thereby exposing "the real face of the Democratic party." SNCC's action was publicly attacked by the SCLC director, Albert Turner. He stated that SNCC's strategy might not influence the outcome of statewide races, but it still might hurt Negro and white moderate candidates in local races—especially in the sheriff's race in Dallas County, where public safety director Wilson Baker was challenging the incumbent segregationist Sheriff Jim Clark. In reply, Stokely Carmichael, senior field secretary of SNCC, said his organization was not concerned with the possibility that this strategy might result in the defeat of some Negro and white moderate candidates. Instead, Carmichael urged Negroes to concentrate on such posts as revenue commissioner and member of the board of education rather than run for sheriff, because a white segregationist sheriff's constant harassment of Negro voters, real or potential, would help foster anti-white attitudes among Negroes and thus strengthen the militancy of LCFO supporters. In short, white segregationist sheriffs would enhance party cohesion.[23]

Carmichael took the position he did because he felt that if blacks participated in the regular Democratic party primary, they would in effect be supporting a party that had denied them their rights and privileges for years. He urged blacks to boycott the regular Democratic primary, hold their own primary on the same day, and nominate their own candidates for public office because he felt this would give black people a sense of dignity, pride, and control over their own political destinies. And he would not support black candidates who were participating in the regular Democratic primary because these blacks were perpetuating the very racist political structure that Carmichael was trying to challenge.

Carmichael's attitude was deplored by many liberals. A *New York Times* editorial, for instance, characterized SNCC's appeal to Negroes to boycott the primaries as "mischief making" and "extremism for the sake of extremism." The *Times* went on to say that SNCC's only concern was to keep Negroes aroused and militant revolutionaries, against government and society, and that SNCC offered neither improvements nor reforms.[24]

To counteract Carmichael's call for a black boycott of the regular Democratic primary and for the holding of a separate black primary, the state office of SCLC asked Dr. Martin Luther King, Jr., to tour the state and urge blacks to participate in the regular primary. Such a call for help was regular procedure. SCLC was an umbrella organization; its staff of about a dozen people kept shop, while Dr. King both answered and generated calls for help. In fact, Dr. King's early successes inspired many black ministers in southern cities to launch their own movements and organizations, most of which affiliated with SCLC. And it was as these local leaders found themselves in need of help that they would sent out a call for Dr. King to come and assist them. So hardly had the uproar over SNCC's action died down than Dr. King began a tour to urge Negroes not only to conquer their fear and vote, but to disregard SNCC's plea and vote as a bloc. He urged Negroes to support all the candidates—black and white—who had been endorsed by Alabama's two major Negro political organizations: ADC and the Confederation of Alabama Political Organizations.

Although Dr. King made a very strong plea for Negro voter turnouts, especially in Dallas and Wilcox counties, he bypassed Lowndes County altogether.[25] Many interpretations could be offered for his bypassing Lowndes County. Perhaps he wished to avoid trouble, even violent protest; perhaps he was respecting SNCC's dominance there; perhaps he was respecting the decision of the county's Negroes to boycott the primary; perhaps he considered SNCC's call for a boy-cott valid for Lowndes County but not elsewhere in the state; perhaps he sought to minimize rivalry between civil rights organizations.

King's appeal had some effect. In all, 54 Negro candidates entered the primary, and a white sheriff who faced Negro opposition hired Negro deputies in the last days before the primary election.[26] King additionally urged Negroes to support Attorney General Richmond Flowers, a moderate, for governor, rather than Mrs. Lurleen Wallace, wife of the current governor. (Alabama law does not permit a gov-ernor to succeed himself. Governor George Wallace sought to bypass this law and retain effective control by having his wife succeed to the governorship.)

After his tour, King's organization, SCLC, made a vigorous at-tempt to effectuate a massive Negro voter turnout by teaching illiter-ates to memorize names, organizing car pools, and canvassing door to door. Also, U.S. Attorney General Nicholas Katzenbach sent in 200 federal observers, promising vigilant observation at the polls.[27] Although some of the 54 Negro candidates were given a better chance than others before the election, the general outlook seemed good.

On the day of the primary, LCFO held its nominating convention on the front lawn of a white frame church on the outskirts of Haynes-ville. More than 800 Negroes appeared at SNCC's makeshift polling place and nominated 7 candidates to seek county offices in November. On the lawn were seven worn wooden tables, one for each candidate; as Negroes filed past, they dropped their small paper ballots into ballot boxes. Immediately tabulated results showed that Sidney Logan, Jr., was one of the first to be nominated—for sheriff.

Elsewhere, early election returns were mixed, but showed heavy Negro voter turnouts in every black-belt county—including Lowndes County. In addition, the size of the Negro voter turnout made it appear early in the day that two Negro candidates were leading for legislative seats and three for sheriff positions. But the vote count revealed that only one of the 54 Negro candidates running for office had won a clear-cut victory; the other leading Negro candidates—24 in all—had to face whites in a runoff election scheduled for May 31. (In Lowndes County, the state attorney general received 613 votes in the regular Democratic primary and political observers said that virtually all of them were from Negroes.) Eight of these contests were for seats in the state legislature, four for sheriff, and the others for tax assessor, tax collector, county commissioner, and local school-board posts.

Despite the relatively heartening showing of Negro candidates in the primary, there was criticism of the sheriff's race in Selma from the Justice Department and criticism of the state's inadequate voting facilities from Dr. King. Federal observers were prevented from keeping watch at some polling places. For example, in Marengo County, Mayor Wille Gay Little of Linden threatened to arrest the federal observers if they got too close to illiterate Negroes being helped by whites when voting. Similar incidents occurred at six polling places in Dallas County, and a federal district court ordered hearings on the Selma situation.[28]

On the other hand, some Negroes and whites said that many Negroes had voted for conservative white candidates; other observers said that the majority of registered Negro voters had failed to turn out at all. Actually, only about 150,000 Negroes voted out of almost 250,000 who were registered to vote. (See Table 10 in the Appendix.) As Albert Gordon, director of the Wilcox County Civic League, an affiliate of SCLC, put it:

> A lot of Negroes were afraid to vote with all of those white people working in the polling places as elected officials. They were afraid they might lose their jobs or something. Others . . . that did go voted for whites because they were afraid to call out the names of the Negro candidates in the presence of whites.[29]

Meanwhile, LCFO had a slate of candidates it had nominated in its own primary. Now it turned its attention to the vigorous campaign it had planned for the November general election.

The 1966 General Election

Shortly after the primary, LCFO's leadership was dealt a blow when Stokely Carmichael was elected national chairman of SNCC.[30] After assuming the national chairmanship, he simply reiterated much of what he had already been saying—that LCFO's efforts would eventually force whites to bargain with Negroes rather than vice versa, and would also make it possible for Negroes to use public funds to equalize schools and other facilities. He went on to assert the need for independent political parties at the city and county levels throughout the South to be controlled by the poor people, because they would not hesitate to destroy the present exploitative political institutions. He added further that these "poor people's parties" were to be organized by Negroes and not by whites. Expressing his general distrust of both major national parties and making clear the militant attitude which was later to become synonymous with SNCC, Carmichael said: "To ask Negroes to get in the Democratic party is like asking [John Lewis, Carmichael's predecessor] to join the Nazi party." [31]

On May 31, a few days after Carmichael became SNCC's national chairman and made his program known, the runoff election involving 25 Negroes took place in every Alabama county except Lowndes.[32] (The original count of 24 runoff candidates had been increased to 25 by the federal district court when it invalidated the extension of one incumbent official's term of office in Bullock County.) Both blacks and whites had readied themselves for the election, and the Justice Department again sent in federal observers.

Early returns showed one Negro, Lucius D. Amersen, leading in the nomination for sheriff in Tuskegee and at least three other Negroes as potential winners. It was at about this time that James Meredith began his march against fear to encourage the "45,000 unregistered Negroes in Mississippi to go to the polls and register." The day after his march began, the final results of the runoff election were announced. Four Negroes were victorious. In Macon County, Amersen won the race for sheriff, L. A. Locklair for tax collector, and Harold Webb for county commissioner; while in Greene County Rev. Peter Kirksey won nomination for a seat on the board of education.

Before SNCC and LCFO could gather themselves for the November election drive, the storm broke. Meredith was ambushed and shot on June 7, 1966, shortly after his march began. Top civil rights leaders immediately converged on Memphis, Tennessee, intent on continuing Meredith's march. While about 40 SNCC members protested at the White House, Carmichael wired Meredith's family deploring the racism and hypocrisy in American society. Carmichael's spirit of militancy continued through the march—and so did public harassment of the marchers.[33] This only served to reinforce the rising militancy among young black radicals in the civil rights movement.

This growing mood of militancy, disillusionment with nonviolent protest and "playing politics," and general pessimism culminated in a slogan born at the conclusion of the march in Jackson, Mississippi, on June 27, 1966. "Black power," the slogan, the credo, the chant—with all its ambiguous meanings—had arrived. Carmichael, author of the phrase, told a crowd of about 12,000 that day: "Negroes must build a power base in this country so strong that we will bring [whites] to their knees every time they mess with us." The statement brought cheers from the crowd; some onlookers burned a Confederate flag. A number of civil rights groups were barred from the platform from which Carmichael spoke because they were not considered militant enough. A new era of civil rights protest was born; militancy was on the rise, accompanied by a new rhetoric and a new kind of leader, typified by Carmichael.

The reverberations of the new phrase, black power, were heard everywhere. The news media amplified and publicized it, forcing people to take sides about it. Some individuals attacked it as reflecting a demagogic and self-defeating reverse racism; others defended it as the introduction of conscious, positive race pride at precisely the right moment; still others were embarrassed or frightened by it. Traditionalists in the movement tended to deny its usefulness, while young militants welcomed and applauded it.

In the long run, the impact of the slogan on the civil rights movement has been immeasurable. In fact, the movement was split over the slogan and what it was taken to mean. Several civil rights organizations and leaders denounced it and issued manifestos against the concept; one Negro leader at first avoided discussing it entirely, while such others as Floyd McKissick of CORE embraced it openly. Major emphasis and concern at first centered around the meaning of the two words—as it still does to some extent. "What does 'black power' mean?" became the major point of departure for every inquiring analyst who sought to understand the new slogan and its ramifications. To find a suitable answer, everybody looked to its originator—not only to *defend* it but to *define* it. Ironically, then, so much of Carmichael's time was spent in answering calls to define the term that he had little left for mustering his full organizational skills to set up the very model he was using to make his definition explicit. In short, all summer long the tremendous task of propelling LCFO forward was left without guidance because its prime mover and major organizer had too little time to perfect it.

In October 1966 Chairman John Hulett announced that LCFO would enter seven black candidates in the November 8 election and predicted that his party, which newspapers first called the Black Panther party and whites now referred to as the Panther party because of the organization's panther emblem, would remake politics in Lowndes County. In his announcement, Hulett emphasized that although the organization had been formed by Carmichael and SNCC, no members of the student committee were members of the executive committee of the Freedom Organization; its officials and candidates were all Lowndes County Negroes. LCFO, he asserted, gave Alabama Negroes their first real opportunity to participate in politics, inasmuch as the actions and attitudes of the Democratic party in the state were actually detrimental to their interests.

Earlier, Carmichael had argued: "If you use the power to tax in Lowndes County, you can get some food, schools, and good roads for blacks. . . . The purpose of this party," he had said, "is to get black people the things they should have, and then they can decide if they want to accept white people in Lowndes County who have brutalized them these many, many years."

The reaction of the county's whites to such rhetoric seemed nonchalant. Many felt safe in assuming that the "good niggers" opposed the Panthers and would help elect the white ticket. One white politician announced with satisfaction and pride that his Negro maid had "chased the civil rights workers away from her house with a butcher knife" and that the Negro schoolteachers had promised him that they would not vote for the Panther party.[34]

As for Negroes' reaction, some said they had little use for the Panthers and even less for the young workers from SNCC. One Negro propertyholder asserted, "The SNCC workers will leave after the election and the rest of us will have to stay. Now, I don't believe in going the third party route. It's a foolish thing to do, and the people that John Hulett has running are unqualified anyway."

On the other hand, some Negroes referred to the Freedom Organization as the "Christian movement" and asserted that they would vote for the LCFO candidates. Nevertheless, in a county with a total population of 15,417 (1960 census figures), 81 percent of them blacks, the count of registered voters stood at 2,681 blacks, all registered under the 1965 Voting Rights Act, and 2,519 whites. Moreover, only 613 pro-black votes had been cast in the county's Democratic primary for Richmond Flowers, whereas pro-white voters had cast 1,443 for Mrs. Wallace.[35] The 813 votes that LCFO had received in its nominating convention and the 613 votes cast for Flowers added up to 1,426 pro-black votes—17 fewer than the pro-white vote total—indicating that at best the general election would be a tossup.

The results of the general election revealed that all the LCFO candidates had been defeated by margins ranging from 200 to 800 votes. What SNCC considered the first test run for black power had failed. (See Table 11 in the Appendix.) The returns suggested that perhaps 300 blacks had voted against the Black Panther candidates. What is more, early returns from Dallas County indicated that the eight black candidates supported by SNCC there were also defeated.[36] Although the young radicals protested the conduct of the election and threatened legal action, LCFO had been dealt a stunning blow. The panther emblem reappeared in the 1968 county election. The national Black Panther party for self-defense that appeared in the 1968 elections is a completely different organization based in California. During the 1968 campaign it formed an alliance with the new Peace and Freedom party and nominated Black Panther Minister of Information Eldridge Cleaver for president. (See Chapter 6.)

The defeat of the LCFO candidates in November 1966 signaled the near failure and collapse of one of the most recent black separate political parties of any importance in the South. Its achievements in Alabama were negligible—at least in terms of electing black officials in Lowndes County. Despite this lack of achievement, however, future applications of the concept remain a distinct possibility, as evidenced by the appearance of a similar all-black party, the Party of Christian Democracy, in Georgia in 1968.[37] The party nominated Hosea L. Williams for the 76th House district seat of Dekalb County, Georgia; Williams was defeated. According to its chairman, John Evans, the party had been organized because the Republican and Democratic parties in this district were insensitive to the needs of black people

In 1969, the LCFO merged with the National Democratic party of Alabama after its candidates made an extremely poor showing during the 1968 county election. And during the 1970 state and local elections, several of the LCFO members won. The party's old chairman, John Hulett, was elected as sheriff of Lowndes County on the NDPA ticket. Alma Miller, a LCFO member, won a position as circuit clerk and Ed McGhee was elected coroner.

The National Democratic Party of Alabama

Alabama is unique in the sense that two distinct black political parties emerged in the state during the sixties: one, the separate LCFO and the other, the satellite National Democratic party of Alabama (NDPA).[38]

Although NDPA received a state charter and officially came into being on January 12, 1968, the party's roots and beginnings go back much earlier. In fact, when the regular state Democratic party failed to open its organization to blacks after the 1964 national convention directed each state party to do so, several blacks and whites in Alabama, led by Charles Morgan, Jr., a white ACLU lawyer, and Dr. John Cashin, a black dentist in Huntsville, proposed such an organization to the Alabama Democratic Conference in Birmingham in November 1965. Moreover, Cashin and Morgan urged ADC to become the nucleus for this proposed party. But Orzell Billingsley, the leader of ADC in 1965, rejected the proposal. As Billingsley put it, he wanted to give the regular state Democratic party more time to comply with the convention's mandate, and compliance could begin with the removal of the white supremacy clause from the party's constitution.[39]

When the executive committee of the state Democratic party met on January 22, 1966, it agreed to strike the white supremacy slogan from the party's constitution and ballot emblem. In fact, the party's emblem, a crowing rooster, had the words on it changed from "White supremacy for the right" to "Democrats of the right." But beyond the removal of such overt signs of white supremacy, the regular party failed to make any changes. In short, blacks were not officially invited to join the party organization.

The combination of the regular Democratic party's failure to institute meaningful reforms and the results of the gubernatorial elections motivated the proposer of a new party to organize one. In the 1966 primary, Governor George Wallace had placed the name of his wife, Lurleen Wallace, on the ballot as candidate for the governorship to circumvent the state law that prevented him from succeeding himself. With his wife in office Wallace would of course still be in control. Running against Mrs. Wallace was Attorney General Richmond Flowers, who had asked ADC for its support. In addition to these major candidates at least six minor candidates were in the race. At this point there was a split among ADC's leadership, with the new head of ADC supporting minor candidate Carl Elliot for governor, while the executive committee threw its support to Flowers. The black electorate received conflicting instruction and split their votes between Flowers and Elliot, and Mrs. Wallace carried the primary.[40]

Mrs. Wallace's subsequent victory in the November 1966 general election moved black and white moderates in the state to action. They had failed to elect Flowers and were now to be governed by another Wallace who had the same extremist views on racial matters. They had witnessed the failure of the regular party to reform and the fragmenting of the black electorate in the gubernatorial election of 1966. They had again witnessed the refusal of the regular Democratic party to initiate reforms in 1967 and bring blacks into the party organization. Now Cashin and Morgan filed for a state charter for NDPA on December 15, 1967,[41] and received it four weeks later.

With the charter in hand and the party officially launched, NDPA issued a call for the first convention to be held in Birmingham on July 20, 1968, and began to prepare for the May 7 primary in which delegates to the national Democratic convention were to be chosen. Alabama is unlike Mississippi in that delegates to the national convention are chosen by the voters in the primary election. (Mississippi delegates are chosen by the state party.) And 45 of Alabama's 50 delegate positions were on the ballot. Five delegates were to be chosen from each of the state's nine congressional districts; the remaining five are statewide delegates whose positions are filled automatically by individuals who hold high office in the state organization: national committeeman, national committeewoman, state party chairman, vice-chairman, and secretary. The regular Democratic party had of course selected candidates to run for each of the 45 elected positions.

In March NDPA announced that it would not put up a slate of candidates for the delegate positions to compete with the regular party candidates in the primary. Instead, NDPA said it would select a delegation at its own July convention to challenge the delegation of the regular party. On the other hand, ADC urged blacks to oppose whites for delegate positions in the primary. And two blacks—Joe Reed, executive director of the predominantly black Alabama State Teachers Association, and Arthur Shores, a Birmingham attorney—were certain of election in the primary because they were unopposed. The two black candidates did win and thereby became part of the delegation to the national Democratic convention.

Alabama election laws require that all candidates for local and state offices not selected in the primary election be nominated by mass meetings on the day of the primary. So NDPA held mass meetings all over the state on primary day and nominated more than a hundred candidates to run for state and local offices in the November general election.

Following the primary, NDPA held its first political convention on July 20. To the convention came old-style white radicals from the old Populist strongholds in the northern part of the state and from the cities, young professional men and women out of academic and scientific communities such as Huntsville and Tuscaloosa, upper-middle-class liberals, black laymen of all economic strains, and black office-holders. Rev. Edwin King of MFDP gave the keynote address, and the convention elected Dr. John Cashin as party chairman, Dr. Mary Pandow as secretary, Joe Gannon as treasurer, and F. Jackson Zylman as executive director; adopted a constitution, a platform, and a statement of goals and objectives; [42] and chose a delegation to challenge the regular state delegation at the national convention.

At the national convention in August, the regular state Democratic party found itself challenged not only by NDPA but also by the Alabama Independent Democratic party (AIDP). Like NDPA, the AIDP organization had been formed early in 1968, but its membership was primarily segregationist whites, who charged that the regular delegation was pledged to Wallace and would not sign loyalty oaths to support the convention nominees. Should the regular delegation fail to sign loyalty oaths, said AIDP chief organizers Robert Vance and David Vann, their group *would* sign the oath and would support the convention's choice of candidates. According to Wieck, on

December 26, 1967, President Johnson promised Vann and Vance that any group they headed would be seated at the 1968 national convention.[43]

When the special subcommittee of the Credentials Committee met to hear the Alabama challenge, representatives of NDPA appeared to present its case. They testified that AIDP had only a delegation at the national convention and a slate of presidential electors pledged to support the national party candidates, whereas NDPA had not only these things but also a slate of candidates for nearly every office in the state. In short, NDPA argued, AIDP was not a true political party because it had no intention of running candidates for office in the general election. Further, NDPA argued, the regular Democratic party delegation was pledged to George Wallace, who was running for president on the American Independent party ticket. Finally, NDPA contended, although the regular delegation included two blacks, it did not reflect the racial balance or the ideological divisions that existed within the state.

Despite the NDPA and AIDP arguments, the special subcommittee voted 33 to 3 to seat the members of the regular Alabama delegation if they would sign a pledge to support the convention ticket. Of the 50 delegates, 13 signed the pledge and were seated by the sergeant at arms on the day of the nomination.

Immediately after the subcommittee voted to reject the challenge, the NDPA delegation began preparations for carrying its fight to the convention floor. NDPA members visited other delegations, explaining the possible consequences of continuing to back the Wallace-supporting regular delegation. Next, NDPA pickets marched in front of the convention hotels, carrying placards asking for a rejection of George Wallace and his racist policies. Other NDPA members distributed leaflets to convention delegates asking them to support the NDPA and vote against the regular delegation.

As these tactics began to attract attention and some support, the NDPA delegates were denied passes into the convention hall. And a few hours before the vote on the challenge was to reach the convention floor, NDPA chairman Cashin later reported, the old political bosses of the national Democratic party and their candidate, Hubert Humphrey, "went from delegation to delegation threatening and promising and demanding that the delegates vote against the NDPA."[44] The possible reasons for this action were suggested earlier by Wieck who reported that "the 11 states of the old confederacy had 527 of the 2,622 convention votes" and that if "300 to 400 southern delegates . . . rally around the favorite son candidacy of Governor John Connally of Texas" . . . it could put an end to Humphrey's hopes for the nomination.[45] Wieck also speculated that if Humphrey supported NDPA he could drive the southern delegates into Connally's camp, and this was a risk Humphrey could not afford to take.

Whatever the political maneuverings at the convention, the full Credentials Committee accepted the report of the subcommittee on the Alabama challenge, and the full convention voted that same day to accept the Credentials Committee's report, which refused to seat the NDPA or AIDP delegates.

At the beginning of September Secretary of State Mabel Amos, a presidential elector on the regular Democratic ticket which was pledged to George Wallace, notified NDPA that a list of its candidates had to be filed and certified by September 5 if their names were to be put on the general election ballot in November. NDPA complied with the request. Under Alabama law the probate judges are responsible for preparing ballots to be used in each of the state's counties, so Mrs. Amos notified the judges that the NDPA candidates were eligible to be placed on the ballot. A short time later Mrs. Amos removed all but two of the NDPA candidates from the November ballot, among them the entire slate of presidential electors.

Mrs. Amos said that her actions were predicated upon the Garrett Act, passed by the Alabama State Legislature in 1967. This act, she argued, stipulated that anyone "who does not file a declaration of intention to become a candidate for such office with the Secretary of State on or before the first day of March of the year in which such general election is held" is to be barred from the ballot.[46] This the party had not done because it did not nominate candidates until the May 7 primary. Nevertheless, NDPA argued that such a law placed an undue burden on the organization and decided to fight it in court.

On September 18, NDPA went into federal district court seeking to have its candidates reinstated on the November ballot. The court issued a temporary restraining order until it could hear oral arguments from both sides; on September 30 the court heard the oral arguments and promised a ruling as soon as possible.

On October 11, 1968, the three-judge Federal District Court in a split decision upheld the Garrett Act. But NDPA appealed the decision to the Supreme Court. And on October 19, the Supreme Court ruled that Alabama officials had to put the racially integrated NDPA slate on the ballot for the November general election.

In making its decision, the Supreme Court held that the Garrett Act violated section 5 of the 1965 Voting Rights Act, which provides that, if any state has "any voting qualification or prerequisite to voting, or standard, practice or procedure with respect to voting different from that in force or effect on November 1, 1964," the state must get a declaratory judgment from the U.S. District Court for the District of Columbia that such changes "will not have the effect of denying or abridging the right to vote on account of race or color." [47] This the state of Alabama had failed to do.

In the November elections seventeen NDPA candidates were elected—eight in Sumter County, five in Marengo County, and four in Etowah County. (See Table 12 in the Appendix.) However, in Greene County none of NDPA's candidates appeared on the ballot despite the Supreme Court's ruling. Therefore, after the election NDPA took the probate judge of that county, James Herndon, to court. And on December 16 the Supreme Court ordered him to show cause why he should not be held in contempt. Herndon responded that he never was officially served with a copy of the High Court's order and thought that the ruling did not apply to candidates in his county.[48]

On March 25, 1969, the Supreme Court ordered that a special election be held in Greene County on July 29 so that the six black NDPA candidates whose names had been left off the ballot could have a chance to run. When the special election was held all six black NDPA candidates won.

At the same time that NDPA was bringing its court case against Judge Herndon, it began a campaign to have the five newly elected representatives and one senator expelled from the Democratic party to reduce their congressional authority—that is, any of them who headed congressional committees were to have the chairmanship taken away from them. The NDPA congressional challenge differed from the MFDP challenge because it sought to expel individuals from the Democratic party and not from Congress itself.

The NDPA challenge began with letters to each congressman explaining that the new representatives and senator from Alabama had supported Wallace's American Independent party and not the Democratic party. This failure to support their own party, NDPA said, should be reason enough for national party officials in Congress to remove them from the party's ranks and strip them of their congressional authority. However, the congressional Democrats failed to act on the request; and NDPA's leadership, realizing that no rules existed for the expulsion of party members, quietly dropped the challenge.[49]

Despite the failure of this challenge, NDPA sent a delegation to the hearing on Democratic party reforms held by a special subcommittee of the Democratic National Committee in May 1969 in Jackson, Mississippi. At the hearing, NDPA chairman John Cashin demanded that the national Democratic party draw up guidelines which would guarantee Alabama's black population a policy-making voice in the state Democratic party. Since the special subcommittee was convened to gather testimony, not to set policy, the impact of Cashin's demands is not yet known.

After the hearings, Cashin traveled throughout Alabama and several other states to publicize and raise money for NDPA. During his tour, Cashin spoke to a mass meeting of Black Panther party supporters in Lowndes County. After the meeting, LCFO decided to run its candidates on the NDPA ticket in the 1970 general elections.

At the NDPA second annual convention in Montgomery on July 12, 1969, it was decided to sponsor Rev. William Branch for national Democratic committeeman from Alabama, although the regular state party had nominated Albert Rains for the position. When NDPA sent Branch's name to the Democratic National Committee, he was turned down by a vote of 57 to 40.

On January 18, 1970, NDPA's executive council decided that its 1970 statewide election strategy would be to concentrate primarily on local offices and endorse no one for governor. The council further agreed to call on the black electorate not to support either Wallace or Albert Brewer in the primary. NDPA's leadership felt that this would prevent Wallace from using the old black bloc vote argument in a runoff election if such an election became necessary. However, NDPA's call upon the black electorate was not as effective as ADC's call urging blacks to support Brewer. Wallace *did* secure enough votes to force a runoff between himself and Brewer, he *did* use the black bloc vote argument to get white voters to support him, and he won in the runoff.

When Wallace won the runoff election, the NDPA at its statewide convention in Montgomery on August 1st, nominated the party chairman, Dr. John L. Cashin, Jr., for governor and Isaiah Hayes, a Black Gadsden labor official and steelworker, for lieutenant-governor as a counterweight in order to give voters in the November general election a real choice.

Moreover, the NDPA members nominated candidates for every state office and numerous local and municipal offices, and a full slate of candidates for the United States Congress. In all, the NDPA nominated 176 candidates for the November general election in 1970.

After the convention, the NDPA leader, Dr. John Cashin, led a whirlwind statewide campaign. The party used the service of such nationally known blacks as Julian Bond who spoke at the convention and telegrams from Mrs. Coretta Scott King and the Rev. Ralph Abernathy to urge black voters in the state to support NDPA candidates.

When the campaign rhetoric and speeches stopped and the election results were in, 21 of the NDPA 176 candidates had won and its gubernatorial candidate, Dr. Cashin, had received more than 106,000 votes. Although he lost to Wallace, he won more than 16 percent of the total black vote in the state. Perhaps the greatest boost to the NDPA efforts was the fact that in Greene County the party won every electoral office. Greene County elected an all black government. (See Table 13 for some of the election results.) Moreover, one of the NDPA black candidates for the state legislature, Thomas Reed (state president of the NAACP), became one of the first blacks to be elected to the Alabama state legislature. The other black elected to the state legislature not on the NDPA ticket was Fred Gray.

Following the election the NDPA entered suits in U.S. Federal District Court contesting election results in Sumter, Perry and Hale counties. In these counties several NDPA candidates lost due to what the party felt was white manipulation of the election returns. At this writing the court has not rendered a verdict.

Besides entering suits, the NDPA leadership assisted numerous blacks in the state to get registered and planned strategy for the 1972 elections. In 1972 the party hoped to capture complete control of several other counties in the black belt, like Sumter, Perry, Hale, etc. To date, the NDPA is the most successful of all black political parties and it seems the most viable. In terms of offices won and votes received, the NDPA is unparalleled. Part of its success seems to be due to the dynamic and powerful leadership of Dr. John Cashin. In his tireless efforts to promote and organize the party he has been able to enlarge its supporters, enhance its image, and make it a relevant competitor in state politics. In addition, the establishing of a monthly newspaper has improved communications among party members, and has spread the news of the party to aspirants, well wishers, and onlookers.

The use of nationally known and popular black leaders as speakers and endorsers has further improved the party's image in the black community. And Cashin's strategy of urging other black political groups and organizations in the state to work with the NDPA has eliminated competition and diminished much of the internal schism and bickering in the black community.

Finally, financial contributions both inside and outside the state have helped the party a great deal, as has the election of numerous candidates. In fact, the kind of political leadership that Dr. Cashin has exemplified may be the force which will move black political parties to newer heights.

At the time of this writing, the NDPA faced one other major problem, the 1972 convention and what the Democratic party would do when NDPA posted a seating challenge to be recognized as the regular party in the state. Much of what happened at the convention could effect the continual viability of the party. In any event, the NDPA has changed the political fortunes of blacks in Alabama.

5

BLACK THIRD PARTIES:

AN ASSESSMENT

Third parties have appeared, disappeared, and reappeared through-out American political history. They have arisen out of a need to proclaim certain principles, doctrines, or philosophies or simply out of a desire to capture the presidency. Whatever their reasons for existence, none has achieved any significant electoral success, except locally. The efforts of George Wallace's American Independent party in 1968 are a notable exception, for the party captured 10 million votes. Most minor parties are short-lived, passing their commitments along to various other institutions, mainly the major parties.[1]

But some, in short glowing periods of brilliance, have advanced notable causes and reforms. Others have served as gadflies, educators, propagandists, promotional agencies, and moralizers. In sum, they have served not only as adjusters of conflict, but also as advertisers of special programs and policies. Still other minor parties have entered presidential races and, according to Key, "doubtless from time to time nourished a belief that they had a chance to win." [2] The Progressive (Bull Moose) party of 1912 is characteristic of these, as are the efforts of Wallace in 1968.

The very existence of minor parties is indicative on the one hand of the flexibility of our political system and, on the other hand, of the failure of the major parties to answer the needs of all sectors of the electorate. This is borne out further by the existence throughout America's political history of two types of minor parties, characterized by Professor Key as the long-lived, recurring party and the short-lived, episodic, nonrecurring party. Activists in "the rather large-scale episodic nonrecurring minor-party movements" [3] have caused both major parties to realign themselves on occasion, thus either narrowing or widening their policy differences. In other cases, minor parties have forced one or the other major party to realign its policies. Such was the intention, for example, of the Dixiecrats in 1948.

But the policy realignment of major parties represents only part of the potential influence of minor parties. Major voter realignment has also occurred from time to time in one or both of the major parties. In this respect, the impact of the Populists in 1896 and the influence of the Progressives in 1912 and 1924 are significant. Populism, primarily a political movement of farmers and rural poor, began in the 1880s in the Midwest and spread rapidly throughout the South. On the national level the Populist party collapsed after the election of 1896, but it continued on the state and local levels for almost a decade more.

Following the Populists came the Progressive movement, which was primarily an attempt by the urban poor to improve their economic condition. Progressivism appeared on the national level in the 1912, 1924, and 1948 presidential elections. Like the Populists, the Progressives had varying degrees of success on the state and local levels.

In 1912 the Progressive party's call for a redistribution of wealth, an end to corruption and graft in municipal and state governments, the elimination of trusts and monopolies in big business, and the creation of new governmental agencies for public purposes brought the party 4,126,000 votes (88 electoral votes) as against the Republican party's 3,484,000 votes (8 electoral votes). Hence the Progressives' platform caused a major voter realignment and put the party in second place in a three-way presidential race that year. In 1968 Wallace's American Independent party caused the Democrats to lose, and the Republican candidate Richard Nixon to take a strong stand on "Law and Order," busing, and the war in Vietnam.

The recurring long-lived minor parties have not had much impact on the major political parties. Because they are usually doctrinaire, more often than not they are isolated and exist outside the mainstream of American political life.[4] They pursue relatively independent courses alongside the major parties without affecting or disrupting the latter's existence or activities.

Despite these differences in national third-party movements, a thread of commonality does exist. In general, these parties espouse points of view deemed too extreme for either major party to uphold, although at times they demonstrate enough support for their ideas to capture the imagination of the established parties. According to Key, however, as a general rule "the minor parties have been national parties, with little substructure of state and local political organizations."[5] (The Socialist party is an exception to this general rule, as was Wallace's 1968 party.)

It is precisely because of this lack of state and local political units to mobilize the electorate that national third parties have continually met defeat at the polls. Yet there *have* been some successful third parties, and "where third parties have discovered more ample support this has usually been sectional."[6] In other words, the most successful third parties have limited themselves to the needs and desires of a given area of the country. Where they are able to rely on local tensions, they may substantially influence the well-entrenched political interests.

"Where solidly founded in their localities," writes Herring, "third parties have been strong and effective over long periods of time."[7] In fact, state and local third-party movements have been much more effective in accomplishing their goals and objectives than have the national movements. Operating independently on local foundations, rather than as offshoots of a nationwide third-party movement, minor state and local parties have on occasion achieved electoral success by championing causes ignored by the two major parties.

State Third Parties: Failures and Accomplishments

The Farmer–Labor party in Minnesota, the American Labor party and the Liberal party in New York, the La Follette movement in Wisconsin, and the Nonpartisan League in North Dakota are excellent illustrations of successful state and local minor parties. For instance, although the Farmer–Labor party never captured full control of the

Minnesota state government, it helped elect governors and wielded tremendous influence on behalf of its supporters—mainly labor and agricultural workers. Many concrete gains were won for these groups because of the party's activities.

In many instances the American Labor party in New York caused voters to realign and caused the major state parties to reorient and redirect their policies, whereas the Nonpartisan League, operating not as a party but as a faction "boring from within" the Republican party, gained control of the government in North Dakota. Both these groups championed local issues and showed little ability to spread to other states. In the case of the La Follette movement, its failure to branch out into other states, after establishing its influence in Wisconsin politics, did not limit its effectiveness on the Wisconsin state level. Such state and local minor parties developed from special circumstances and needs within their localities and, by answering these needs, insured themselves a degree of continued existence.

Nevertheless, state minor parties, like national minor parties, have usually been transitory or at best semipermanent. The aforementioned parties, even though they fall into the semipermanent category, did not achieve anything like the stability of either major party.

Another factor that can greatly limit the scope and activities of the small independent state or local party is its inability either to obtain or to grant patronage; such an inability can even force a minor party to merge with another party or to give up its activities altogether. Lacking the power to grant regular rewards to its loyal followers— political favors and appointed positions, for instance—a minor party cannot long continue to operate. If a minor party promises and can deliver a significant number of votes to a major party in a national election, some degree of patronage may be forthcoming; but if, as in several states, the election procedures render it impossible to ascertain the nature and extent of a local party's contribution in a national election, the minor party's claim to such patronage is tenuous. In some states—New York, for example—a single candidate can run on the ballot of several parties, in which case the contribution of a minor party can easily be determined. But only a few states permit such a procedure.

Still another factor affecting the success and longevity of minor state and local parties is the extent of their organizational cohesiveness. If victories at the polls are required to sustain the organization and victories are not forthcoming, party survival rests on precarious grounds. If, on the other hand, the party leader can rely on a solid bureaucracy—similar to that in trade unions—continuation of the party is more likely.

Over and above the problems of patronage, organizational consolidation, and electoral handicaps, there may exist an even more formidable obstacle: the overt hostility of the government itself. If the state government is hostile to a minor party—as have been the governments of Mississippi and Alabama to black third parties—the success or failure of the party, even its very survival, depends largely on its resilience in withstanding the state's suppressive measures.[8] But here again, the support or opposition of the populace remains a significant factor in determining the fate of the party. In the face of governmental hostility, other factors must weigh heavily in the party's favor if meaningful goals are to be achieved.

Briefly, then, national, state, and local minor parties have grown out of social and economic discontent, challenging the wielders of power in many elections throughout American history, with varying degrees of success. Their chances for electoral victory have depended upon their bases of support—financial as well as popular—their programs, policies, and goals, and the adaptive ability of the major-party competitors. And on the whole, the local or sectional minor parties have proved much more successful than the national ones.

In perspective, we can clearly see that the MFDP and LCFO movements dealt with in Chapters 3 and 4—their plans for expansion notwithstanding—are examples of state and local movements. Before we consider the political significance of these movements, we must examine a bit more closely the nature of the regular parties in the states where these two movements were active.

The existence of a national two-party system does not in itself mean that individual states will have analogous two-party systems. In fact, in the words of Lawson, "state parties in general are highly independent of national party control." [9] Since neither of the major parties has a highly centralized and well-disciplined organization, state Democratic and Republican parties develop more or less freely, in accordance with the local political culture. This is true even though the national parties depend on state parties for fund-raising and election campaigning and state parties in turn depend on the national parties for political rewards in the form of patronage and other favors as well as for financial support. The relationship may be described as one of limited cooperation, sometimes even noncooperation. The classic examples are the relationships between the national Democratic party and the state parties of Alabama and Mississippi, both of which decided in 1948 and 1964 not to back the national party because of the civil rights planks in its platform.

State parties display not only varying degrees of autonomy from the national party but also different natures and characteristics altogether. Furthermore, the politics in some states is dominated by one particular party, while other states are two-party in makeup. In the one-party state, bifactionalism or multifactionalism within the dominant party can further enhance the uniqueness of this system, while vigor of competition is the most notable characteristic of the true two-party state. But whatever the nature of the state's politics, local issues are its driving force: sectionalism and localism provide the background for and foundation of state parties' existence.

The politics of the states we are concerned with here, Alabama and Mississippi, are not only dominated by sectional and local issues, but are also controlled by a single party—in both cases the Democratic party.[10] The respective natures of these two state parties have in part led to the creation of MFDP, LCFO, and NDPA, discussed earlier.

Mississippi Politics and the Rise of MFDP

In Mississippi, one-party politics began when the black-belt white plantation owners, with the aid of impoverished hill farmers, restored white supremacy in the 1875 elections. Because the Republican party, which had dominated southern state legislatures during Black Reconstruction, was widely identified with emancipated Negroes and carpetbaggers, for all intents and purposes the Democratic party became the party of the white southerner. The Democratic party, it was hoped, would ensure southern white supremacy forever: it was to be the be-all and end-all for the white man in southern politics. But before the party was well entrenched, its solidarity began to crumble.

To understand why, it must first be understood that Mississippi whites reorganized the old Democratic party out of dire necessity. Its existence was originally predicated on the overthrow of "nigger domination"; in practical terms, this meant that the party remained solidly welded together so long as it was made to appear that Negroes represented a continual political threat. Once this threat was diminished, however, party cohesion faltered. Then, since Mississippi is a region with heterogeneous political, social, and economic conditions, political activities inevitably reflected such divertities.

To go back to the days of slavery, Key says "a lively two-party competition prevailed in the south before the Civil War." [11] The larger planters, financiers, urban merchants, and slaveholders identified with the Whig party.[12] The small farmers, hill people, and others who were not slaveholders found comfort in the Jeffersonian and Jacksonian traditions of the Democratic party. In short, the few wealthy whites opposed the many poor and illiterate whites. Class politics dominated the antebellum South, most notably in Mississippi and Alabama; in both states class differences reflected and were further accentuated by geography, the lowlands (black belt) being where most rich whites lived and the uplands being inhabited mostly by poor whites.

The power struggle between these two groups first arose in the 1830s over such issues as whether slaves should be counted in determining representation in the state legislature and in the party convention, and whether to stiffen or repeal property qualifications for officeholding and voting. The lowland whites, as was to be expected, favored counting slaves and stiffening property qualifications, while the hill whites took the opposite side on these questions. In terms of currently fashionable labels, the black-belt whites were basically conservative, opposing welfare legislation and radical change, while the hill whites were generally speaking liberal and favored a welfare form of government.

These antebellum forces never engaged in a meaningful clash, for the secessionist issue and the impending crisis created a "stilling silence," a shaky yet sacrosanct social order. As the Civil War approached, party lines became blurred as white propaganda from the black belt proved sufficient to convince the upland whites that "outsiders" were trying to disturb their peculiar way of life and that secession was not only inevitable but desirable. It is noteworthy that despite the urgency of such arguments, there remained many opponents of secession among the hill whites, mainly those who had little material wealth and few or no slaves. In at least one Mississippi county, whites refused to serve in the Confederate army, maintaining that the conflict was a "rich man's war and a poor man's fight." [13] When the debate was over, the black-belt white slaveholders had carried the day by dint of their unity and superior political skills. They carried their states to war, and the ignorant and illiterate white masses fell into line.

The victory of the North in the Civil War and the excesses of the forces of occupation forged a certain degree of unity and cooperation between whites of substance and poor whites. For example, although a number of poor Mississippi whites worked with the Freedmen and Republicans during Reconstruction, rich Delta whites ultimately succeeded in winning the support of the majority of poor hill whites to overthrow the black-dominated governments.

When the Reconstruction government was finally eliminated with the help of the poor whites from the hills, the black-belt whites from the Delta region—chiefly planters—regained political power. Mississippi Democrats led the way by managing what amounted to violent recapture of the state government and the institution of white supremacy in 1875, and other southern states played follow the leader.

Once in power, the black-belt Democrats sought to ensure the absolute security of their position. Since the only plausible basis for maintaining white solidarity was the fear of Negro domination, this fear was conscientiously nurtured. On the other hand, the Democrats further strengthened their hand by repressing poor whites, employing for this purpose the very methods and techniques that had been used to eliminate the Reconstruction government. Thus from the inception of the one-party system in Mississippi, party unity has depended on the suppression of all other economic, social, and political issues in order to keep Negroes politically impotent. Consequently, party solidarity has been threatened only when other questions have overshadowed the race issue in the public eye.

Because party unity in Mississippi breaks down—to any measurable degree—only when the so-called Negro question is quiescent, much of Mississippi's political history since 1875 has to do with keeping the Negro issue in the limelight. In fact, Mississippi politics since then is mainly an attempt to perfect this technique. But even before the turn of the century, economic issues soon came to outweigh the race issue, leading to political complications; that is, legal and illegal methods of suppressing Negro political activity had proved so effective that economic and class conflict surfaced in the form of an intraparty battle. Later, poor agrarian hill whites, seeking to improve their economic situation, formed or joined independent political movements such as the Jeffersonian Democrats or Populists and sought to remove the white-supremacist Democrats from power.[14] But the black-belt Delta whites, helped in part by Negro votes gained through fraud and manipulation, defeated this Populist movement. Moreover, the black-belt whites moved swiftly to forestall future agrarian movements by calling for a constitutional convention in 1890.

The convention was suspect to begin with, having been authorized on a mixture of clandestine and fraudulent activity with the Negro as supposedly the primary concern. In fact, the 1890 Mississippi constitutional convention effectively disfranchised many thousands of whites along with virtually all the state's Negroes. The intent of the convention, to redress the "gross irregularity of representation that penalized the white counties," was primarily why the poor whites "gave their tacit approval and submitted to the poll tax and disfranchisement plan." Perhaps unknowingly, their submission amounted to guaranteeing the perpetuation and solidification of the power of the black-belt oligarchy.

When it became clear that the final draft of the 1890 constitution would disfranchise the majority of poor whites along with most Negroes, it was bitterly attacked by more than a third of the state's newspapers. Faced with such hostility, the black-belt oligarchs, instead of submitting the new constitution to the electorate for ratification, audaciously proclaimed it to be the law of the land.[15]

During the 1890s Populism flourished everywhere in the South except in Mississippi, where the immediate effect of the new constitution was to stultify the agrarian revolt. The Populist party in the state was at best peripheral and never constituted a major threat to the oligarchs. In fact, Populism almost bypassed the state altogether. Nevertheless, the limited agrarian insurgency had the effect of intensifying the political conflict in the state. The struggle between the planters and the yeomen was widened when the Delta cotton planters increased their strength by forging a political alliance with the growing industrial class, hoping thereby to make their power secure forever. But this new alliance failed to resolve the basic problem underlying the class cleavage: the impoverished condition of the hill whites.

Thus by the turn of the century, with the decline of the Negro as a political factor, the stark economic gap between rich and poor served to rekindle the conflict between hill whites and Delta whites. The poverty of Mississippi hill whites soon came to express itself in terms of neo-Populism under the leadership of such political characters as James Vardaman (governor from 1902 to 1908 and senator from 1913 to 1919) and Theodore Bilbo (governor from 1915 to 1919 and again from 1927 to 1932 and senator from 1934 to 1947).[16] These men exploited the hill whites' envy of the Delta planters and resented the latter's welfare programs providing education and hospital care for Negroes. For the most part, the campaigns of the Vardamans and Bilbos, waged at the expense of the black-belt aristocracy, have hardly been unsuccessful. The few Delta politicians who have since been able to capture major political posts in the state were forced in one way or another to appeal to the "red-neck" hill whites.[17]

Since the 1890 constitution disfranchised all of Mississippi's Negroes and most of its poor whites, agrarian and aristocratic whites have continued their struggle virtually unabated. Whenever the threat of Negro political activity has arisen, whether with or without outside help, intraparty competition among whites—regardless of their economic and social status—has declined. Party unity and cohesion were the order of the day whenever the race issue became paramount. Thus the establishment of the federal Fair Employment Practices Commission and the passage of such federal legislation as anti-poll-tax, anti-lynching, and civil rights bills have won for Bilbo and politicians of his ilk the grudging (and somewhat self-defeating) but wholehearted support of the rich Delta whites.[18]

Intent on perpetuating white supremacy, and grounded in fear of Negro political activity, one-party politics in Mississippi has created a political life characterized by frustrated abilities, colorful personalities, fiery oratory, and shameless demagoguery. Geographically speaking, the politics of the Delta and hill regions have to some extent coalesced, although the two areas continue to reflect different states of mind that are rooted in the past. Thus the continuing regional conflict is not clearly delineated by—or even within—the state's one-party structure. Mississippi politics is too poorly organized to permit the effective expression of these (or any other) viewpoints. Neither group is represented by a political organization anything like a party machine, nor can one clearly identify candidates' campaign proposals with particular viewpoints. The factions that arise before election time are of a transient nature, and lines are drawn somewhat confusedly, largely according to localities.

In the main, candidates rely on organizations that lack formal discipline, but maintain a great amount of cohesion through personal loyalty. For all intents and purposes a candidate's supporters are his neighbors; and their attachment to him rests on his expression of their personal hopes and aspirations. This aspect of Mississippi politics further limits solidarity within the one-party structure; candidates for state offices cannot count on support—on the basis of party alone—from candidates on the county level, nor can county candidates be sure of local support, and so on. No one wants to antagonize his close followers, and so only a very few risk their political careers for the sake of principles. In these instances, Mississippi one-party politics tends to disintegrate into multificationalism, with the advantage going primarily to the lawyer–planter–merchant groups.[19] On the other hand, the hill whites, who normally lack formal organization and interest-group unity, require the emergence of such demagogues as Theodore Bilbo to express their interests.

Sometimes, in a one-party state, party solidarity exists and political fortunes are made at the expense of a segment of the population that represents a threat, real or imagined. When this group is effectively suppressed, the major cohesive force of the party is undermined, and it no longer has any basis for unity. In the continuing political dialogue between the agrarian and aristocratic classes in Mississippi, the Negro has been the eternal overriding issue. The threat he represents has been kept in the forefront, if only superficially. His political, economic, and social rights have been sternly suppressed, his "place" defined and redefined. Even when politically dormant and posing no overt threat, he has come to be the perennial whipping boy.

By the middle of this century, Negroes had virtually disappeared from Mississippi politics. Their right to vote had been limited both legally and illegally, sometimes by means of the state constitution, sometimes in violation of both state and federal constitutions. Those few Negroes who surmounted legal obstacles to the franchise have found it extraordinarily difficult to overcome fear, violent repression, and crippling economic sanctions. Even if they could vote, their choice would be limited to white Democratic candidates, all of whom were inimical to Negroes' interests. Thus what expectations could political participation fulfill? Desperation and frustration eventually begot apathy, and Negro voter participation in Mississippi ground to a halt. To be sure, the Supreme Court's abolition of all-white primaries in one-party states [20] dispelled some of the deepening apathy, but the vast majority of Mississippi Negroes remained politically ineffective and uninterested.

The federal voting rights acts of 1957, 1960, and 1963 represented much-needed help from outside the state, but white Mississippians reacted by reuniting and repressing the small but rising number of Negro voters. Indigenous Negro leaders, harkening to the sounds of the Negro revolution of the 1960s, launched their own voter registration drive in 1961 in synchronization with outside efforts. Accompanying these efforts was the desire to remake the regular, all-white Mississippi state Democratic party and to reverse its ultraconservatism.

Out of these first efforts came COFO. Although COFO was made up of five black civil rights organizations, youthful SNCC volunteers did much of the canvassing and grassroots work, and some of the individual members of SNCC thereby gained a disproportionate amount of influence, prestige, and direction over the emerging MFDP leaders. This gave SNCC a little more leverage in MFDP than other COFO members had. But in general it was as a result of COFO's efforts that MFDP came into being.

Having no place to turn or party to affiliate with, and suffering repression at the hands of the only party existing in the state, Mississippi Negroes formed their own independent state party: the Mississippi Freedom Democratic party. At first, the chief aim of the organization was to unseat the regular state delegation to the 1964 Democratic national convention and gain recognition as the official Mississippi delegation.

After rejection of MFDP's challenge by the convention, the organization became more of a separate state party. Specifically, MFDP became a satellite party, an organized party within a major party (in this case, the national Democratic party) whose future rested upon its being recognized as the legitimate successor to the regular party.

MFDP hoped that the federal government would offer help in the party's attempt to register Mississippi Negroes, whose votes would determine the party's future. COFO's massive voter drive during the 1964 freedom summer had proved disappointing, having added fewer than 90,000 Negro voters to the rolls. Thus it became apparent that additional help would be needed if the MFDP challenge of the political power of the regular Democratic party was to succeed. In view of massive statewide resistance to replacing the regular state party, appealing to the federal government seemed the logical move.

From late 1964 on, the coalition of Delta and hill whites that had controlled Mississippi's political institutions for more than a half-century sought to crush MFDP through constitutional and other means. Thus to a large extent the history of MFDP has been an unending struggle to overcome the repressive measures aimed at the party during each election. Every conceivable method—from questionable laws and administrative restraints to violence—has been used to halt MFDP activities, and these measures have not been without effect. During the period from late 1964 to early 1966 the party was almost forced out of existence, and its image and political effectiveness consequently were at low points. One major factor—if not the essential one—that enabled MFDP to continue was the passage of the Voting Rights Act in August 1965, after (and perhaps partly because of) the failure of the party's convention challenge. The act's provision for sending federal registrars to areas of low voter enrollment, such as Mississippi, rendered the party's position more tenable inasmuch as it represented a means whereby it could broaden its base of support. With the arrival of federal help, the party believed that Negroes who had been merely sympathizers would become voters and would increase the party's chances for continued existence.

The internal problem of party unity and the external one of state repression were not the only threats to the survival of the newly emerging MFDP; the danger always existed of being absorbed into the regular state Democratic party. The regular party membership has always included some moderate whites who, if only out of self-interest, have sought to improve schools and health facilities for the state's Negroes.[21] After the 1964 challenge had failed, these moderates joined white liberals, state labor leaders, and the state NAACP in forming the Mississippi Democratic Conference (MDC) for the purpose of gaining control of the regular party and winning the allegiance of potential Negro voters. These efforts brought it into direct competition with MFDP.

Within the MFDP hierarchy, SNCC radicals had risen to ascendancy after the 1964 Democratic national convention. It was this group that dominated much of the party's ideology, rejected out of hand all coalitions with white liberals, and kept MFDP representation out of MDC. Charging that the white allies had ultimately undermined the convention challenge and that, furthermore, the entire establishment was morally bankrupt, the SNCC faction determined that the party should adopt a go-it-alone program.[22] Armed with such a program and its attendant ideology, MFPD emerged as the arch-competitor of the NAACP—the state's only other predominantly black organization—in seeking the support of the state's newly enfranchised Negroes. The 1965 Natchez boycott of white merchants can thus be viewed in part as a battle in which each of the two organizations sought to boost its image among Mississippi's black people.

Further conflict between the organizations was avoided primarily because the two were obliged to limit their activities to different areas of the state. A combination of insufficient funds, limited numbers of organizers, and state repression forced both organizations to concentrate their activities in order to achieve even minimal success. Nevertheless, events surrounding the election of several black candidates by both groups in 1967 led to a degree of cooperation between them. Repressive measures taken by the state, culminating in the controversy over the bonding of newly elected black officeholders, served to forge an alliance between the two organizations. The resultant cooperative spirit was reinforced when NAACP state secretary Charles Evers, running for Congress in a special election, succeeded in enlisting MFDP chairman Lawrence Guyot as his campaign manager. Furthermore, in 1968, both NAACP and MFDP joined white liberals to form the Loyal Democrats of Mississippi, which sent a delegation to the 1968 Democratic national convention and successfully challenged the regular state Democratic delegation.

Whether MFDP will be absorbed by either the NAACP or LDM, or whether LDM will simply break up, or whether the state NAACP will leave future political action to either or both of the other organizations depends on many factors. Competition between MFDP and

NAACP may break out again, although limited cooperative efforts that allow each to retain its identity are also possible. In any event, the success of any future merger will obviously depend upon the ability and foresight of the leadership and the other strengths and weaknesses of the united organization, as well as upon the degree of success or failure of inevitable white repression.

Two major problems that MFDP has always faced concern finances and patronage. Money to run campaigns, to print literature, to strengthen the party organization, and to fight legal battles has always been in short supply. For the most part, supporters and potential supporters have been poverty-stricken because the party's activities have centered on the Delta region—part of Mississippi's black belt, where poverty among Negroes is most pronounced. (In its competition with MFDP over voter registration, the NAACP chose to concentrate on the state's southwestern area, where a small Negro middle-class population resides.) Thus MFDP has had to depend heavily on outside contributions, and party candidates have often been forced to draw upon their own resources to finance their campaigns. In many instances, therefore, campaigns have been hampered, voter registration drives have been limited or even abandoned, and party literature has been available only in limited quantities.

During COFO's short existence, each member organization contributed funds to support MFDP; and during the freedom summer of 1964, the ranks of party organizers and workers were swollen by volunteer college students, black and white, from the North. But the 1964 Democratic national convention was something of a psychological and emotional watershed. After the convention COFO was disbanded, and the subsequent blossoming of SNCC's radical black power philosophy alienated many liberal whites who had been among MFDP's strongest contributors and supporters. In addition, when SNCC withdrew most of its workers from MFDP in order to create LCFO in Alabama, MFDP, unlike the NAACP, was left with no national organization to call upon for funds or personnel. Thus during 1965 and 1966 the party dwindled to little more than a spiritual union. Until the 1967 election it existed, for the most part, in name only. Whether the election of six MFDP candidates in 1967, six in 1968, and eight in 1969 can strengthen the party to the extent of adding to its coffers remains to be seen.

MFDP has not been alone in achieving electoral victories; the NAACP under Charles Evers' tutelage has also been successful. After the 1968 national Democratic convention the NAACP began a major drive in the six southwestern counties to win municipal and local offices. Although the NAACP backed candidates in all the cities throughout the area, major effort was concentrated on the city of Fayette. This was done because in this one-main-street town with a population of 2,000, blacks numbered 1,200.

For the 1969 primary, the NAACP backed Charles Evers for mayor and six blacks for executive committeemen (election officials). On May 13, primary day, Evers and his entire slate were victorious. In fact, Evers defeated incumbent white Mayor R. J. Allen, who had held that office for 18 years, by a vote of 433 to 264. Evers and his entire slate were unopposed in the June 3 general election, and they of course carried the day and were formally inaugurated into office. With this victory, Evers became the only black mayor of a previously white-run town in Mississippi (the all-black town of Mound Bayou has always had a black mayor). Concomitant with Evers' electoral victory and major showing in the 1971 gubernatorial campaign, the NAACP rose in prestige. Whether its election victories will make it more popular with the black voters in the state than MFDP only time will tell.

Regarding MFDP's problem of patronage, since neither the national Democratic party nor the state party is disposed to reward MFDP, the party itself can offer little in the way of patronage as a means of building a well-disciplined and tightly knit organization. So far, then, MFDP has been unable to reward its supporters or followers. Not until 1967 were any of its candidates victorious; then, the election successes of 1967, 1968, and 1969 raised another question. Will MFDP candidates continue to identify with the party after they are elected—not only in name but in policies, principles, and political rewards—or will they exploit their power and prestige primarily to build personal organizations? The lack of finances and patronage that might otherwise bring MFDP a small measure of independence and a secure economic base undoubtedly has its damaging effects. Federal surplus food and contributions from white liberals certainly help, but they represent only a fraction of what is needed.

Finally, the problem of overcoming the fear and apathy of the black community, reinforced by years of exclusion from politics, is ever present. Whether all or even a majority of eligible black voters eventually will support MFDP or whether, out of fear of economic reprisal and concerted violence, they will shrink from such activity and support white conservative candidates depends largely on whether MFDP—or similar organizations—can overcome the major obstacles with a clear-cut strategy. The election of six MFDP candidates in one year is a heartening sign, but the defeat of more than 40 others in the same elections is, by comparison, somewhat discouraging.

Certainly not all is bleak for MFDP. Surely it has inherent strong points; otherwise, the party probably would have failed to elect any candidates up to now—or would even have collapsed altogether. One of the basic strengths of MFDP rests in the special circumstances of its creation and the special needs of the localities in which and for which it was created. The long-unfulfilled need of Mississippi Negroes for political expression and for the rewards that political power grants is certainly a major force to be creatively channeled. The continued and increasingly severe repression of Negro political activity in the state, after black politics came to an end following Reconstruction, eventually led to its re-emergence and in part accounted for the radical form it took when it re-emerged. The anger and alienation, the bitterness and resentment, the hopes and aspirations of the many—especially those in the poverty areas—were so intense that a mere handful were able to coalesce and weld together this unique political vehicle. Since the adoption of SNCC's radical philosophy in 1964, perhaps the party speaks for few and will continue mainly in spirit or name to represent the special views and interests of poverty-stricken blacks, their new sense of defiance. For the most part, the party could not have survived under the harsh state repression had the spirit and will to exist been missing. It was this will, this spirit, this hope that enabled the party to survive if only in the minds of its supporters. And it is likely to survive for some time, until the anger and bitterness and idealism that brought it into being have spent themselves.

The spirit of the MFDP leadership, like the spirit of the organization itself, is one of its essential fine points, and this spirit has been vigorously expressed in the charismatic personality of Mrs. Fannie Lou Hamer and in the rugged determination of its chairman, Lawrence

Buyot. Both have embodied the will to struggle and to go on, regardless of obstacles.[23] The inspiring examples of these dedicated leaders enabled the organization to survive some of its early crises, and such leadership may prove to ensure its survival.

Another source of support has been the whites who contributed money, legal advice, and personal service to build up the party. Without their encouragement and support during the early stages of the party's existence, it probably would not have fared so well as it has. After SNCC's black power philosophy radicalized the party, however, most of this support disappeared, except for some continued legal advice. The help of whites in the beginning was crucial, and possibly their help in the future may likewise be crucial.

When all is said and done, however, the most important factor affecting the future success or failure of MFDP is the response of blacks in the areas of most concentrated Negro population in Mississippi—the black-belt areas. This concentration represents the party's best chance of electoral victory, provided the obstacles can be overcome. Inasmuch as the effects of slavery and segregation have served more or less to leave Negroes in areas of isolation—whether they be urban slum ghettos or rural pockets of poverty—the potential political power that remains as a byproduct of these infamous institutions is incalculable. Releasing this power effectively, tapping this human resource and using it to the advantage of the people of the ghettos and pockets of poverty, is the as yet unfinished part of the MFDP story. The attempt to release the energy of these Negro areas in Mississippi in politically constructive forms is the essence of the history of MFDP, nothing more nor less. The story continues because the problems and their creators remain.

Alabama Politics and the Rise of LCFO

In Alabama, as in Mississippi, Negroes were elected to state and national offices during Black Reconstruction. Blacks sat in both houses of the state legislature, and three Negroes represented Alabama in Congress; but the Negro population of Alabama was proportionally too small for blacks to gain the sort of significant leadership and power there that they held in Mississippi. Thus the brutal restoration of white rule in Alabama, which followed Mississippi's lead in 1875, was completed in a much shorter period of time.

Like Mississippi, Alabama before the Civil War had a two-party system that broke along class lines. The Whig party was the party of the slaveholders and men of means, while the Democratic party received most of its support from the less-affluent whites in the northern and southeastern parts of the state. After Lincoln's election in 1860 the Republican party became identified with opposition to slavery. So during Alabama's debate over secession, the black-belt plantation owners became Democrats and dragged the state's reluctant northern and southeastern whites into the Confederacy. After the war, black-belt whites successfully solicited the aid of northern whites in overthrowing the Black Reconstruction government. Considering that Montgomery was the capital of the Confederacy, it is perhaps no surprise that the black-belt whites who regained power following Reconstruction had little trouble in establishing white supremacy as the basis for one-party (Democratic) solidarity. To many, the "lost cause" could be revived if the Negro was effectively suppressed politically and otherwise; but before the mortar in the walls of the house of party solidarity could dry, Negroes had been so vigorously suppressed that the threat of blacks' regaining power—the major basis for party unity—disappeared, old party lines reappeared, and sectional rivalries were revived. Several independent agrarian movements appeared in the 1880s; but the ingenuity of black-belt conservatives, the use of violence and fraud, and the effect of such outside forces as the Lodge Bill restored the spirit in the house that white supremacy had built. The Lodge Bill, sponsored by Henry Cabot Lodge (R. Mass.) in 1890, provided for federal supervision of national elections, especially in the South.

Only briefly suppressed, agrarian radicalism re-emerged in the 1890s as Populist and Independent movements. The Independent movement, organized by Reuben F. Kolb, mounted a challenge to the black-belt conservative Democrats in the 1892 election, with Kolb as the gubernatorial candidate. Although quixotic, Kolb's challenge was a serious effort. The election results showed that the black-belt white candidate, Thomas G. Jones, defeated Kolb by a margin of only 11,000 votes out of a total of 250,000 cast. But close examination of the vote totals revealed that Kolb had carried eight more counties than Jones and had received a majority of the votes in white counties (which outnumbered the black-belt counties). Kolb supporters were convinced that he had been swindled out of a victory by a Democratic faction that controlled the election machinery. Nevertheless, the Democratic-controlled legislature refused to provide for lawful redress, and so the election results stood.

Kolb refused to give up. Between 1892 and 1894 his Independent and Populist forces crusaded for the movement in systematic and unremitting fashion. For an entire year prior to the 1894 election, the conservative Democrats were under constant attack. During this period, the predominantly Democratic legislature retaliated by passing the Sayre Election Law, which disfranchised thousands of illiterate voters, both white and black. Refusing to despair, Kolb's supporters met threats with counterthreats and violence with violence, and they attempted to strengthen their position by merging with the local Republicans; but Kolb lost again. Fraud at the polls and the refusal of the legislature to order a new, honest election again permitted the black-belt Democratic candidate to take his seat as governor. In 1896, the fusion of Populists and Democrats on the national level crippled state and local agrarian movements. The final blow was struck by Alabama's disfranchising convention of 1901. Under such pressure, the Independent–Populist movement died.

While the movement was faltering, however, Democrats continually charged that the Negroes, whom the Populists and Independents sought to help, were defeating the Populists and Independent political movements. This propaganda was not without its effect. For example, although the constitution of 1901 disfranchised just as many whites as it did Negroes, the document was actually approved by the electorate (which had not been the case with Mississippi's similar 1890 constitution).

Since 1901, one-party politics has prevailed in Alabama. But class cleavages have expressed themselves through factions within the one-party structure. These factions, much like those in Mississippi, are mostly temporary and generally highly personalized. Factions appear, align themselves for an election, and disappear, only to reappear for the next election.

Stable, distinguishable viewpoints rarely exist, a situation in which the large planter–industrialist–business group reaps benefits while rural elements generally suffer—until the emergence of a highly magnetic spokesman, such as George Wallace.[24] But even the Wallaces can do little more than promise the impossible and try their best to keep the black below the poor hillbilly in terms of status and rights. And if Vardaman and Bilbo represent poor whites in Mississippi, Wallace has come to represent the same people in Alabama and has expanded this appeal nation wide.

Here again, it should be obvious that the voting rights and political activities of Alabama Negroes have been vigorously suppressed since the end of Reconstruction. Negro political activity in the state finally surfaced again not in the form of a party but as a political referral and endorsing agency, such as the Alabama Democratic Conference. Later the first independent Negro political party in Alabama was organized in 1960: the Afro-American party. Operating before the inception of MFDP, this party attracted 1,480 votes in the 1960 national election for its presidential and vice-presidential nominees, and afterward faded from the scene.[25]

The next attempt by Alabama Negroes to enter state politics in this century was not primarily inspired by indigenous leadership, as in the case of MFDP (although SNCC did help these leaders bring their ideas to fruition). Instead, SNCC announced plans to develop a county-level political party in Alabama after parting company with MFDP. In addition to representing a narrowing of focus from the state to the county level, LCFO was predicated on a philosophy different from that of MFDP. It was both hailed and denounced as a separatist movement sponsored mainly by a radical organization (SNCC) that had grown distrustful of establishment whites and coalition politics ever since MFDP's unsuccessful 1964 convention challenge and unsuccessful 1965 congressional seating challenge.

Armed with little more than a theory, SNCC workers led by Stokely Carmichael entered Lowndes County in March 1966 to solicit the aid of local leaders in enlisting support and inspiring enthusiasm for the idea of organizing an all-Negro party in a southern black-belt area.[26] In fact, part of the history of LCFO is the history of the selling of an idea. First, a strategy had to be developed to legitimize the party's activities and at the same time to dramatize the extent of its support. The strategy adopted for this purpose—a statewide boycott of the

May primary and a concurrent mock primary—immediately alienated such civil rights groups as the Alabama SCLC. This was because many blacks were running for office on the Democratic ticket in the primaries, and if SNCC's boycott succeeded it would mean certain defeat for these candidates throughout the state. The resultant antagonism that developed between the two groups did not pose a direct problem for LCFO, however, for SCLC refrained from venturing into Lowndes County. Thus the major difficulty facing LCFO was posed by state and local repression, not by black political competition in the county.

Official repression was directed at LCFO both by the state legislature and by white Lowndes County public officials. The legislature attempted to redistrict the county and to extend the terms of incumbent white Lowndes County officials; for their own part, county officials increased the filing fees for prospective candidates tenfold, making it that much more difficult for impoverished blacks to obtain a place on the ballot. These repressive measures were overcome by the party with varying success (see Chapter 4).

What finally overwhelmed the party was the problem of organizational development. SNCC's coffers were nearly empty when it founded LCFO; in other words, financial backing for LCFO was virtually nonexistent from the beginning. The launching of the party was characterized by nothing like the efforts that went into building COFO and, subsequently, MFDP. Moreover, because SNCC's newly adopted policy barred whites from participating in its projects, LCFO operated without benefit of white student volunteer help of the sort that MFDP received during the summer of 1964. Thus, lacking the requisite funds, time, and manpower to conduct an adequate campaign, the party failed to advance its ideas and concepts to any meaningful extent.

Certainly LCFO received a setback—perhaps its major setback—when Stokely Carmichael, the party's chief organizer and tactician, was elected national chairman of SNCC in May 1966. Because Carmichael was forced to turn his attention away from the fledgling county organization in order to attend to the problems of a rapidly deteriorating national one, SNCC was helped at the expense of LCFO. Furthermore, after his black power speech in Jackson, Mississippi, Carmichael was compelled to devote much of his time to defending, defining, and clarifying the meaning of the slogan and the purpose and objectives of his black power philosophy. Ironically, then, the time Carmichael spent in traveling and making speeches to explain SNCC's philosophy was time taken away from the very model on which this philosophy was based.

Lacking an adequate staff of organizers and sufficient financial backing, LCFO was bound to run into difficulties. In Alabama, according to one writer, "counties with Negro majorities are the poorest economically, educationally, and otherwise in the poorest section of the country. Getting control of them in view of the poverty and continuous migration would be governing ghost towns or cemeteries." [27] Lowndes County is no exception, being among the poorest counties in Alabama:

> Of all the black belt counties, Lowndes is the very heart of darkness. There are four times as many Negroes as whites (12,000 to 3,000) but the blacks live in poverty, subservience and fear. The median family income for Negroes is $935, for whites it is $4,000. Until [1965] not a single Negro was registered to vote. In 1964, about 118 percent of 1,900 eligible whites were registered. There are a lot of dead souls [voting] in Lowndes County.[28]

Because the median educational level for Negroes in Lowndes County was then 5.1 years of schooling and because 80 percent of the people, black and white, were illiterate, political education of the county's Negroes was particularly difficult. SNCC tried to overcome this problem by printing and circulating "political comic books" and by creating a readily identifiable symbol for the party—the black panther. But centuries of illiteracy could not be overcome in the short time preceding elections.

In such a situation, what could a financially handicapped party expect to achieve? Playing upon the anti-white feelings of Negroes— SNCC's strategy, in the eyes of those who disapproved of it—was by itself not enough to inspire party solidarity. In this view, the party ultimately offered blacks little more than the opportunity to participate in a protest forum, and supporters could not expect much in return except the wrath of the plantation owners. Even Carmichael later conceded that LCFO

> . . . must begin thinking of ways to build a patronage system, some . . . mechanism for offering day-to-day bread-and-butter help to the black people's immediate needs. . . . Otherwise, only so many black people

will rush to the banner of "freedom" and "blackness" without seeing some way to make ends meet to care for their children.[29]

SNCC's politics of emotion and protest, without benefit of a system of patronage, failed to produce a well-structured and continuing organization, and LCFO fell easy prey to violence and other forms of white retaliation, such as threatened eviction and similar economic reprisals. Internally, then, LCFO was much more limited than MFDP. On the other hand, the white minority of Lowndes County organized more intensely against LCFO than Mississippi whites did against MFDP. This was the case because whites had been used to doing it since Reconstruction—that is, keeping blacks from entering politics or from gaining political power. In short, it was standard practice. Before the primary election, plantation owners, intent on undermining LCFO's announced boycott, assembled "their" Negroes to make sure they registered to vote.[30] A similar procedure was repeated during the November general election. So once again blacks were used to keep other blacks from gaining political power. The Populists had done the same thing much earlier. At that time black-belt whites sometimes distorted the election returns to show blacks voting against blacks and supporting the plantation-owning whites.

MFDP and LCFO: Similarities and Differences

Despite major differences in the MFDP and LCFO structures, circumstances, and accomplishments, there are some striking similarities between the two. For one thing, SNCC played a major role in organizing both parties, particularly LCFO. Consequently, both parties eventually expressed to some extent the radicalism that SNCC came to represent. Since LCFO was founded after MFDP's 1964 convention challenge and 1965 congressional seating challenge, it was much more radical than MFDP. This is not to suggest that there was anything conservative about MFDP. In its struggle for political existence, MFDP has also exhibited a growing radical spirit—with a bit more success than LCFO.

The two parties faced similar obstacles, among them state repression, the illiteracy of their potential supporters, inadequate organizational strength, and insufficient financial resources. MFDP fared much better in solving its problems partly because, in its initial stages, COFO provided a broad base of organizational support. The NAACP, SCLC, SNCC, and CORE all backed MFDP's early efforts. In addition, in the crucial summer of 1964 COFO supplied MFDP with hundreds of student volunteers who canvassed and organized prospective voters.[31] (The number of summer volunteers in Mississippi during the COFO experiment almost surpassed the total number of votes received by the least successful LCFO candidate in the 1966 election.) Thus the ideas and concepts of MFDP were more widely disseminated. One consequence of this was that the resistance of the Negro middle class was less of a problem in Mississippi, whereas LCFO was opposed from the beginning by Alabama's Negro professionals and middle class.[32] In sum, then, large group support and massive volunteer help moved MFDP through its initial stages, which was not the case with LCFO. Whites were permitted and even encouraged to aid in the organizational efforts of MFDP but—because of SNCC's policy, adopted largely because of its experiences with MFDP—not in the organizational efforts of LCFO. From the start LCFO was an all-black effort, and the inadequate finances of both its organizers and its supporters seriously hampered it. Although MFDP later dropped many of its white supporters, the important point is that they were available to help in the crucial early days.

The problem of finances plagued LCFO more than it did MFDP, which raised money jointly through COFO during the initial stages. Thus, although less money was available after the 1964 challenge and the demise of COFO, by then the party had established a base strong enough to continue on, whereas LCFO suffered severe problems from its inception.

Although the whites in both Alabama and Mississippi reacted to the resurgence of Negro political activity in much the same fashion, MFDP has suffered repression over a longer life span and has achieved greater internal unity than LCFO.

What finally emerges as the most significant difference is that MFDP has been successful in electing candidates and seems to have a future, whereas the defunct LCFO failed in its efforts at the polls. (Although it received enough votes to continue operating as a legal county party in Alabama, it has not appeared on the ballot since 1968. But it has recently agreed to place its candidates on the NDPA ticket.) Why did one organization fail and the other one succeed? Although the similarities and differences are illuminating, two factors are outstanding. One is that the activities of COFO proved invaluable in laying the necessary groundwork for MFDP, while no comparable organization existed to back up LCFO. Second is the shift in SNCC's policy regarding the role of whites in such organizational activity. MFDP may well prove to be a force to reckon with in Mississippi politics. In that event, MFDP, and not LCFO, may end up the working model for black power.

Satellite and Separate Black Parties: A Comparison

Beyond the actual similarities and differences between LCFO and MFDP, there also are theoretical and structural differences that exist in a broader and more general sense.

For instance, inherent in the nature of the black satellite party is a twofold quest for national party acceptance and for the acquisition of power, whereas the black separate party is primarily concerned with a single goal: the acquisition of power. To be sure, both types of parties seek to be accepted by the voters. If the black satellite party is to be accepted as a national political organization's representative in the state, it must convince the national party that the state party is now dysfunctional and a detriment rather than an asset. The specific cases of MFDP, NDPA, and SCPDP suggest that the persuasive arguments of the black satellites include such ideas as these: (1) The state party is disloyal to the national organization; (2) the state party is not representative of all the people in the state; (3) the state party represses certain elements within the state and thus is not committed to the democratic principles of equality and representative government; and (4) the state party's refusal to put an end to repression is immoral. On the other hand, in the black satellite party's quest for recognition and acceptance it not only attempts to discredit the regular state party but seeks to prove that its own new party is more loyal, more representative, more fully committed to the democratic principles of equality and representative government, and more moral (that is, even though the new party's members have suffered at the hands of the state party, they hold firm to their belief in the national organization). In short, the black satellite party seeks to persuade the national party organization that the regular state party should be reformed because it is too corrupt or replaced because it is beyond repair. In addition, the satellite argues that *it* is the organization to reform or replace the state party.

A black satellite party does not include these points merely to persuade the national organization; it uses them in conjunction with a particular political strategy to attract the national party's attention. Its tactics and strategy include seating challenges at national conventions, congressional challenges on the national level, and efforts to expel state elected officials from the national party. Seen in perspective, the seating challenges of MFDP, the Black and Tan Republican party, NDPA, and SCPDP, the congressional challenges of MFDP, and the party expulsion tactics of NDPA were attempts to achieve acceptance and recognition, the first steps on the road to power. With recognition and acceptance come patronage and organizational help from the national party as well as some degree of security and permanence. Moreover, recognition from the national organization attracts individual voters and supporters who are wary of casting protest votes or throwing their votes away on a fly-by-night political party. Recognition of the satellite party gives state voters the sense that the organization is permanent. And with more supporters, the possibility of electoral victories throughout the state is considerably improved.

If the new black satellite party fails in early attempts to achieve national party recognition, it goes back to running numerous candidates for office and trying to achieve significant electoral victories. In this way it seeks to prove that the electorate recognizes it as a legitimate reform party. In this drive for power through electoral victories, new black satellite parties have the black-majority areas to rely on for support. Even if there is competition within the black community, such as MFDP faced in Mississippi from the NAACP, some measure of victory still can be achieved because of the sheer size of the black electorate in certain areas.

However, the electoral victories of the new black satellite party may not be convincing enough or significant enough to persuade the national party to accept or recognize it. One of the major problems of the black satellite parties—especially in the South—is that they tend to be predominantly black. And the credentials committee at a national party convention is likely to balk at the idea of replacing an all-white delegation with one that has few whites in its ranks. Moreover, old convention rules and regulations are not necessarily binding upon a new convention and its presidential contenders. For example, the Democratic convention of 1948 made certain promises to SCPDP but failed to keep them in the 1956 convention. Each contender for the presidency at the convention seeks to maximize his own chances of getting the nomination and deals with contesting delegations in that light. In other words, members of the credentials committee are pressured by the chief contenders for the nomination to support certain delegations favorable to each particular candidate. The experiences of the Black and Tan contesting delegations from the South at the 1928 Republican convention are evidence of this.[33] Their success or failure depended not upon the strength or validity of their case, but upon their usefulness to each individual seeking the presidential nomination. When Herbert Hoover felt that he no longer needed the group, he failed to recognize it any more. In the final analysis, then, party and convention rules and regulations, as well as their application, fail to set forth in precise terms the conditions under which a state party should be reformed or replaced. In addition, the rules say little about the type of organization that should replace the regular state party. Nevertheless, implicit in the drive for power of the black satellite parties is the desire for acceptance and recognition. And whether these organizations will be content with electoral victories alone, though they lack national acceptance and recognition, is as yet unclear. Repeated rejection could mean that the black satellite party will lose most of its zeal and simply disperse.

On the other hand, the focus of black separate parties is on the fruits of power. In other words, they are not concerned with election victories as a means of winning recognition from a national organization. Victories for a separate party mean viability and continued existence. They mean that voters and supporters have been won over to the separate party's principles and objectives, not to some national party's policies. Since a separate party acts on the belief that it can compete effectively with any other party because of a certain distinctiveness in goal, objectives, and policies, it seeks no affiliation with another party. Separate parties do not strive for recognition and acceptance by a national party, as satellite parties do. Black separate parties do not resort to seating challenges or congressional challenges; they do not expend their energies on tactical maneuvers aimed at recognition. Instead, separate parties strive to win at the polls because only in this way can they exist as viable political organizations. Winning is essential for black separate parties because it is from their elected officials that they expect the financial resources and policy spokesmen they need if they are to continue to exist. Without victories to sustain them, black separate parties such as the Negro Protective party, the Afro-American party, LCFO, and the Party of Christian Democracy quickly fade from the political scene, because organizational needs such as patronage and prestige with voters outweigh sheer determination and courage.

In another sense, the black separate party's rejection of national party recognition and its drive for distinctiveness give it a certain degree of flexibility, which the black satellite party does not have. For instance, separate black parties can operate on the national, state, or local level, whereas the black satellite party can operate only on the state or regional level; should it throw its support to anyone other than a party candidate, it would become a rival rather than a satellite of the national body.

But black separate parties have been active at all levels. For example, the Freedom Now party, National Liberty party, and Peace and Freedom party have backed candidates on the national level. LCFO appeared on the county level, the Party of Christian Democracy appeared on the district level, and the Afro-American party operated on the state level. Black satellite parties such as SCPDP and NDPA have existed on the state level, and MFDP, because of political competition from the NAACP, has become a regional party concentrated chiefly in central Mississippi.

In addition to operating on different levels, black separate parties can run their own candidates for the presidency, whereas black satellite parties *must* support the presidential electors of the national party organization. As we have seen, NDPA and MFDP backed the presidential candidates chosen at the Democratic national conventions even though these satellites had not been accepted by the Democrats as their representatives within the state.

Moreover, black separate parties are free to concentrate on state elections before the separate party turns its attention to national offices. In this context, Michigan's Freedom Now party of 1964, which is discussed in the next chapter, is an excellent example.

If black separate parties have been more flexible because of their distinctiveness and aloofness, they also face a much greater risk of defeat for the same reason. Being separate and aloof, these parties are easily tagged as radicals or dissenters or militants who work outside the system and against it. They are open to the accusation that they believe the existing political organization is corrupt or evil. And those who support the party are likely to be seen in the same light, which may frighten or confuse the community and drive away support. The aloofness of black separate parties also suggests that they are transient and at best will not last long. Therefore, for many voters the separate party is merely a temporary organization that they do not want to associate with. Many of the problems faced by LCFO are characteristic of these general problems of black separate parties.

Yet, in spite of these difficulties, the mere fact that black separate parties exist implies the need for reform in the regular state or national parties which the separate parties compete with and in the areas which these regular parties control. In the final analysis (unless the separate black parties are ideologically motivated seeking to impose a particular doctrine) they are primarily reformist in nature because they too seek to change things in our society. And in this respect they are very much like black satellites parties. But there is a difference in their reformist approaches. The satellite seeks to reform or replace the major state party and then to reform the state or region in question, whereas the black separate party bypasses state and national parties and goes directly to the people in its geographical region. Hence, a significant difference in black parties rests in their approaches to reform.

On the other hand, a major similarity of black political parties, be they satellite or separate, state, national, or local, is that they have all attempted to bring the black man to a position of power within the American political system and secure for him the benefits and fruits of political power that so long have been denied him.

6

THE FUTURE OF BLACK POLITICAL

PARTIES

Even before the Lowndes County Freedom Organization was formed, its chief organizer, Stokely Carmichael, said he envisioned moving out all across the black-belt counties of the South—and even into northern ghetto areas such as those in Philadelphia, Cincinnati, and Chicago—to create new and independent all-black political parties based on his Lowndes County model. In areas where Negroes constituted majorities or near-majorities, he argued, they should not hesitate to seek political power and, once having gained it, to remake the social, economic, and cultural institutions in their own image.[1] Only in this way, Carmichael said, could blacks overcome, or at least cope with, the racism rampant in American society.

Inasmuch as Carmichael's "new forms" (that is, independent movements) would have to address themselves to the growing needs of the alienated black people in America, he maintained, the initiative for change would have to come from the black community itself; after 300 years of neglect, white America has forfeited its chance to act in this regard. The blacks of the ghettos and the rural pockets of poverty, according to Carmichael, should stop regarding the color of their skin as a handicap and instead make it the basis for a new solidarity. Thus the exclusion of whites and the avoidance of coalitions with whites was a matter of tactics stemming from Carmichael's bitter experiences with MFDP, which had instilled in him a distrust of all whites, even so-called liberals. But even more, it was also a matter of psychology.

What are the prospects for such movements in light of the facts about the two types of black political parties which have appeared in this country and the nature of American political and social institutions? Certainly neither the Negro parallel or satellite political party nor the Negro separate party can yet be described as representing a solution to the Negro's problems in this country; nor should either be completely ruled out. Either view would constitute an oversimplification.

After Goldwater's defeat in the 1964 election, party-switching seemed to have proved as unsuccessful as the strategy of choosing unpledged independent electors. For example, in late 1967 George Wallace of Alabama launched the American Independent party, the first major national third-party effort since the 1948 Progressive party. Wallace's appeal was so strong that his third party set new records; it received some 10 million popular votes and 46 electoral votes from five southern states in 1968. (Because the Dixiecrat party appeared on the ballot in only four states, it is more accurately termed a regional third-party movement. Wallace's American Independent ticket appeared on the ballot in all 50 states.) The tactics of the South had now shifted from regional third-party movements and independent electors to the first national third-party movement in two decades. Despite Wallace's glib oratory concerning meaningful alternatives, states' rights, and law and order, his party, like the Dixiecrats, thrived on anti-Negro sentiment.[2] Wallace has found strong support not only in the South but throughout the country. In fact, the widespread favorable response to his appeals has exposed undercurrents of anti-Negro attitudes in American society that many had not suspected were present. In 1972 Wallace became a contender for the Democratic Presidential election and captured several Presidential primaries with generally the same appeal that he had made in 1968 on the AIP ticket.

Has support for Wallace's party in any way encouraged the numerous spokesmen who are currently pushing for the creation of an all-black party? If so, this development may in part provide a rationale for an independent black political party, wherever it may arise. It may even be that all-black parties will emerge out of the desire of some whites to legalize or institutionalize their anti-Negro behavior.

Although racially separatist political parties exist in the white community, their emergence in the black community faces numerous obstacles. First, many Negroes, in common with many whites in the South and elsewhere, simply do not respond to the idea of separatist movements. Not all blacks feel that existing political mechanisms have failed—or, for that matter, are incapable of solving black problems and achieving equality for blacks. In fact, the annals of black history are filled with the names of blacks who sought to change the form of American society by working within existing social and political institutions. And the many black office seekers who currently run on the tickets of the two major political parties attest to the fact that some blacks, perhaps a majority, still have faith in these institutions.[3]

Moreover, Negro class cleavages constitute a major obstacle to the forming of both separate and parallel Negro political organizations. The constituencies of LCFO and MFDP, for example, were almost exclusively lower-class Negroes, whereas middle-class Negroes in both Alabama and Mississippi had much earlier formed Negro civic associations and voter leagues which usually endorsed the most moderate of the regular Democratic candidates.[4] In addition, the Negro middle class in both states had already obtained the vote (or could have obtained it fairly easily) and more or less accepted the regular party.

Wherever the Negro middle class is relatively large and broadly based—that is, where it has an independent base of financial support, as do Negro professionals in northern cities—the gulf separating the middle class from the lower class is almost unbridgeable.[5] The values, life patterns, and goals of the two strata are so different that bringing them together for common political action might be a near-impossible task.[6] But where the black middle class is narrowly based, this gap may not be so wide. If, however, a narrowly based Negro middle class is relatively small and depends upon the white power structure for jobs and other forms of security, as in many areas of the South, the problem arises once more. Negro schoolteachers in southern rural communities, for instance, usually refrain from criticizing the status quo, by word or deed, for fear of losing their jobs.

The Mississippi black middle class, mainly in the six southwestern counties where Charles Evers has concentrated NAACP activity, has been persuaded by Evers to form a coalition with moderate Mississippi Democrats and forsake the idea of creating or joining an independent Negro political party. Evidently, many middle-class Negroes in this area believe that there is still hope for remaking the state Democratic party. In short, they still retain a faith in existing political structures. On the other hand, the Negro middle class in Alabama's Lowndes County, mostly schoolteachers, supported local white politicians against the LCFO candidates or failed utterly to participate in election activity out of fear of reprisals, economic and otherwise. Elsewhere in Alabama, various Negro civic associations and voter leagues, following SCLC's lead, supported such moderate white candidates as Attorney General Richmond Flowers, instead of adopting a militant go-it-alone strategy as advocated by SNCC or NDPA. Basically, however, independent Negro political efforts in Alabama have been concentrated in rural counties that lack a broadly based Negro middle class. Even the satellite black party—NDPA—has achieved success only in the rural counties of Alabama.

These examples suggest that class cleavages may create disunity among the supporters of black parties and even represent obstacles to establishing such parties. In addition, the gulf between classes deprives lower-class Negroes of the potentially helpful organizational skills of the Negro middle class, skills that lower-class Negroes have had neither the time nor the opportunity to develop. Individuals of low educational and occupational levels are, generally speaking, not very active in politics. In conditions of extreme poverty the struggle to survive is of overriding importance; this struggle in turn saps both the energy and the motivation to engage in political activity.[7] As political scientist Seymour Lipset points out, the individual in the lowest socioeconomic stratum has little leisure time—especially psychic leisure free from anxiety and frustration—to invest in political problems.[8] Moreover, the lower on the socioeconomic scale a man is, the narrower his contacts and the more provincial his world is likely to be.[9]

In short, differences in attitudes, values, needs, skills, and awareness separate lower-class Negroes from middle- and upper-class Negroes in terms of political participation. Because lower-class Negroes lack the requisite time and training, they are ill-equipped to act as political leaders.[10] Desire and determination can overcome certain deficiencies in skills, but in a climate of repression it becomes especially difficult for an all-black organization comprising mainly lower-class Negroes to sustain itself. In the case of LCFO, for example, the indigenous leadership was unprepared to cope with the factors that ultimately caused its downfall.

These are basically environmental problems in establishing independent or parallel black political parties in the South. In the North the problem is somewhat different. The major problem there grows out of existing strong political affiliations, although class differences also represent a factor. The social distance between the two groups in the North—as well as in the South—is aggravated by the desire of many middle-class Negroes to dissociate themselves from the life style of the lower class.[11] Politically, they are even further separated in regard to voting power, political participation, and political efficacy in local and state elections.

According to Professor Wilson, Negro politics in the North cannot be understood apart from the city in which it is formed. . . . The Negro political organization is created and shaped by the political organization of the city." [12] The existence of such Negro political machines as the one in Chicago usually depends upon the existence of a white machine; in such a situation, the black machine relies on the white machine for patronage and organizational support, and it must therefore operate according to the rules of the game.

Where the white machine is caught up in factional strife or where temporary coalitions are made at election time, Negro political groupings must seize opportunities as they appear. Ordinarily, only when Negroes represent the largest single group in a political unit do they stand a chance of gaining control of that unit. Even then, however, race prejudice may so dominate the political scene that the Negro's advance into the political life of the city will lag.[13]

To overcome the difficulties inherent in city politics, a potential black leader may try to create his own machine. According to Wilson, however, "no Negro boss can spring up where there is not already a white boss." [14] The very existence of a Negro political machine, then, spells trouble for the budding independent Negro political organization, for the fledgling group will be seen as a threat not only to the white machine in power but also to the subservient Negro machine. In addition, the potential Negro leader's constituency in most cities has a bigger proportion of the lower class than any comparable group. Because the average income and educational levels of lower-class Negroes are usually among the lowest in the city and because many of them have a rural background, which hardly equips them with the sophistication necessary to fathom the intricacies of city politics, it has never ceased to be difficult to organize the black community politically on a scale large enough to gain power.

Nevertheless, some Negroes have succeeded in establishing relatively independent political organizations, most notably Democratic Representatives William Dawson in Chicago and the late Adam Clayton Powell in New York's Harlem.[15] But Dawson, who built his own political machine as a race man, was later co-opted into the white party machine and turned conservative on the race issue, the price he had to pay to be able to reward his followers with patronage from the machine. Powell built a large following in Harlem as a race man and remained a race man thereafter, but his flamboyance in Congress temporarily cost him his job.[16] His radical speeches on race during the forties, fifties, and early sixties caused so much resentment among his fellow congressmen (especially white southerners) that eventually they began playing up the slightest hints of suspected misconduct on his part. The House voted to exclude him in 1967, but he was readmitted after his re-election in 1968. He was defeated again in 1970, and died in 1972.

While Negro middle-class aspirations and security in general militate against the desire for recognition and against the welfare needs of the Negro lower classes, the precarious nature of Negro organizations created in ghetto areas itself militates not only against some of their needs and aspirations but also against any new and radical Negro political organizations. For instance, all attempts by blacks to dislodge entrenched urban machines have so far been unsuccessful. Martin Luther King, Jr., attempted in 1964 and 1965 to oust Mayor Richard Daley in Chicago, but this proved futile, as have early black candidates' attempts against Dawson. Now that Dawson is dead, the entire character of black politics in Chicago may change. The story in Harlem is quite similar. James Meredith's attempt to unseat Powell in 1966 proved futile, as did many other attempts. Powell's failure to win the Democratic primary in 1970 was indicative of the changes taking place in Harlem. In short, the broad-based organizations of Powell and

Dawson, which seemed impregnable in their heyday, are now vulnerable because of the rising needs of their constituencies which neither Powell nor Dawson fulfilled.

There are now in the North many Negro state legislators, city councilmen, and even mayors, most of them Democrats from predominantly Negro areas. Thus an all-Negro political organization, independent of either Democrats or Republicans, faces the task of defeating these incumbent black Democrats or bringing them into the new party.

Another important factor which must be taken into account in any consideration of black voter support for black parties and black candidates is the cohesiveness of the black electorate. Two views have been widely held among political scientists on this matter. One put forth by Wilson argues that in the absence of an intense and well-organized campaign, black voters will not vote strictly along racial lines in a black–white contest for positions at the bottom of the ticket, as in the seemingly unimportant races for county committeeman and district leader.[17] In other words, Wilson sees the black electorate as cohesive only in supporting blacks in state and local elections when major political officers are involved.

The other position, put forth by Professor Ladd, is this: "Race advancement dominates Negro electoral participation as no issue dominates the participation of white voters. . . . No other group ever has had to look to government for so much assistance affecting such vital interests as Negro Americans must. . . ."[18] In essence then, Ladd holds that the majority of blacks can be expected to vote as a bloc when racial progress is an issue in any electoral campaign, especially at the national level.

Today, both views are dated because they represent conclusions drawn before the impact of the 1965 Voting Rights Act was felt and before the full emergence of the black cultural awareness movement, which stresses a certain unity and pride in blackness. Since these two events, more than 1,400 black public officials have been elected. In fact, several major northern cities—Flint, Michigan; Gary, Indiana; Newark, New Jersey; and Cleveland, Ohio—have elected black mayors and many minor state and local officials. In the South, blacks hold political office in cities such as Atlanta, Georgia; Chapel Hill, North Carolina; and Fayette, Mississippi.

In other words, the cohesiveness among the black electorate in support of black candidates can only be guessed at because some of the aforementioned black officeholders ran on the Republican or Democratic ticket, others ran as independents, and still others campaigned as candidates of black political parties. Moreover, in some cases black candidates contested for the same position, while in other contests several blacks ran against one or more whites for the same position. In each case the black electorate was faced with the problem of choosing the person or political organization to support. Current responses suggest that there is a great deal of flexibility in black voting—both North and South. Although the present cohesiveness of the black electorate may not always approach some desired level of political sophistication, this cohesiveness has helped to elect the largest number of black officeholders in state and local races in American political history.

Moreover, both Ladd's and Wilson's observations pertained to the black middle-class voter and not to the lower class. The latter group of black voters did not really emerge in any significant numbers until after the Voting Rights Act of 1965 and the black social revolution of the 1960s. Hence, little is really known about the voting behavior of the lower class of black voters. Furthermore, with these new changes, many of the old ideas about black middle-class voters will also have to be modified.

To sum up, in the North the factors that militate against the evolution of independent or parallel Negro political organizations are the existence of class cleavages, the apathy of lower-class Negroes, well-entrenched Negro machines and politicians, and long-standing party allegiances. In the South the relevant factors are class cleavages, Uncle-Tom attitudes, the fear of economic reprisal, state repression, the apathy of Negro voters and potential voters, an absence of trained political leadership, and a distrust or fear of outside radical leadership.

Ironically, race prejudice and discriminatory practices tend to solidify Negro communities, North and South, perhaps making independent political organizations more workable. Thus anti-Negro violence, police oppression and brutality, the denial of public services, other forms of repression stemming from race hatred, and even the continual denial of access to normal political channels for redress of specific grievances—all militate for new parties. In this regard, the nation's relatively small Negro middle class *is* included in the regular political parties. But the exclusion of the Negro lower class is often tantamount to total Negro exclusion, inasmuch as the Negro middle class seeks to disown the lower class. Furthermore, ambiguous governmental concessions to the Negro political subcommunity can be just as effective as total exclusion in stimulating a desire for independent action, because the Negro lower class has an immediate need for unambiguous solutions to its problems.[19]

The high unemployment rate and wretched living conditions among lower-class Negroes can also generate political pressures. The 1968 Poor People's March (which included "token whites") is an example. Whether such an ad hoc pressure group can be converted into an all-black political poor people's party is debatable. Perhaps LCFO and MFDP are such organizations. That the blacks of Alabama, South Carolina, and Mississippi were compelled to form independent parties in order to express themselves politically demonstrates that the same conditions that hinder all-black political movements also make their formation more likely.

Unless potential leaders among radical blacks opt for revolutionary goals, they may turn their abilities to organizing independent Negro political movements. In Carmichael's case, his knack for radical innovation transformed the independent ethnic party from a theoretical construct into a reality—a workable reality, some would insist, despite its lack of success. But after leaving SNCC he rejected the idea of reforming the American political system on the ground that American society is too racist, and he moved on to a belief shared by many militants: that the system must be destroyed and rebuilt before any meaningful progress can be achieved. Yet there are other militant blacks—and black militancy is on the rise—who do not completely reject the system, only the argument that it can be reformed by working from within the two major parties. The black militants' emphasis on all-black organizations to control black communities increases the possibilities for all-black political organizations.

This brings us to a consideration of perhaps the most important factor of all affecting the success of black political organizations: the concentration of the black population, both North and South. In the southern states more than 80 counties have black majorities, while in the North a heavy and increasing concentration of Negroes in the core cities of metropolitan areas will soon make blacks a majority in some cities; Newark, New Jersey, for example, is already more than 50 percent Negro. In this regard, the push-pull effect that is moving blacks from rural areas to urban areas has given Negroes tremendous potential political power.[20] The "push" aspect of white violence and economic deprivation that has driven so many blacks from southern rural areas to the urban ghetto, North and South, is now about to reap another kind of harvest. The "pull" aspect—the hopes, often unfulfilled, of finding better living and working conditions and less discrimination—largely accounts for the high concentration of blacks in northern cities and for their growing dissatisfaction, manifested in the ghetto riots of recent years. Even now, this concentration accounts for a tremendous increase in Negro political representation in both the North and the South.[21]

So far, Negro politicians have generally worked within the traditional political parties in order to gain power; perhaps they will continue to do so, or perhaps they will move toward creating all-Negro parties. Another possibility is that, because of the white middle-class flight to suburbia and the continual Negro migration from rural areas, Negroes may in time gain control of major or minor urban political parties by default.[22] In fact, a parallel party with a style of its own (such as the Black and Tan Republican party in the South early in this century) may arise in due time. Because of the special problems of cities (such as rising welfare rolls and the refusal of certain areas to be annexed for the purpose of taxation) Negro leaders may force such a parallel party to take a different stand from that of the major party, thereby making it independent in style, if not in organization.[23]

In any event, black political power is bound to be enhanced by the implementation of the Supreme Court's 1965 one-man-one-vote ruling.[24] That is, the consequent reapportionment of state legislatures, which should result in greater representation of urban areas, makes possible a greater number of Negro politicians and more effective representation of Negroes. A similar high-court ruling extended to include county and municipal governments would further strengthen the political power of Negroes in the cities and heighten prospects for all-Negro political organizations.

The strategic location of areas of concentrated Negro population, coupled with the low socioeconomic position of Negroes, gives them both the power and the incentive to be simultaneously politically flexible and innovative. Thus one observer contends that "Negro politics will continue to be . . . more visible and more volatile throughout the country than the politics of other minorities." [25] In the main, Negro political parties represent a protest against the political status forced upon Negroes as a group. The group wants in, and genuine political rewards from a regular party might be enough to draw them into that party's organization. As Professor Spindler has suggested, voting rights have certain other dimensions, such as psychological and practical ones, which should be acknowledged and satisfied if Negroes are to become equal citizens.[26] The longer they are denied these necessary preconditions to equal citizenship, the more insistent and radical the protest against their status will be. Their protest may not always take the form of independent political parties, but in certain localities and in certain situations this is a distinct possibility. Yet it must be kept in mind that Negro political parties have usually been attuned to the needs, aspirations, and hopes of relatively small areas of concentrated Negro population, and they will probably continue to be limited to such areas and thus limited in terms of influence.

The Freedom Now Party, 1963–1964

Nationally, recent black political parties have not fared well. One, the Freedom Now party, was organized in Washington, D.C., in August 1963, during the march for jobs and freedom. At that time the party's national chairman, New York lawyer Conrad L. Lynn, announced that party candidates would run for office in the New York, Connecticut, and California 1963 elections. All these candidates were badly defeated; consequently, the party made little impression on the black electorate or on the public at large.

After these defeats in 1963, the party decided to concentrate on one state, Michigan, in the 1964 elections. Under the leadership of state chairman Albert Cleage, a Congregationalist minister, the party entered 39 black candidates in contests for offices ranging from U.S. senator to Wayne County drain commissioner. Although Cleage believed that there was only a slight chance for victory, he indicated that he expected the party to capture at least 100,000 of the 750,000 black votes in the state, which would vividly demonstrate to state Democrats and Republicans that his organization was a force to be reckoned with. Moreover, the purpose of the party, according to Cleage, was not only to elect more militant blacks and to make a show of black political power, but also to educate blacks to use their political power effectively.[27]

Since the Freedom Now party had predicated its future on this election, it canceled campaigns projected for 1966 in 13 other states when all the Freedom Now candidates made a very poor showing in the Michigan election. (See Table 13 in the Appendix.)

The Peace and Freedom Party, 1968

In 1968, another black party indirectly competed in the national elections when Eldridge Cleaver, the Black Panther party's minister of information, ran for president (his running mate was Douglas F. Dowd, a professor of economics at Cornell) in almost 20 states on the Peace and Freedom party ticket, receiving 195,135 votes.

However, the Peace and Freedom party should not be confused with the Freedom and Peace party, which ran Dick Gregory as its presidential candidate in some states but had no presidential candidate in others. Although the two parties were similar in platform and policy, they did differ significantly in terms of black supporters and allies. The Peace and Freedom party formed a coalition with the Black Panthers—the California group, not the Lowndes County Freedom Organization, even though Carmichael was involved in both—but the Freedom and Peace party had no major black group involved with it.

The coalition of the Black Panthers and the Peace and Freedom party was another attempt by blacks to establish a national political party, although it marked the first time that a post-LCFO militant black group entered into a coalition with whites. This shift in tactics was necessary, according to Cleaver, because black militants had failed to work out a meaningful program and had attempted to "camouflage this failure by emphasizing 'cultural nationalism' rather than 'political revolution.' "[28] Cultural nationalism, Cleaver asserted, was secondary to the real needs of the black community: a political revolution that would change the social and economic structure and thereby achieve social justice for blacks and other oppressed minorities. Since the New Left embraces the same basic concept, Cleaver went on, whites and blacks should cooperate in bringing about the revolution.

For the Black Panthers, a black nationalist/white leftist coalition promised additional support for their program, which included demands for land, adequate food and housing, proper education, social justice (including a halt to police brutality), and an end to American military involvement abroad. For the New Left, this new coalition avoided an old stumbling block: the touchy issue of black cultural identity. The Black Panthers and the New Left entered into the coalition as equal partners. In addition, both groups hoped that the coalition would help solve the old problem of capturing enough votes to win elections. Perhaps another reason for this alliance was the fact that Black Panther leader Huey Newton was in jail, and if he was to be freed, funds and legal aid were necessary, all of which the New Left could supply.

During the 1968 presidential campaign, Cleaver introduced some new twists by asking the United Nations to accord the Black Panthers status as a nongoverning organization and to assign U.N. observers to report on police brutality in major black communities. He also declared his opposition to Adam Clayton Powell because of Powell's middle-class posture and his lack of militancy in seeking justice for blacks.[29] In addition, the Peace and Freedom party's platform called for a radical economic program, black freedom, and peace in Vietnam.

Inasmuch as Cleaver's showing on the Peace and Freedom ticket in the 1968 election was far from encouraging, and key Panther officers across the country were either in jail on vague and suspicious charges or (as in Cleaver's case) in involuntary exile, it is difficult to forecast the future of the Black Panthers. One critical factor is sure to be the nature of their coalition with the New Left, which will dictate whether this coalition will concentrate on national politics, whether the history of the alliance between radicals and blacks in the thirties will be repeated (see Chapter 2), or whether some totally new political form will emerge. In 1970 the Peace and Freedom party ran twelve candidates for several state offices in California ranging from the gubernatorial position to the state assembly. However, as far as is known, the party didn't have any Black Panther members as candidates. This could indicate that the 1968 coalition is either dissolving or that the Black Panthers are under so much repression by the state and federal agencies that they have dropped electoral politics and become primarily a revolutionary organization.

*   *   *

Summing up, then, until recently the American black political party has for the most part been a byproduct of the one-party system prevalent in many southern states, just as national third parties have been byproducts of the national two-party system. Black parties so far seem to be much more successful on the local and district levels than on the national and state levels. Mainly instruments for protest, black parties express the desire of Negroes to be included in the mainstream of American political life. Unique primarily in their almost totally ethnic composition, they are basically small third parties created because of the miscalculation or neglect of the major parties. Like other third parties, they will arise when the need presents itself, call attention to the difficulties and aspirations and goals of the excluded, and then perhaps—if they fail to overcome internal or external organizational difficulties—fade from the political scene. Black political parties, like third parties in general, are part of a continuing phenomenon in our political system and will probably appear now and again for some time to come.

Epilogue

THE ROLE OF BLACK POLITICAL

PARTIES IN BLACK POLITICS

In 1972, Black Americans, especially in politics, were trying to achieve two basic goals: (1) to become an independent force in American politics and (2) to use politics as a tool to remove much of the burdens upon blacks in this country. The two goals, which are interrelated and complement each other, are outgrowths of the now defunct Civil Rights movements. In fact, the political activities of blacks in the seventies are a continuation of the pressure or nonelectoral tactics of blacks in the sixties.

If true equality and liberation from the problems which plague black Americans are to occur, then, as numerous black leaders have advocated, blacks must use politics as a means to that end. The new black politics, however, entails the regeneration of the politics of old, or the creation of a new political strategy.

The politics of old for black Americans has left much undone in black America and much to be desired. The politics of old embraced bossism, token rewards to black bosses, and limited outputs to the black electorate, while few meaningful public policies for blacks emerged from reliance upon white politics, white political leaders, and the white political structure and organizations. Therefore, to make the politics of old—of yesterday—functional for a politically conscious black community, the present reform efforts of the white political structure will have to be more comprehensive, more relevant, and more useful. Otherwise, the needs of black communities will force their representatives to abandon the politics of yesteryear.

The new black politics which the 1972 National Black Political Convention in Gary spoke of and represented demands a move toward independence and community orientation. Since the old politics called for dependence and limited reforms, the new politics not only seeks substantive changes but also tries vainly to make them itself. The new black politics strives for self-control and a voice, as well as a hand, in black people's own destiny. Hence, black liberation, community control, and independence became the watchwords as the seventies began to emerge.

Therefore, in this drive for a new type of politics (i.e., a relevant type of politics) for the black community, the black political parties became very clear and meaningful. Whereas in the past black parties tried hard to bring attention to and generate concern for black problems (in addition to attempting to make changes within the political structure and system of the country), they did signal a growing movement toward independent politics.

Today, the Mississippi Freedom Democratic party is over nine years old; the National Democratic party of Alabama is more than four years old; and the United Citizens' party of South Carolina is more than three years old—facts that are indicative of a growing tendency to remain independent. Each party has struggled for its existence, and none is completely sure of its continued existence. But the longer each party stays in public view, the more confidence it generates, and the more public support it will likely gain. Even yet the future is not rosy, for the MFDP is losing luster, the NDPA is having some financial difficulties, and the UCP is still looking for some dramatic electoral victories. With these handicaps and weaknesses, each organization is hanging on in the political arena. And several black leaders are constantly talking about creating newer and more black political parties.

In a way, some of the black political parties represent the politics of old in that they sought limited reforms (i.e., within certain political structures); they also in part represent the new black politics due to their emphasis upon black control and black-led organizations. Therefore, it is this potential, i.e., *the opportunities which black parties give blacks for self-determination and independence in politics*) that makes black parties play such an important role in the new black politics.

This potential for independence and the use of politics as a tool or solution, then, are the unique roles which black parties give blacks. But black political independence must overcome the black power enclave in each and every black community. Numerous black leaders, real or self-styled, and their organizations exist, North and South, in every county or locality where blacks are numerous, and they deal with the white power structure on their own terms and particular arrangements. These enclaves of black power resist the new black political independence of black parties, for the black parties pose more threats to them and their entrenched power than any other force by working for a shift of power to the community and away from the individual or clique.

In Alabama, John Cashin, leader of the NDPA, has overcome the black political elite in numerous localities due to his near charismatic leadership and unique organizing technique. His frequent meetings on a regular basis, the party newspaper, *The Eagle Eye* (which gives the party a communication arm), and the tremendous diversified activities of the party from social to economic programs simply enable the party to bypass or encircle and isolate the old line black political elite.

The destruction of this black political elite may be the key to the new black politics, the politics of black independence via black political parties. As these black political independent forces develop on the local, regional, and state level, one can expect that a national black political party will emerge to express this new politics on the national level. The new party may join the already existing black parties and black voting leagues, or it may create its own subnational units. But no matter how a national black party deals with the problems of nomenclature, it will be exalting the notions of black control, liberation, and black independence. In many ways it will bolster the urge in black Americans to become an independent force in American politics and use the American political system to remove some of the disabilities of black Americans. When the national black party will arrive, no one can say, but there is much talk of one—it could, however, die stillborn.

No matter what happens, black parties will continue to assume the role of being an independent force in black politics.

Notes

Introduction

[1] Gabriel Almond and Sidney Verba, *The Civic Culture* (Boston, Little Brown and Company, 1965), p. 117.

[2] *Ibid.*, p. 138.

[3] Gunnar Myrdal, *An American Dilemma* (New York: Harper & Row, 1962), p. 28.

Chapter 1

[1] W. C. Abbott, "The Origin of English Political Parties," *The American Historical Review,* Vol. 24, No. 3 (July 1919), 578–602.

[2] James R. Owens and P. J. Staudenraus (eds.), *The American Party System* (New York: Macmillan, 1965), p. 21; Pendleton Herring, *The Politics of Democracy* (New York: Holt, 1940).

[3] *The Federalist* (No. 10).

[4] E. E. Schattschneider, *Party Government* (New York: Holt, 1942), p. 7.

[5] W. E. Binkley, *American Political Parties* (New York: Knopf, 1944), pp. 3–72.

[6] Clinton Rossiter, *1787: The Grand Convention* (New York: Macmillan, 1966), pp. 257–274.

[7] Binkley, *American Political Parties,* pp. 72–93.

[8] Rossiter, *1787,* p. 300.

[9] Binkley, *American Political Parties,* pp. 5–16.

[10] Dixon Ryan Fox, "The Negro Vote in Old New York," *Political Science Quarterly,* Vol. 32 (1917), 253–256.

[11] Binkley, *American Political Parties,* pp. 72–87.

[12] Noble E. Cunningham, Jr., *The Jeffersonian Republicans in Power* (Chapel Hill: University of North Carolina Press, 1960), Chapter 9.

[13] Richard P. McCormick, *The Second American Party System* (Chapel Hill: University of North Carolina Press, 1966), pp. 3–8. 13–16.

[14] Peter H. Odegard, *American Politics* (New York: Harper, 1949), pp. 1–2.

[15] See Sigmund Neumann, "Toward a Comparative Study of Political Parties," in Sigmund Neumann (ed.), *Modern Political Parties* (Chicago: University of Chicago Press, 1956), pp. 395–405.

[16] Samuel J. Eldersveld, *Political Parties* (Chicago: Rand McNally, 1965), pp. 8–10.

[17] See the Report of the Committee on Political Parties of the American Political Science Association, *Toward a More Responsible Two-Party System* (New York: Holt, 1950).

[18] Stephen K. Bailey, *The Condition of Our National Political Parties* (Santa Barbara, Calif.: Center for the Study of Democratic Institutions, 1959), pp. 1–10.

[19] David Truman, *The Governmental Process* (New York: Knopf, 1951), Chapter 9. See also Harmon Ziegler, *Interest Groups in America* (Englewood Cliffs, N.J.: Prentice-Hall, 1965); A. E. Bentley, *The Process of Government,* ed. Peter Odegard, Cambridge, Mass.: Harvard University Press, 1967), Chapters 14–16.

[20] Odegard, *American Politics,* pp. 2–4.

[21] See W. B. Hesseltine, *The Rise and Fall of Third Parties* (Washington, D.C.: Public Affairs Press, 1959); and *Third Party Movements in the United States* (Princeton, N.J.: Van Nostrand, 1962). See also Howard P. Nash, Jr., *Third Parties in American Politics* (Washington D.C.: Public Affairs Press, 1959).

[22] V. O. Key, Jr., *Politics, Parties, and Pressure Groups* (New York: Thomas Y. Crowell, 1958), pp. 280–282. See also Herring, *The Politics of Democracy,* Chapter 13.

[23] Elizabeth Howze, "Minor Parties as Catalysts of Social Change: Their Influence on the Policies of the Major Parties in the United States" (Atlanta University, M.A. thesis, 1964), pp. 3–9.

[24] Herring, *The Politics of Democracy,* p. 184.

[25] Allan Spindler, *Political Parties in the United States* (New York: St. Martin's Press, 1966), pp. 51, 52, 61–69.

[26] See Frank T. Sorauf, *Party Politics in America* (Boston: Little, Brown, 1968), p. 43.

[27] Robert K. Merton, *Social Theory and Social Structure* (New York: The Free Press, 1957), Chapters 4 and 5.

[28] Richard Cloward and Lloyd Ohlin, *Delinquency and Opportunity* (New York: The Free Press, 1960).

[29] Charles Wesley, *Neglected History: Essays in Negro-American History* (Wilberforce, Ohio: Central State College Press, 1965), pp. 57–58.

[30] Fox, "The Negro Vote in Old New York," pp. 264, 273–274.

[31] Charles Wesley, "The Participation of Negroes in Anti-Slavery Political Parties," *Journal of Negro History* (January 1941), 39–41.

[32] *Ibid.* See also Leon Litwack, *North of Slavery: The Negro in the Free States, 1790–1860* (Chicago: University of Chicago Press, 1961), pp. 81–84.

[33] *Ibid.,* p. 80–87.

[34] Sister M. Theaphane, *A History of Third Parties in Pennsylvania* (Washington, D.C.: Catholic University Press, 1938), pp. 1–51.

[35] Charles Wesley, "Negro Suffrage in the Period of Constitution Making, 1787–1865," *Journal of Negro History* (April 1947), 153–167. See also Wesley, *Neglected History,* pp. 50–54; and Litwack, *North of Slavery,* pp. 87–88.

[36] Roger Shuggs, "Negro Voting in the Ante-Bellum South," *Journal of Negro History* (October 1936), 351–356, 357–364; and Litwack, *North of Slavery,* pp. vii–ix.

[37] John Hope Franklin, *The Free Negro in North Carolina, 1790–1860* (Chapel Hill: University of North Carolina Press, 1943), pp. 105–120.

[38] William Lloyd Ames, "The Legal Status of Free Negroes and Slaves in Tennessee," *Journal of Negro History* (July 1919), 254–272. See also James W. Patton, "The Progress of Emancipation in Tennessee," *Journal of Negro History* (January 1932), 71–73.

[39] Shuggs, "Negro Voting in the Ante-Bellum South," 360–362.

[40] Litwack, *North of Slavery,* pp. 87–88, 99–101. See also Wesley, *Neglected History,* pp. 47–54.

[41] *Ibid.,* pp. 86–87. For a list of Negro petitions for the return of suffrage rights, see Herbert Aptheker (ed.), *A Documentary History of the Negro People in the United States* (New York: Citadel Press, 1951). See also Wesley, "Negro Suffrage in the Period of Constitution Making," 159–160, 162–165.

[42] See Hanes Walton, Jr., *The Negro in Third Party Politics* (Philadelphia: Dorrance, 1969); and Walton, "The Negro in Early Third Party Movements," *Negro Educational Review* (April–July 1968), 73–82.

[43] Walton, *The Negro in Third Party Politics,* Chapter 2; Wesley, *Neglected History,* pp. 59–75; and T. C. Smith, *The Liberty and Free Soil Parties in the Northwest* (Cambridge, Mass.: Harvard University Press, 1897).

[44] Eric Foner, "Politics and Prejudices: The Free Soil Party and the Negro, 1849–1852," *Journal of Negro History* (October 1965), 239–256.

[45] See Wesley, "Participation in Anti-Slavery Parties," 58.

[46] Walton, *The Negro in Third Party Politics,* Chapter 2. See also Nash, *Third Parties,* pp. 23–24; and Wesley, "Negro Suffrage in 1787–1865," 162–168.

[47] Wesley, *Neglected History,* p. 76.

[48] See Samuel D. Smith, *The Negro in Congress* (Chapel Hill: University of North Carolina Press, 1940); Monroe Work, "Some Negro Members of Reconstruction Conventions and Legislatures and Congress," *Journal of Negro History* (January 1920), 63–91; and W. E. B. DuBois, *Black Reconstruction* (New York: Harcourt, 1935).

[49] See V. O. Key, Jr., *Southern Politics in State and Nation* (New York: Knopf, 1949); and C. V. Woodward, *Origins of the New South: 1877–1913* (Baton Rouge: Louisiana State University Press, 1951).

[50] See C. G. Woodson, *A Century of Negro Migration* (Washington, D.C.: Associated Publishers, 1918); Walter Fleming, " 'Pap' Singleton, The Moses of the Colored Exodus," *American Journal of Sociology* (July 1937), 61–71; and R. Garvin, "Benjamin or 'Pap' Singleton and His Followers," *Journal of Negro History* (January 1948), 7–23.

[51] Walton, *The Negro in Third Party Politics,* pp. 38–45. See also Jack Abramowitz, "The Negro in the Populist Movement," *Journal of Negro History* (July 1953), 257–289.

[52] This is the argument of certain historians and political observers. For example, see Henry Lee Moon, *Balance of Power: The Negro Vote* (Garden City, N.Y.: Doubleday, 1948). p. 79; and H. Walton, Jr., and J. Taylor, "Blacks, the Prohibitionists, and Disfranchisement," *Quarterly Review of Higher Education Among Negroes* (April 1969), 66–69.

[53] John Hope Franklin, *From Slavery to Freedom* (New York: Knopf, 1967), pp. 435, 441–443. See also S. M. Scheiner, "President Theodore Roosevelt and the Negro," *Journal of Negro History* (July 1962), 169–182.

[54] See Walton, *The Negro in Third Party Politics,* pp. 48–52; Walton, "The Negro in the Progressive Party Movements," *Quarterly Review of Higher Education Among Negroes* (January 1968), 17–21; and A. S. Link, "The Negro as a Factor in the Campaign of 1912," *Journal of Negro History* (January 1947), 89.

[55] Samuel Lubell, *White and Black: Test of a Nation* (New York: Harper, 1964), pp. 46–52.

[56] *Ibid.;* and Walton, *The Negro in Third Party Politics,* pp. 61–72.

[57] Samuel Lubell, *The Future of American Politics* (New York: Anchor Books, 1956), pp. 100–105.

[58] Martin Luther King, Jr., *Why We Can't Wait* (New York: Signet Books, 1964), pp. 143–144. See also Arthur Schlesinger, Jr., *A Thousand Days* (Boston: Houghton Mifflin, 1965).

[59] See W. D. St. James, *National Association for the Advancement of Colored People: A Case Study in Pressure Groups* (New York: Exposition Press, 1957). See also Gilbert Ware, "Lobbying as a Means of Protest: The NAACP as an Agent of Equality," *Journal of Negro Education* (Spring 1964), 103–110; Clement E. Vose, "Litigation as a Form of Pressure Group Activity," *Annals of the American Academy of Science* (September 1958), 20–31.

[60] See Aptheker (ed.), *A Documentary History,* pp. 1–28. See also Benjamin Quarles and Leslie Fishel, *The Negro American: A Documented History* (Atlanta: Scott, Foresman, 1967), pp. 44–45.

[61] "David Walker's Appeal to the Colored Citizens of the World—1829–1830," in Herbert Aptheker (ed.), *One Continual Cry* (New York: Humanities Press, 1965), pp. 62–147.

[62] Franklin, *From Slavery to Freedom,* p. 249.

[63] Truman, *The Governmental Process,* pp. 362–368.

[64] See Samuel Unger, "A History of the National Woman's Christian Temperance Union" (Ohio State University, Ph.D. thesis, 1933); James Knout, *The Origins of Prohibition* (New York: Knopf, 1925); and Ida Harper, *The History of Woman's Suffrage* (New York: National American Woman Suffrage Association, 1922).

[65] There is a wealth of articles, pamphlets, and books on the origin of the NAACP. Among the best books are Robert L. Jack, *History of the National Association for the Advancement of Colored People* (Boston: Meador, 1943); Langston Hughes, *Fight for Freedom: The Story of the NAACP* (New York: Norton, 1962); and Charles Flint Kellogg, *NAACP: A History of the National Association for the Advancement of Colored People* (Baltimore: Johns Hopkins Press, 1967), Vol. 1, 1909–1920.

[66] St. James, *NAACP: A Case Study,* pp. 105–108.

[67] *Ibid.,* pp. 109–110.

[68] *Ibid.* See also Gunnar Myrdal, *An American Dilemma* (New York: Harper, 1962; first edition, 1944), pp. 833–835.

[69] Foner, "Politics and Prejudices," 239–250.

[70] Walton, *The Negro in Third Party Politics,* pp. 30–45.

[71] *Ibid.,* pp. 79–81.

Chapter 2

[1] Quoted in Aptheker (ed.), *A Documentary History,* pp. 59–60.

[2] Quoted in Bella Gross, *"Freedom's Journal* and the Rights of All," *Journal of Negro History* (July 1932), 241–286.

[3] See Bella Gross, "The First National Negro Convention," *Journal of Negro History* (October 1946), 435–443.

[4] Quoted in Aptheker (ed.), *A Documentary History,* pp. 176–177.

[5] See H. Bell, "National Negro Convention of the Middle 1840's: Moral

Suasion vs. Political Action," *Journal of Negro History* (October 1957), 247–260. See also his "The Negro Convention Movement, 1830–60: New Perspectives," *Negro History Bulletin* (February 1951), 103–105, 114; and Bella Gross, *Clarion Call: The History and Development of the Negro Convention Movement in the United States from 1817 to 1840* (New York: N.P., 1947).

[6] See Foner (ed.), *Life and Writings,* Vol. 2, p. 27.

[7] See Aptheker (ed.), *A Documentary History,* pp. 499–500.

[8] *Ibid.,* p. 523.

[9] *Ibid.,* pp. 527–530.

[10] See Foner (ed.), *Life and Writings,* Vol. 4, pp. 16–20.

[11] *Ibid.,* p. 41. See also Benjamin Quarles, "Frederick Douglass and the Woman's Rights Movement," *Journal of Negro History* (January 1940), 39.

[12] See Foner (ed.), *Life and Writings,* Vol. 4, p. 44, and Quarles, "Frederick Douglass . . . ," 41–42.

[13] See Aptheker (ed.), *A Documentary History,* pp. 526–532.

[14] Emma Lou Thornbrough, "The National Afro-American League, 1887–1908," *Journal of Southern History* (November 1961), 498.

[15] See Aptheker (ed.), *A Documentary History,* pp. 786–791.

[16] Walton, *The Negro in Third Party Politics,* pp. 38–45.

[17] See Aptheker (ed.), *A Documentary History,* p. 852.

[18] See Bernard Eisenberg, "Kelly Miller: The Negro Leader as a Marginal Man," *Journal of Negro History* (July 1960), 186–193.

[19] Sterling D. Spero and Abram L. Harris, *The Black Worker* (New York: Columbia University Press, 1931), pp. 425–427.

[20] See Eisenberg, "Kelly Miller . . . ," 188.

[21] Lester B. Granger, "The National Negro Congress: An Interpretation," *Opportunity* (May 1936), 151–153; and Myrdal, *An American Dilemma,* pp. 817–818.

[22] *Ibid.*

[22a] Imamu Amiri Baraka, "Strategies and Factors of an Afro-American Party," *The Black Politician* (Fall, 1971), pp. 40–43.

[23] See Granger, "Negro Congress . . . ," 164.

[24] See Lerone Bennett, Jr., *The Negro Mood* (Chicago: Johnson Publishing, 1964), Chapter 5.

[25] See Clinton Rossiter, *Parties and Politics in America* (Ithaca, N.Y.: Cornell University Press, 1960), pp. 141–144.

[26] Myrdal, *An American Dilemma,* especially, "The Negro Problem as a Moral Issue," pp. xix–xxi.

[27] See Lerone Bennett, Jr., *Confrontation: Black and White* (Chicago: Johnson Publishing, 1965), pp. 3–14.

[28] See Key, *Southern Politics,* pp. 15–17.

[29] See "Negroes Vote at the GOP Convention," Little Rock, Arkansas, *Gazette* (April 29, 1920), 1.

[30] See Paul Casodorph, *The Republican Party in Texas* (Austin: Pemberton, 1965), pp. 70–127.

[31] For a detailed discussion of the Negro in the Populist party in Texas, see Rosco C. Martin, *The People's Party in Texas: A Study in Third Party Politics* (Austin: University of Texas Press, 1933).

[32] See Phillip D. Uzee, "Republican Party in Louisiana 1877–1900" (Baton Rouge: Louisiana State University, Ph.D. dissertation, 1950); Lawrence Dixon

Clepper, Jr., "A History of the Republican party in Louisiana 1900–1952" (Baton Rouge: Louisiana State University, M.A. thesis, 1963), pp. 28–47; Frederick Joseph Dumas, "The Black and Tan Faction of the Republican Party in Louisiana 1908–1936 (New Orleans: Xavier University, M.A. thesis, 1943).

[33] V. O. Key, *Southern Politics*, pp. 288–289.

[34] Levinson, *Race, Class and Party*, p. 181.

[35] *Ibid.*, p. 185.

[36] See W. P. Robinson, Sr., "Democracy's Frontiers," *Journal of Human Relations*, Vol. 2 (Spring 1954), 63–71; and A. Heard, *A Two-Party South* (Chapel Hill: University of North Carolina Press, 1952), pp. 192–194. However, for much of the data used in this discussion, the author relied upon materials sent to him in a letter from the party's chairman, John McCray.

[37] For insight into the economic plight of blacks in South Carolina and how the New Deal programs began to help them see E. Hoffman, "The Genesis of the Modern Movement for Equal Rights in South Carolina, 1930–1939," *Journal of Negro History* (October 1959), 363–369.

[38] Robinson, "Democracy's Frontiers," 65.

[39] *Ibid.*

[40] Quoted in Robinson, "Democracy's Frontiers," 69.

[41] For a different estimate see Moon, *Balance of Power,* p. 194.

[42] Luther P. Jackson, "Race and Suffrage in the South Since 1940," *New South* (June–July 1948), 4–5.

[43] "South Carolina Blacks Plan New Party," *NYT* (November 24, 1969), 30.

[44] *Ibid.*

[45] *Ibid.*

[46] H. Walton, Jr., "Black Politics in the South," *Ebony* (August 1971), 142.

Chapter 3

[1] See Leslie Burl McLemore, "The Freedom Democratic Party and the Changing Political Status of the Negro in Mississippi" (hereafter "The MFDP") (Atlanta University, M. A. thesis, 1965), p. 44; Jack Minnis, "The Mississippi Freedom Democratic Party," *Freedomways* (Spring 1965); and Lawrence Guyot and Mike Thelwell, part I, "The Politics of Necessity and Survival in Mississippi," *Freedomways* (Spring 1966), and part II, "Toward Independent Political Power," *Freedomways* (Summer 1966).

[2] See Donald R. Matthews and James Prothro, *Negroes and the New Southern Politics* (New York: Harcourt, 1966), pp. 203–235; and William Keech, *The Impact of Negro Voting* (Chicago: Rand McNally, 1968), pp. 34–36.

[3] See Smith, *The Negro in Congress*, pp. 4–5.

[4] McLemore, "The MFDP," 6–9; Lerone Bennett, Jr., *Black Power* (Chicago: Johnson Publishing, 1968), Chapter 8.

[5] Vernon L. Wharton, *The Negro in Mississippi, 1865–1890* (New York: Harper, 1965), pp. 189–192, 202–204.

[6] For insight on the constitutionality of the grandfather clause, see *Guinn and Beal v. U.S.* 238 U.S. 347 (1914)

[7] William Alexander Mabry, "Disfranchisement of the Negro in Mississippi," *Journal of Southern History*, Vol. 4 (August 1938), 319.

[8] McLemore, "The MFDP," 12–14.

[9] Key, *Southern Politics*, p. 229.

[10] McLemore, "The MFDP," p. 16.

[11] Key, *Southern Politics*, pp. 15–18.

[12] McLemore, "The MFDP," 17–18. See also Myrdal, *An American Dilemma*, p. 1358.

[13] *Smith, v. Allwright*, 321 U.S. 649 (1944).

[14] McLemore, "The MFDP," 18–21.

[15] Pat Watters and Reese Cleghorn, *Climbing Jacob's Ladder: The Arrival of Negroes in Southern Politics* (New York: Harcourt, 1967), p. 246.

[16] Guyot and Thelwell, "The Politics of Necessity and Survival."

[17] U.S. Commission on Civil Rights, *Voting in Mississippi* (Washington, D.C.: U.S. Government Printing Office, 1965).

[18] Rayford W. Logan, *The Betrayal of the Negro* (New York: Collier Books, 1965), pp. 23–104.

[19] Key, *Politics, Parties, and Pressure Groups*, pp. 293–296; Guyot and Thelwell, "The Politics of Necessity and Survival," 123.

[20] See Samuel Dubois Cook, "Political Movements and Organizations," *Journal of Politics*, Vol 28. (February 1964), 130–153.

[21] McLemore, "The MFDP," 22–28.

[22] Watters and Cleghorn, *Climbing Jacob's Ladder*, pp. 124–129.

[23] McLemore, "The MFDP," 20–21, 39–40.

[24] Several books describe the summer project of 1964 and the COFO experiment. The best accounts are Len Holt, *The Summer That Didn't End* (New York: Morrow, 1965), pp. 31–42; Sally Belfrage, *Freedom Summer* (New York: Viking, 1965), pp. 3–55; William McCord, *Mississippi: The Long, Hot Summer* (New York: Norton, 1965), pp. 50–80; Elizabeth Sutherland (ed.), *Letters from Mississippi* (New York: McGraw-Hill, 1965), pp. 1–34. On the violence which took place, see W. B. Huie, *Three Lives for Mississippi* (New York: WCC Books, 1965), and N. Hoffman, *Mississippi Notebook* (New York: David White, 1964).

[25] McLemore, "The MFDP," 39–40. For further insight on this point see Watters and Cleghorn, *Climbing Jacob's Ladder*, pp. 65–67.

[26] McLemore gives 88,000 ("The MFDP," 41); Watters and Cleghorn give 90,000 (*Climbing Jacob's Ladder*, p. 67); and Holt gives 93,000 (*The Sumer That Didn't End*, p. 153).

[27] Quoted in Reese Cleghorn, "Who Speaks for Mississippi," *The Reporter* (August 13, 1964), 32.

[28] McLemore, "The MFDP," 41.

[29] *Ibid.*, 42.

[30] *Ibid.* See also McCord *Mississippi: The Long, Hot Summer*, pp. 113–118.

[31] *Ibid.*, p. 48. See also Holt, *The Summer That Didn't End*, pp. 160–161.

[32] *Ibid.*, pp. 49–50; and Watters and Cleghorn, *Climbing Jacob's Ladder*, p. 32.

[33] *Ibid.*, pp. 52–53.

[34] *Ibid.*, p. 55. See also "Johnson Cautions Delegates," *National Observer* (August 3, 1964), 1.

[35] See Holt, *The Summer That Didn't End*, pp. 339–340.

[36] *Ibid.*, pp. 58, 167.

[37] *Ibid.*, pp. 169–178.

[38] See McLemore, "The MFDP," 54.

[39] "Mississippi Blocs Vie Before Panel," *NYT* (August 23, 1964), 18.

[40] Holt, *The Summer That Didn't End*, pp. 169–170, 174–177.

[41] "GOP Is Extolled by Mississippians," *NYT* (September 10, 1964), 22. See also "Mississippi: What's in a Name?" *Newsweek* (September 21, 1964), 34.

[42] "Mississippi Seats Under Challenge," *NYT* (December 5, 1964), 19.

[43] Richard Rovere, "Letter from Washington," *The New Yorker* (October 16, 1965), 233–234.

[44] George Slaff, "Five Seats in Congress: The Mississippi Challenge," *The Nation* (May 17, 1965), 527.

[45] *Ibid.*, 528.

[46] *Ibid.*, 526.

[47] Rovere, "Letter from Washington," 240–241.

[48] *Ibid.*, 238. See also "Mississippi Challengers," *The New Republic* (October 2, 1965), 8.

[49] *Ibid.*, 240–241.

[50] Andrew Kopkind, "Seat Belts for Mississippi Five," *The New Republic* (July 24, 1965), 16.

[51] Rovere, "Letter from Washington," 242.

[52] "The Challenge Is Real," *The Nation* (June 21, 1965), 659.

[53] Simeon Booker, "50,000 March on Montgomery," *Ebony* (May 1965), 53.

[54] Watters and Cleghorn, *Climbing Jacob's Ladder*, p. 257.

[55] "Mississippi Challengers," 8.

[56] See Stokely Carmichael and Charles Hamilton, *Black Power: The Politics of Liberation in America* (New York: Random House, 1967), Chapters 3 and 4; John Herber, "Mississippi Freedom Democrats to Run Own Slate for Congress," *NYT Supplement* (September 23, 1965), 1.

[57] See Watters and Gleghorn, *Climbing Jacob's Ladder*, pp. 258–259.

[58] "Mississippi and the NAACP," *Crisis* (June–July 1966), 31.

[59] *Ibid.*, 31.

[60] Althea Simmons. "50,000 New Voters," *Crisis* (October 1965), 498.

[61] "Over 5,000 Registered in Mississippi," *Crisis* (January 1966), 39. See also Charles Derber, "Registration Tactics in Mississippi," letters to the editor, *NYT* (August 26, 1965), 32.

[62] On the MFDP–NAACP rivalry, see "Deacons in Mississippi Visit, Implore Negroes to Wake Up," *NYT* (August 30, 1965), 18; "Aide of Dr. King Sent to Natchez to Weigh the Next Rights Move," *NYT* (September 4, 1965), 22; and "Troop Withdrawal Is Urged in Natchez," *NYT* (September 6, 1965), 7.

[63] See "Mississippi Negroes Ask Federal Court to Redistrict State," *NYT* (October 20, 1965), 1; "$1,000 in Food Collected by Students for Mississippi," *NYT* (November 26, 1965), 1; and "Freedom Party Enters Race," *NYT* (January 7, 1966), 34.

[64] "Mississippi Vote Is Won by Whites," *NYT* (March 6, 1966), 75.

[65] See "Court to Review Mississippi's Plan," *NYT* (April 11, 1966), 39; "Delta Negroes Threaten Whitten's Seat in House," *NYT* (April 3, 1966), 52; and "Mississippi Primary Faces a Challenge," *NYT* (May 1, 1966), 55.

[66] See Edward Burke, "Meredith Began Vote March Today," *NYT* (June 5, 1966), 78; "U.S. Files Suit," *NYT* (June 17, 1966), 1; "Mississippi Backs Negro Voter Curbs," *NYT* (June 10, 1966), 34; "Mississippi Session Ends,"

NYT (June 13, 1966), 31; "Eastland Wins Mississippi Race," *NYT* (June 8, 1966), 27; and Table 5 in the Appendix.

[67] Roy Reed, "Negroes and Liberal Whites Score Big Gains in Mississippi," *NYT* (July 17, 1966), 61.

[68] See "Four in Mississippi See Election Ban," *NYT* (October 6, 1966), 41; "Miss. Negroes Lose Election Suit," *ibid.*, 23; "Court Refuses to Review Order Backing NAACP," *NYT* (October 11, 1966) 32; and "U.S. Court Orders Mississippi to Grant NAACP Charter," *NYT* (October 29, 1966), 17.

[69] See "Negroes Sue to Win Ballot Place Denied by Mississippi," *NYT* (October 22, 1966), 14; "Mississippi's Curb on Ballot Lifted," *NYT* (October 27, 1966), 34; "Eastland Facing Battle Against Strong GOP Rival and Black Vote," *NYT* (November 2, 1966), 24; "Eastland Chosen for Fifth Term," *NYT* (November 9, 1966), 33; and "Democrats Sweep Miss. Slate," *NYT* (November 10, 1966), 36.

[70] See "Mississippi Handed a Districting Plan," *NYT* (March 29, 1967), 32.

[71] See "Negro Is Hopeful in Mississippi Bid," *NYT* (April 30, 1967), 84; "U.S. Election Aides Sent to Mississippi," *NYT* (May 2, 1967), 23; and "2 All-Negro Tickets Defeated in Mississippi Delta," *NYT* (May 3, 1967), 32.

[72] See "Miss. Will Start 3-Way Governorship Primary," *NYT* (August 6, 1967), 55; "Evers Conducting Negro Vote Drive," *NYT* (June 25, 1967), 54; "Miss. Posts Won by 11 Negroes," *NYT* (August 10, 1967), 1; "A Negro Congressman Urges Mississippians to Vote," *NYT* (August 29, 1967), 23; "Race in Mississippi Won by Williams, Negroes Lose Test," *NYT* (August 30, 1967), 1; "Miss. Test Lost by Negroes," *NYT* (August 31, 1967), 23; "Setback in Mississippi," *NYT* (August 31, 1967), 32.

[73] See "At Least 3 Negroes Win Miss. Contest," *NYT* (November 8, 1967), 38; "Negroes Elected to All-White Mississippi Legislature." *NYT* (November 9, 1967), 33; and *Pittsburgh Courier* (January 13, 1968).

[74] See "Negro Challenged on Seat in Mississippi Legislature," *NYT* (December 6, 1967), 53; and "Sutton Asks Aid for Negroes in Fight for Mississippi Seat," *NYT* (December 15, 1967), 43.

[75] "Negro Office Winners Ask Federal Help in Miss." *NYT* (December 16, 1967), 4; "Negroes Plan Drive on Bonding Office," *NYT* (December 20, 1967), 32.

[76] "6 More Negroes Get Bonds in Miss." *NYT* (December 21, 1967), 23; "Surety Bond Denial May Spur Boycott," *NYT* (December 24, 1967), 48; "3 More Negroes Get Surety Bonds," *NYT* (December 28, 1967), 24.

[77] "Protest Withdrawn: Miss. Negro Is Set to Take Seat," *NYT* (January 2, 1968) 22; "Miss. Seats First Negro Legislator in 74 Years," *NYT* (January 3, 1968), 1.

[78] "Miss. Seat Sought by Evers," *NYT* (January 26, 1968), 17; Walter Rugaber, "Black Political Power," *NYT* (March 17, 1968), 6; "Mississippi Acts to Block Evers from Gaining Seat," *NYT* (March 28, 1968), 17; "Mississippi's House Acts to Bar Evers," *NYT* (March 29, 1968), 27; "Evers Decides to Pass Up Another Try for Congress," *NYT* (April 6, 1968), 22.

[79] See "Democratic Unit Lays Racial Bias to Mississippians," *NYT* (August 19, 1968), 1; "Democrats Clash over Credentials," *NYT* (August 20, 1968), 27; "Mississippi Rebels Reject Compromise Seating Plan," *NYT* (August 21, 1968), 32; and "Delegate Fights Transform Party," *NYT* (August 28, 1968), 1. See also Map 1 in the Appendix.

Chapter 4

[1] Charles Brown, "Reconstruction Legislators in Alabama," *Negro History Bulletin* (March 1963), 198–199.

[2] Alrutheus Taylor, "Negro Congressmen a Generation After," *Journal of Negro History* (April 1922), 127, 171.

[3] Malcolm C. McMillan, "A History of the Alabama Constitution of 1901" (University of Alabama, M.A. thesis, 1940), 35.

[4] *Ibid.,* 1–5.

[5] *Ibid.,* 5–7. See also Taylor, "Negro Congressmen," 171; and Smith, *The Negro in Congress,* Chapter 3.

[6] *Ibid.,* pp. 6–7.

[7] *Ibid.,* p. 8.

[8] Key, *Southern Politics,* pp. 45–47, 535–541; see also McMillan. "Alabama Constitution of 1901." On the role of the Negro in the Populist movement in Alabama, see W. Rogers, "The Negro Alliance in Alabama," *Journal of Negro History* (January 1960), 38–44; and Joseph H. Taylor, "Populism and Disfranchisement in Alabama," *Journal of Negro History* (October 1949), 410–427.

[9] Woodward, *Origins of the New South,* pp. 321–322.

[10] *Ibid.* See also McMillan, "Alabama Constitution of 1901," 35–37, 183–184.

[11] Woodward, *Origins of the New South.* See also Joseph M. Brittain, "Some Reflections on Negro Suffrage and Politics in Alabama—Past and Present," *Journal of Negro History* (April 1962), 127–138.

[12] "Rights Group Plans Drive in Alabama," *NYT* (November 4, 1965), 36.

[13] "Formation of Alabama Party Is Urged by Moderate Democrats," *NYT* (November 8, 1965), 18.

[14] Gene Roberts, "Student Rights Group Lacks Money and Help but Not Projects," *NYT* (December 10, 1965), 37.

[15] See John Hulett, Stokely Carmichael, and J. Benson, *The Black Panther Party* (New York: Merit Publishers, 1966); Joanne Grant (ed.), *Black Protest* (New York: Fawcett, 1968), pp. 402–407; Carmichael and Hamilton, *Black Power,* Chapter 5.

[16] Roberts, "Students Rights Group Lacks Money and Help but Not Projects," 37.

[17] "New Election Asked in Alabama: Negroes Call White Rule Illegal," *NYT* (January 7, 1966), 34.

[18] "Democrats Raise Alabama Filing Fee," *NYT* (February 5, 1966), 33.

[19] Gene Roberts, "Alabama Sheriff Opposed by Negro," *NYT* (February 20, 1966), 68. For insight into the campaign, see G. Roberts, "A Remarkable Thing Is Happening in Wilcox County, Alabama," *NYT* (April 17, 1966), 26.

[20] Carmichael and Hamilton, *Black Power,* pp. 118–119.

[21] "Alabama Vote Test Voided by U.S. Court," *NYT* (March 30, 1966), 28.

[22] "Negroes Urge Court to Bar Alabama Law," *NYT* (March 9, 1966), 81; "Negroes Lose Fight to Oust All Officers in Lowndes County," *NYT* (April 1, 1966), 24.

[23] Gene Roberts, "Alabama Negroes Urged Not to Vote," *NYT* (April 20, 1966), 27.

[24] "Sabotage in Alabama," *NYT* (April 21, 1966), 38.

[25] Gene Roberts, "Dr. King Bids Alabama Negroes Conquer Fears and Vote as Bloc," *NYT* (April 30, 1966), 1.

[26] "Negro Nominations Seen," *NYT* (May 1, 1966), 72.

[27] John Herbers, "U.S. Outlines Plan to Safeguard Negroes During Alabama Vote," *NYT* (April 27, 1966), 29.

[28] Roy Reed, "Alabama Negro Candidates Lead in 2 Legislative, 3 Sheriff's Votes," *NYT* (May 4, 1966), 28; Roy Reed, "U.S. Observers Restricted," *NYT* (May 7, 1966), 1; "Hearing Ordered on Vote in Selma," *NYT* (May 7, 1966) 1; Gene Roberts, "U.S. Rule Upheld in Selma Voting," *NYT* (May 18, 1966), 24.

[29] Gene Roberts, "Negroes in Alabama Explain Defections," *NYT* (May 8, 1966), 78; see also, "New Voters in Alabama," *NYT* (May 8, 1966), 1.

[30] Gene Roberts, "Militants Take Over Student Coordinating Group," *NYT* (May 17, 1966), 22.

[31] Gene Roberts, "New Leaders and New Course for 'Snick,'" *NYT Magazine* (May 22, 1966), 4.

[32] Gene Roberts, "Alabama Whites Brace for Runoffs," *NYT* (May 30, 1966), 8.

[33] Gene Roberts, "Troopers Shove Group Resuming Meredith March," *NYT* (June 8, 1966), 1.

[34] John Corry, "The Changing Times in Lowndes County: An All Negro Ticket," *NYT* (October 31, 1966), 1, 22.

[35] Gene Roberts, "Wife of Wallace Wins in Alabama: Negro Vote Heavy," *NYT* (May 4, 1966), 22.

[36] "Negro Candidates Lose in Alabama," *NYT* (November 9, 1966), 25.

[37] "Forming a New Political Party," *The Herald* (November 1, 1968), 1.

[38] See Paul R. Wieck, "Southern Democrats: Not What They Used to Be," *The New Republic* (August 3, 1968), 13–15, and NDPA's official newspaper, *The Eagle Eye*, which was published each month from January to June 1970 with the exception of a convention issue published at its first convention in July 1969.

[39] "Formation of Alabama Party Is Urged by Moderate Democrats," *NYT* (November 8, 1965), 18.

[40] John Cashin, "Black Judases' Handicraft," *The Eagle Eye* (May 1970), 4.

[41] "Ala. Demos Fake Reform," and "Mrs. Cashin Calls Party Reform 'Farce,'" *The Eagle Eye* (February 1970), 1.

[42] See Documents 1–3 in the Appendix.

[43] Wieck, "Southern Democrats," 14.

[44] "Chicago: NDPA at the Democratic Convention," *The Eagle Eye* (July 1969), 4.

[45] Wieck, "Southern Democrats," 15.

[46] *Sallie M. Hadnott* v. *Mabel S. Amos, The United States Law Week* (March 3, 1969), p. 4257.

[47] *Ibid.,* p. 4258.

[48] "High Court Case Accuses a Judge," *NYT* (December 17, 1968), 33.

[49] Walter Rugaber, "Negro Group Bids Democrats Oust 6," *NYT* (November 24, 1968), 30.

Chapter 5

[1] See Hesseltine, *Third Party Movements in the United States*, Chapters 1–9; Nash, *Third Parties in American Politics*, Chapters 1–11; and Walton, *The Negro in Third Party Politics*, Chapters 1–8.

[2] Key *Politics, Parties, and Pressure Groups*, pp. 281–301.

[3] *Ibid.*, p. 307.

[4] *Ibid.*, pp. 300–301.

[5] *Ibid.*, p. 302.

[6] Herring, *The Politics of Democracy*, p. 182.

[7] *Ibid.*, p. 185.

[8] See U.S. Civil Rights Commission, *Political Participation* (Washington, D.C.: U.S. Government Printing Office, 1968), pp. 19–152.

[9] Kay Lawson, *Political Parties and Democracy in the United States* (New York: Scribner's, 1968), p. 51.

[10] Key, *Southern Politics*, Chapters 3 and 11.

[11] *Ibid.*, p. 551.

[12] See A. C. Cole, *The Whig Party in the South* (Gloucester, Mass.: Peter Smith, 1962).

[13] See Key, *Southern Politics*, pp. 41–46, 280–285.

[14] See W. D. McCain, "The Populist Party in Mississippi" (University of Mississippi, Master's thesis, 1931).

[15] Woodward, *Orgins of the New South*, p. 391.

[16] Key, *Southern Politics*, pp. 230–253.

[17] *Ibid.*, pp. 246–253.

[18] *Ibid.*, p. 244.

[19] *Ibid.*, p. 246.

[20] *Smith* v. *Allwright*, 321 U.S. 649 (1944).

[21] See Key, *Southern Politics*, pp. 235–236, 240; and Hodding Carter, *So the Heffners Left McComb* (Garden City, N.Y.: Doubleday, 1965).

[22] See Carmichael and Hamilton, *Black Power*, Chapter 3.

[23] On Mrs. Hamer's determination and resiliency see the description of the "Winona incident" in Watters and Cleghorn, *Climbing Jacob's Ladder*, pp. 363–375.

[24] Key, *Southern Politics*, pp. 52–57.

[25] "Presidential Candidates from 1788 to 1960," *Congressional Quarterly* (special report, 1961), 23–24.

[26] See Grant, *Black Protest*, pp. 402–403; R. Analavage, "A Victory in Defeat in Lowndes," *National Guardian* (November 19, 1966); and E. Barnes, "Independent Politics: The Significance of the Black Panther Party," *Young Socialist* (October–November 1966).

[27] Samuel Dubois Cook, "The Tragic Myth of Black Power," *The New South* (Summer 1966), 61.

[28] Andrew Kopkind, "Lair of the Black Panther," *New Republic* (August 13, 1966), 10.

[29] Carmichael and Hamilton, *Black Power*, pp. 119–120.

[30] *Ibid.*, pp. 118–119.

[31] Holt, *The Summer That Didn't End*, pp. 37–54.

[32] Carmichael and Hamilton, *Black Power*, pp. 101–102.

[33] See Hanes Walton, Jr., *The Politics of the Black and Tan Republicans* (forthcoming).

Chapter 6

[1] Stokely Carmichael, "What We Want," *New York Review of Books* (September 22, 1966), 5–7.

[2] Walton, *The Negro in Third Party Politics,* Chapter 8. See also Walton, "Blacks and the 1968 Third Parties," *Negro Educational Review* (January 1970), 19–23.

[3] See Bailey (ed.), *Negro Politics in America,* pp. 235–236, 311–313, 419–420.

[4] See Prothro and Matthews, *Negroes and the New Southern Politics,* pp. 204–232.

[5] *Ibid.,* pp. 178–210. On Negro voting behavior, see Johnnie Daniel, "Changes in Negro Political Mobilization and Its Relationship to Community Socioeconomic Structure," *Journal of Social and Behavioral Sciences* (Fall 1968), 41–46.

[6] *Ibid.,* 59–63.

[7] Edward Banfield, *The Moral Basis of a Backward Society* (New York: The Free Press, 1958).

[8] S. M. Lipset, *Political Man* (Garden City, N.Y.: Doubleday, 1960).

[9] W. Warner and Paul Lund, *The Social Life of a Modern Community* (New Haven: Yale University Press, 1941).

[10] Everett C. Ladd, Jr., *Negro Political Leadership in the South* (Ithaca, N.Y.: Cornell University Press, 1966), pp. 63–64.

[11] See E. Franklin Frazier, *The Black Bourgeoisie* (New York: The Free Press, 1957); and Nathan Hare, *The Black Anglo-Saxons* (New York: Marzani and Munsell, 1965).

[12] James Q. Wilson, *Negro Politics: The Search for Leadership* (New York: The Free Press, 1965), p. 23.

[13] Bailey (ed.), *Negro Politics in America,* pp. 315–317.

[14] Wilson, *Negro Politics,* p. 24.

[15] See James Q. Wilson, "Two Negro Politicians: An Interpretation," *Midwest Journal of Political Science* (November 1960), 346–369.

[16] Jack Anderson, *Washington Exposé* (Washington, D.C.: Public Affairs Press, 1967).

[17] Wilson, *Negro Politics,* p. 24.

[18] Ladd, *Negro Political Leadership in the South,* pp. 36–37.

[19] Daniel, "Changes in Negro Political Mobilization," pp. 42–44, offers statistical evidence that these factors in Alabama operated to increase Negro political mobilization throughout the state from 1960 to 1966.

[20] Pat Watters, "The Negroes Enter Southern Politics," *Dissent* (July– August 1966), 365–367; Chuck Stone, *Black Political Power in America* (Indianapolis: Bobbs-Merrill, 1968).

[21] See U.S. Civil Rights Commission, *Political Participation.*

[22] Watters and Cleghorn, *Climbing Jacob's Ladder,* pp. 75–109.

[23] Hesseltine, *Third-Party Movements in the United States,* pp. 98–101; Harold M. Rose, "The All-Negro Town: Its Evaluation and Function," *The Geographical Review* (July 1965), 362–381.

[24] Joseph C. Haugh, "Reapportionment and Present Negro Politicians," *The Christian Century* (February 9, 1964), 30.

[25] Bailey (ed.), *Negro Politics in America,* p. 420.

[26] See Allan P. Spindler, "Protest Against the Political Status of the Negro,"

The Annals of the American Academy of Political and Social Science (January 1965), 49–51.

[27] See "Negro Party Files in Michigan," *NYT* (May 3, 1964), 70; and David R. Jones, "Negro Party Puts Strength to Test," *NYT* (October 4, 1964), 70.

[28] See Harold Cruse, "The Fire This Time," *New York Review of Books* (May 8, 1969), 13.

[29] Walton, *The Negro in Third Party Politics,* p. 81.

Appendix

Table 1-A Returns of an Election Held November 2, 1920 for President and Vice-President—Black-Tan Republican

COUNTIES	ELECTORS AT LARGE		DISTRICT ELECTORS																	
	T. H. Adkins	Geo. W. Burkitt	Dist. No. 1	Dist. No. 2 H. Troutman	Dist. No. 3 R. O. Spence	Dist. No. 4 L. H. Crawford	Dist. No. 5	Dist. No. 6 A. W. Conitz	Dist. No. 7 E. E. Danna	Dist. No. 8 R. E. Hanney	Dist. No. 9 Ed. Tracey	Dist. No. 10	Dist. No. 11 W. H. Pierce	Dist. No. 12 J. E. B. Stewart	Dist. No. 13 L. V. Lindsey	Dist. No. 14 J. H. Duffner	Dist. No. 15	Dist. No. 16	Dist. No. 17 Jas. Jenkins, Jr.	Dist. No. 18 Mack B. Bybee
Anderson	906	906	—	906	906	906	—	906	906	906	906	—	906	906	906	906	—	—	906	906
Andrews	—	—	—	—	—	—	—	—	—	—	—	—	—	—	—	—	—	—	—	—
Angelina	119	119	—	119	119	119	—	119	119	119	119	—	119	119	119	119	—	—	119	119
Aransas	—	—	—	—	—	—	—	—	—	—	—	—	—	—	—	—	—	—	—	—
Archer	—	—	—	—	—	—	—	—	—	—	—	—	—	—	—	—	—	—	—	—
Armstrong	1	1	—	1	1	1	—	1	1	1	1	—	1	1	1	1	—	—	1	1
Atascosa	7	7	—	7	7	7	—	7	7	7	7	—	7	7	7	7	—	—	7	7
Austin	87	87	—	87	87	87	—	87	87	87	87	—	87	87	87	87	—	—	87	87
Bailey	—	—	—	—	—	—	—	—	—	—	—	—	—	—	—	—	—	—	—	—
Bandera	—	—	—	—	—	—	—	—	—	—	—	—	—	—	—	—	—	—	—	—
Bastrop	147	147	—	147	147	147	—	147	147	147	147	—	147	147	147	147	—	—	147	147
Baylor	—	—	—	—	—	—	—	—	—	—	—	—	—	—	—	—	—	—	—	—
Bee	—	—	—	—	—	—	—	—	—	—	—	—	—	—	—	—	—	—	—	—

County																
Bell	168	168	168	168	168	168	168	168	168	168	168	168	168	—	168	168
Bexar	597	596	556	555	556	556	557	557	558	557	556	557	597	—	558	557
Blanco	14	13	13	13	14	14	13	13	13	14	13	13	13	—	14	14
Borden	—	—	—	—	—	—	—	—	—	—	—	—	—	—	—	—
Bosque	28	28	28	28	28	28	28	28	28	28	28	28	28	—	28	28
Bowie	255	254	254	254	254	254	254	254	254	254	254	254	254	—	254	254
Brazoria	25	25	25	25	25	25	25	25	25	25	25	25	25	—	25	25
Brazos	502	502	502	502	502	502	502	502	502	502	502	502	502	—	502	502
Brewster	—	—	—	—	—	—	—	—	—	—	—	—	—	—	—	—
Briscoe	—	—	—	—	—	—	—	—	—	—	—	—	—	—	—	—
Brooks	—	—	—	—	—	—	—	—	—	—	—	—	—	—	—	—
Brown	14	14	14	14	14	14	14	14	14	14	14	14	14	—	14	14
Burleson	458	458	458	458	458	458	458	458	458	459	459	459	459	—	458	459
Burnett	—	—	—	—	—	—	—	—	—	—	—	—	—	—	—	—
Caldwell	218	218	218	218	218	218	218	218	218	218	218	218	218	—	218	218
Calhoun	34	34	34	34	34	34	34	34	34	34	34	34	34	—	34	34
Callahan	—	—	—	—	—	—	—	—	—	—	—	—	—	—	—	—
Cameron	1	1	1	1	1	1	1	1	1	1	1	1	1	—	1	1
Camp	442	442	442	442	442	442	442	442	442	442	442	442	442	—	443	443
Carson	—	—	—	—	—	—	—	—	—	—	—	—	—	—	—	—
Cass	184	184	184	184	184	184	184	184	184	184	184	184	184	—	184	184
Castro	—	—	—	—	—	—	—	—	—	—	—	—	—	—	—	—
Chambers	2	2	2	2	2	2	2	2	2	2	2	2	2	—	2	2

Table 1-A (Cont.)

COUNTIES	ELECTORS AT LARGE		DISTRICT ELECTORS																	
	T. H. Adkins	Geo. W. Burkitt	Dist. No. 1	Dist. No. 2 H. Troutman	Dist. No. 3 R. O. Spence	Dist. No. 4 L. H. Crawford	Dist. No. 5	Dist. No. 6 A. W. Conitz	Dist. No. 7 E. E. Danna	Dist. No. 8 R. E. Hanney	Dist. No. 9 Ed. Tracey	Dist. No. 10	Dist. No. 11 W. H. Pierce	Dist. No. 12 J. E. B. Stewart	Dist. No. 13 L. V. Lindsey	Dist. No. 14 J. H. Duffner	Dist. No. 15	Dist. No. 16	Dist. No. 17 Jas. Jenkins, Jr.	Dist. No. 18 Mack B. Bybee
Cherokee	260	260	—	260	260	260	—	260	260	260	260	—	260	260	260	260	—	—	260	260
Childress	1	1	—	1	1	1	—	1	1	1	1	—	1	1	1	1	—	—	1	1
Clay	3	3	—	3	3	3	—	3	3	3	3	—	3	3	3	3	—	—	3	3
Cochran	—	—	—	—	—	—	—	—	—	—	—	—	—	—	—	—	—	—	—	—
Coke	—	—	—	—	—	—	—	—	—	—	—	—	—	—	—	—	—	—	—	—
Coleman	4	4	—	4	4	4	—	4	4	4	4	—	4	4	4	4	—	—	4	4
Collin	31	31	—	31	31	31	—	31	31	31	31	—	31	31	31	31	—	—	31	31
Collingsworth	1	1	—	1	1	1	—	1	1	1	1	—	1	1	1	1	—	—	1	1
Colorado	346	346	—	346	346	346	—	346	346	346	346	—	346	346	346	346	—	—	346	346
Comal	2	2	—	2	2	2	—	2	2	2	2	—	2	2	2	2	—	—	2	2
Comanche	—	—	—	—	—	—	—	—	—	—	—	—	—	—	—	—	—	—	—	—
Concho	1	1	—	1	1	1	—	1	1	1	1	—	1	1	1	1	—	—	1	1
Cooke	89	89	—	89	89	89	—	89	89	89	89	—	89	89	89	89	—	—	89	89
Coryell	8	8	—	8	8	8	—	8	8	8	8	—	8	8	8	8	—	—	8	8

County																
Cottell	2	2	2	2	2	2	2	2	2	2	—	2	2	2	2	2
Crane	—	—	—	—	—	—	—	—	—	—	—	—	—	—	—	—
Crockett	—	—	—	—	—	—	—	—	—	—	—	—	—	—	—	—
Crosby	2	2	2	2	2	2	2	2	2	2	—	2	2	2	2	2
Culberson	—	—	—	—	—	—	—	—	—	—	—	—	—	—	—	—
Dallam	—	—	—	—	—	—	—	—	—	—	—	—	—	—	—	—
Dallas	1,637	1,637	1,637	1,637	1,637	1,637	1,637	1,637	1,637	1,637	—	1,637	1,637	1,637	1,637	1,637
Dawson	—	—	—	—	—	—	—	—	—	—	—	—	—	—	—	—
Deaf Smith	—	—	—	—	—	—	—	—	—	—	—	—	—	—	—	—
Delta	51	50	50	50	50	50	50	50	50	50	—	50	50	50	50	50
Denton	82	82	82	82	82	82	82	82	82	97	—	82	82	82	82	82
De Witt	394	394	394	394	394	394	394	394	394	394	—	394	394	394	394	394
Dickens	—	—	—	—	—	—	—	—	—	—	—	—	—	—	—	—
Dimmit	—	—	—	—	—	—	—	—	—	—	—	—	—	—	—	—
Donley	—	—	—	—	—	—	—	—	—	—	—	—	—	—	—	—
Duval	—	—	—	—	—	—	—	—	—	—	—	—	—	—	—	—
Eastland	—	—	—	—	—	—	—	—	—	—	—	—	—	—	—	—
Ector	—	—	—	—	—	—	—	—	—	—	—	—	—	—	—	—
Edwards	—	—	—	—	—	—	—	—	—	—	—	—	—	—	—	—
Ellis	321	321	321	321	321	321	321	321	321	321	—	321	321	321	321	321
El Paso	8	8	8	8	8	8	8	8	8	8	—	8	8	8	8	8
Erath	15	15	15	15	15	15	15	15	15	15	—	15	15	15	15	15
Falls	731	731	731	731	731	731	731	731	731	731	—	731	731	731	731	731

Table 1-A (Cont.)

	ELECTORS AT LARGE		DISTRICT ELECTORS																	
COUNTIES	T. H. Adkins	Geo. W. Burkitt	Dist. No. 1	Dist. No. 2 H. Troutman	Dist. No. 3 R. O. Spence	Dist. No. 4 L. H. Crawford	Dist. No. 5	Dist. No. 6 A. W. Conitz	Dist. No. 7 E. E. Danna	Dist. No. 8 R. E. Hanney	Dist. No. 9 Ed. Tracey	Dist. No. 10	Dist. No. 11 W. H. Pierce	Dist. No. 12 J. E. B. Stewart	Dist. No. 13 L. V. Lindsey	Dist. No. 14 J. H. Duffner	Dist. No. 15	Dist. No. 16	Dist. No. 17 Jas. Jenkins, Jr.	Dist. No. 18 Mack B. Bybee
Fannin	319	319	—	319	319	319	—	319	319	319	319	—	319	319	319	319	—	—	319	319
Fayette	355	356	—	355	355	355	—	356	356	356	356	—	356	356	356	356	—	—	356	356
Fisher	1	1	—	1	1	1	—	1	1	1	1	—	1	1	1	1	—	—	1	1
Floyd	1	1	—	1	1	1	—	1	1	1	1	—	1	1	1	1	—	—	1	1
Foard	—	—	—	—	—	—	—	—	—	—	—	—	—	—	—	—	—	—	—	—
Fort Bend	67	—	—	—	—	—	—	—	—	—	—	—	358	—	—	—	—	—	—	67
Franklin	—	—	—	—	—	—	—	—	—	—	—	—	—	—	—	—	—	—	—	—
Freestone	630	630	—	630	630	630	—	630	630	630	630	—	630	630	630	630	—	—	630	630
Frio	2	2	—	2	2	2	—	2	2	2	2	—	2	2	2	2	—	—	2	2
Gaines	—	—	—	—	—	—	—	—	—	—	—	—	—	—	—	—	—	—	—	—
Galveston	111	109	—	109	109	109	—	109	109	109	109	—	108	108	108	108	—	—	108	108
Garza	—	—	—	—	—	—	—	—	—	—	—	—	—	—	—	—	—	—	—	—
Gillespie	—	—	—	—	—	—	—	—	—	—	—	—	—	—	—	—	—	—	—	—
Glasscock	—	—	—	—	—	—	—	—	—	—	—	—	—	—	—	—	—	—	—	—

224

County	1	2	3	4	5	6	7	8	9	10	11	12	13
Goliad	66	66	—	66	66	66	66	66	66	66	66	65	66
Gonzales	167	167	—	167	167	167	167	167	167	167	167	167	167
Gray	—	—	—	—	—	—	—	—	—	—	—	—	—
Grayson	351	351	—	351	351	351	351	351	351	351	351	351	351
Gregg	177	177	—	177	177	177	177	177	177	177	177	177	177
Grimes	4	4	—	4	4	4	13	13	13	13	13	13	13
Guadalupe	69	69	—	69	69	69	69	69	69	69	69	82	82
Hale	—	—	—	—	—	—	—	—	—	—	—	—	—
Hall	1	1	—	1	1	1	1	1	1	1	1	1	1
Hamilton	5	5	—	5	5	5	5	5	5	5	5	5	5
Hansford	—	—	—	—	—	—	—	—	—	—	—	—	—
Hardeman	—	—	—	—	—	—	—	—	—	—	1	1	1
Hardin	58	58	—	58	58	58	58	58	58	58	58	58	58
Harris	5,289	5,289	—	5,289	5,289	5,289	5,289	5,288	5,262	5,262	5,264	5,263	5,263
Harrison	576	576	—	576	576	576	576	576	576	576	576	576	576
Hartley	—	—	—	—	—	—	—	—	—	—	—	—	—
Haskell	—	—	—	—	—	—	—	—	—	—	—	—	—
Hays	16	16	—	16	16	16	16	16	16	16	16	16	16
Hemphill	—	—	—	—	—	—	—	—	—	—	—	—	—
Henderson	124	124	—	124	124	124	124	124	124	124	124	124	124
Hidalgo	2	2	—	2	2	2	2	2	2	2	2	2	2
Hill	48	48	—	48	48	48	48	48	48	48	48	48	48
Hockley	—	—	—	—	—	—	—	—	—	—	—	—	—

Table 1-A (Cont.)

| COUNTIES | ELECTORS AT LARGE | | DISTRICT ELECTORS | | | | | | | | | | | | | | | | | |
	T. H. Adkins	Geo. W. Burkitt	Dist. No. 1	Dist. No. 2 H. Troutman	Dist. No. 3 R. O. Spence	Dist. No. 4 L. H. Crawford	Dist. No. 5	Dist. No. 6 A. W. Conitz	Dist. No. 7 E. E. Danna	Dist. No. 8 R. E. Hanney	Dist. No. 9 Ed. Tracey	Dist. No. 10	Dist. No. 11 W. H. Pierce	Dist. No. 12 J. E. B. Stewart	Dist. No. 13 L. V. Lindsey	Dist. No. 14 J. H. Duffner	Dist. No. 15	Dist. No. 16	Dist. No. 17 Jas. Jenkins, Jr.	Dist. No. 18 Mack B. Bybee
Hood	27	27	—	27	27	27	—	27	27	27	27	—	27	27	27	27	—	—	27	27
Hopkins	99	99	—	99	99	99	—	99	99	99	99	—	99	99	99	99	—	—	99	99
Houston	451	451	—	451	451	451	—	451	451	451	451	—	451	451	451	451	—	—	451	451
Howard	—	—	—	—	—	—	—	—	—	—	—	—	—	—	—	—	—	—	—	—
Hudspeth	—	—	—	—	—	—	—	—	—	—	—	—	—	—	—	—	—	—	—	—
Hunt	204	204	—	204	204	204	—	204	204	204	204	—	204	204	204	204	—	—	204	204
Hutchinson	—	—	—	—	—	—	—	—	—	—	—	—	—	—	—	—	—	—	—	—
Irion	—	—	—	—	—	—	—	—	—	—	—	—	—	—	—	—	—	—	—	—
Jack	—	—	—	—	—	—	—	—	—	—	—	—	—	—	—	—	—	—	—	—
Jackson	5	5	—	5	5	5	—	5	5	5	5	—	5	5	5	5	—	—	5	5
Jasper	37	18	—	29	29	18	—	18	18	18	18	—	18	18	18	18	—	—	18	18
Jeff Davis	—	—	—	—	—	—	—	—	—	—	—	—	—	—	—	—	—	—	—	—
Jefferson	802	802	—	802	802	802	—	802	802	802	802	—	802	802	802	802	—	—	802	802
Jim Hogg	—	—	—	—	—	—	—	—	—	—	—	—	—	—	—	—	—	—	—	—

226

County																
Jim Wells	—															—
Johnson	46	—	46	46	46	46	—	46	46	46	46	46	46	—	46	46
Jones	—		—				—							—		
Karnes	16	—	16	16	16	16	—	16	16	16	16	16	16	—	16	16
Kaufman	573	—	573	573	573	573	573	573	573	573	573	—	573	573	573	573
Kendall	2	—	2	2	2	2	2	2	2	2	2	—	2	2	2	2
Kent	1	—	1	1	1	1	1	1	1	1	1	—	1	1	1	1
Kerr	—											—				
Kimble	—											—				
King	—											—				
Kinney	—											—				
Kleberg	10	—	10	10	10	10	10	10	10	10	10	—	10	10	10	10
Knox	—											—				
Lamar	459	—	459	459	459	459	459	459	459	459	459	—	459	459	459	459
Lamb	—											—				
Lampasas	5	—	5	5	5	5	5	5	5	5	5	—	5	5	5	5
La Salle	—											—				
Lavaca	144	—	144	144	144	144	144	144	144	144	144	—	144	144	144	144
Lee	331	—	331	332	332	332	332	332	332	332	332	—	332	332	333	333
Leon	74	—	74	74	74	74	74	74	74	74	74	—	74	74	74	74
Liberty	—											—				
Limestone	401	—	401	401	401	401	401	401	401	401	401	—	401	401	401	401
Lipscomb	—											—				

Table 1-A (Cont.)

COUNTIES	ELECTORS AT LARGE		DISTRICT ELECTORS																	
	T. H. Adkins	Geo. W. Burkitt	Dist. No. 1	Dist. No. 2 H. Troutman	Dist. No. 3 R. O. Spence	Dist. No. 4 L. H. Crawford	Dist. No. 5	Dist. No. 6 A. W. Conitz	Dist. No. 7 E. E. Damn	Dist. No. 8 R. E. Hanney	Dist. No. 9 Ed. Tracey	Dist. No. 10	Dist. No. 11 W. H. Pierce	Dist. No. 12 J. E. B. Stewart	Dist. No. 13 L. V. Lindsey	Dist. No. 14 J. H. Duffner	Dist. No. 15	Dist. No. 16	Dist. No. 17 Jas. Jenkins, Jr.	Dist. No. 18 Mack B. Bybee
Live Oak	15	—	—	—	—	—	—	—	—	—	—	—	—	—	—	—	—	—	—	—
Llano	1	1	—	1	1	1	—	1	1	1	1	—	1	1	1	1	—	—	1	1
Loving	—	—	—	—	—	—	—	—	—	—	—	—	—	—	—	—	—	—	—	—
Lubbock	7	7	—	7	7	7	—	7	7	7	7	—	7	7	7	7	—	—	7	7
Lynn	1	1	—	1	1	1	—	1	1	1	1	—	1	1	1	1	—	—	1	1
Madison	144	144	—	144	144	144	—	144	144	144	144	—	144	144	144	144	—	—	144	144
Marion	304	304	—	304	304	304	—	304	304	304	304	—	304	304	304	304	—	—	304	304
Martin	—	—	—	—	—	—	—	—	—	—	—	—	—	—	—	—	—	—	—	—
Mason	—	—	—	—	—	—	—	—	—	—	—	—	—	—	—	—	—	—	—	—
Matagorda	61	61	—	58	58	58	—	58	58	58	58	—	58	58	58	58	—	—	58	58
Maverick	1	1	—	1	1	1	—	1	1	1	1	—	1	1	1	1	—	—	1	1
McCulloch	1	1	—	1	1	1	—	1	1	1	1	—	1	1	1	1	—	—	1	1
McLennan	192	192	—	192	192	192	—	192	192	192	192	—	192	192	192	192	—	—	192	192
McMullen	—	—	—	—	—	—	—	—	—	—	—	—	—	—	—	—	—	—	—	—

County	1	2	3	4	5	6	7	8	9	10	11	12	13	14	15	16	17	18	19
Medina	2	2	—	2	2	2	2	—	2	2	2	2	2	—	2	2	2	2	2
Meard	—	—	—	—	—	—	—	—	—	—	—	—	—	—	—	—	—	—	—
Midland	—	—	—	—	—	—	—	—	—	—	—	—	—	—	—	—	—	—	—
Milam	407	407	—	407	407	407	407	—	407	407	407	407	407	—	407	407	407	407	407
Mills	—	—	—	—	—	—	—	—	—	—	—	—	—	—	—	—	—	—	—
Mitchell	—	—	—	—	—	—	—	—	—	—	—	—	—	—	—	—	—	—	—
Montague	—	—	—	—	—	—	—	—	—	—	—	—	—	—	—	—	—	—	—
Montgomery	144	144	—	144	144	144	144	—	144	144	144	144	144	—	144	144	144	144	144
Moore	—	—	—	—	—	—	—	—	—	—	—	—	—	—	—	—	—	—	—
Morris	68	68	—	68	68	68	68	—	68	68	68	68	68	—	68	68	68	68	68
Motley	—	—	—	—	—	—	—	—	—	—	—	—	—	—	—	—	—	—	—
Nacogdoches	276	276	—	276	276	276	276	—	276	276	276	276	276	—	276	276	276	276	276
Navarro	248	248	—	248	248	248	248	—	248	248	248	248	248	—	248	248	248	249	249
Newton	30	30	—	30	30	30	30	—	30	30	30	30	30	—	30	30	30	30	30
Nolan	—	—	—	—	—	—	—	—	—	—	—	—	—	—	—	—	—	—	—
Nueces	49	49	—	49	49	49	49	—	49	49	50	50	49	—	49	49	49	48	47
Ochiltree	—	—	—	—	—	—	—	—	—	—	—	—	—	—	—	—	—	—	—
Oldham	—	—	—	—	—	—	—	—	—	—	—	—	—	—	—	—	—	—	—
Orange	21	21	—	21	21	21	21	—	21	21	21	21	21	—	21	21	21	63	63
Palo Pinto	11	11	—	11	11	11	11	—	11	11	11	11	11	—	11	11	11	11	11
Panola	95	95	—	95	95	95	95	—	95	95	95	95	95	—	95	95	95	95	95
Parker	6	6	—	6	6	6	6	—	6	6	6	6	6	—	6	6	6	6	6
Parmer	—	—	—	—	—	—	—	—	—	—	—	—	—	—	—	—	—	—	—

Table 1-A (Cont.)

COUNTIES	ELECTORS AT LARGE		DISTRICT ELECTORS																	
	T. H. Adkins	Geo. W. Burkitt	Dist. No. 1	Dist. No. 2 H. Troutman	Dist. No. 3 R. O. Spence	Dist. No. 4 L. H. Crawford	Dist. No. 5	Dist. No. 6 A. W. Conitz	Dist. No. 7 E. E. Danna	Dist. No. 8 R. E. Hanney	Dist. No. 9 Ed. Tracey	Dist. No. 10	Dist. No. 11 W. H. Pierce	Dist. No. 12 J. E. B. Stewart	Dist. No. 13 L. V. Lindsey	Dist. No. 14 J. H. Dufner	Dist. No. 15	Dist. No. 16	Dist. No. 17 Jas. Jenkins, Jr.	Dist. No. 18 Mack B. Bybee
Pecos	1	1	—	1	1	1	—	1	1	1	1	—	1	1	1	1	—	—	1	1
Polk	55	55	—	55	55	55	—	55	55	55	55	—	55	55	55	55	—	—	55	55
Potter	1	1	—	1	1	1	—	1	1	1	1	—	1	1	1	1	—	—	1	1
Presidio	—	—	—	—	—	—	—	—	—	—	—	—	—	—	—	—	—	—	—	—
Rains	26	26	—	26	26	26	—	26	26	26	26	—	26	26	26	26	—	—	26	26
Randall	—	—	—	—	—	—	—	—	—	—	—	—	—	—	—	—	—	—	—	—
Real	1	1	—	1	1	1	—	1	1	1	1	—	1	1	1	1	—	—	1	1
Reagan	—	—	—	—	—	—	—	—	—	—	—	—	—	—	—	—	—	—	—	—
Red River	326	326	—	326	326	326	—	326	326	326	326	—	326	326	326	326	—	—	326	326
Reeves	1	1	—	1	1	1	—	1	1	1	1	—	1	1	1	1	—	—	1	1
Refugio	1	1	—	1	1	1	—	1	1	1	1	—	1	1	1	1	—	—	1	1
Roberts	—	—	—	—	—	—	—	—	—	—	—	—	—	—	—	—	—	—	—	—
Robertson	134	134	—	134	134	134	—	134	134	134	134	—	134	134	134	134	—	—	134	134
Rockwell	3	3	—	3	3	3	—	3	3	3	3	—	3	3	3	3	—	—	3	3

230

Runnels	4	4	—	4	4	4	4	—	4	4	4	—	4	4	4	4	4
Rusk	284	284	—	284	284	284	284	—	284	284	284	—	284	284	284	284	284
Sabine	27	7	—	10	10	10	10	—	10	10	10	—	10	10	7	7	9
San Augustine	7	7	—	7	7	7	7	—	7	7	7	—	7	7	7	7	7
San Jacinto	173	173	—	173	173	173	173	—	173	173	173	—	173	173	173	173	173
San Patricio	—	—	—	—	—	—	—	—	—	—	1	—	—	—	—	—	—
San Saba	3	3	—	3	3	3	3	—	3	3	3	—	3	3	3	3	3
Schleicher	—	—	—	—	—	—	—	—	—	—	—	—	—	—	—	—	—
Scurry	—	—	—	—	—	—	—	—	—	—	—	—	—	—	—	—	—
Shackelford	1	1	—	1	1	1	1	—	1	1	1	—	1	1	1	1	1
Shelby	174	174	—	174	174	174	174	—	174	174	174	—	174	174	174	174	174
Sherman	—	—	—	—	—	—	—	—	—	—	—	—	—	—	—	—	—
Smith	553	553	—	553	553	553	553	—	553	553	553	—	553	553	553	553	553
Somervell	—	—	—	—	—	—	—	—	—	—	—	—	—	—	—	—	—
Starr	—	—	—	—	—	—	—	—	—	—	—	—	—	—	—	—	—
Stephens	1	—	—	1	—	—	—	—	1	1	—	—	—	—	—	—	—
Sterling	—	—	—	—	—	—	—	—	—	—	—	—	—	—	—	—	—
Stonewall	1	1	—	1	1	1	1	—	1	1	1	—	1	1	1	1	1
Sutton	—	—	—	—	—	—	—	—	—	—	—	—	—	—	—	—	—
Swisher	1	1	—	1	1	1	1	—	1	1	1	—	1	1	1	1	1
Tarrant	833	833	—	833	833	833	833	—	833	833	833	—	833	833	833	833	833
Taylor	8	8	—	8	8	8	8	—	8	8	8	—	8	8	8	8	8
Terrell	1	1	—	1	1	1	1	—	1	1	1	—	1	1	1	1	1

Table 1-A   (Cont.)

COUNTIES	ELECTORS AT LARGE		DISTRICT ELECTORS																	
	T. H. Adkins	Geo. W. Burkitt	Dist. No. 1	Dist. No. 2 H. Troutman	Dist. No. 3 R. O. Spence	Dist. No. 4 L. H. Crawford	Dist. No. 5	Dist. No. 6 A. W. Conitz	Dist. No. 7 E. E. Dana	Dist. No. 8 R. E. Hanney	Dist. No. 9 Ed. Tracey	Dist. No. 10	Dist. No. 11 W. H. Pierce	Dist. No. 12 J. E. B. Stewart	Dist. No. 13 L. V. Lindsey	Dist. No. 14 J. H. Duffner	Dist. No. 15	Dist. No. 16	Dist. No. 17 Jas. Jenkins, Jr.	Dist. No. 18 Mack B. Bybee
Terry	—	—	—	—	—	—	—	—	—	—	—	—	—	—	—	—	—	—	—	—
Throckmorton	—	—	—	—	—	—	—	—	—	—	—	—	—	—	—	—	—	—	—	—
Titus	144	144	—	144	144	144	—	144	144	144	144	—	144	144	144	144	—	—	144	144
Tom Green	19	19	—	19	19	19	—	19	19	19	19	—	19	19	19	19	—	—	19	19
Travis	379	379	—	379	379	379	—	379	379	379	379	—	379	379	379	379	—	—	379	379
Trinity	51	51	—	51	51	51	—	51	51	51	51	—	51	51	51	51	—	—	51	51
Tyler	69	69	—	69	69	69	—	69	69	69	69	—	69	69	69	69	—	—	69	69
Upshur	107	107	—	107	107	107	—	107	107	107	107	—	107	107	107	107	—	—	107	107
Upton	—	—	—	—	—	—	—	—	—	—	—	—	—	—	—	—	—	—	—	—
Uvalde	—	—	—	—	—	—	—	—	—	—	—	—	—	—	—	—	—	—	—	—
Val Verde	—	1	—	—	—	—	—	—	—	—	—	—	—	—	—	—	—	—	—	—
Van Zandt	34	34	—	34	34	34	—	34	34	34	34	—	34	34	34	34	—	—	34	34
Victoria	66	66	—	66	66	66	—	66	66	66	66	—	66	66	66	66	—	—	66	66
Walker	148	148	—	148	148	148	—	148	148	148	148	—	148	148	148	148	—	—	148	148

County																
Waller	224	224	224	224	224	224	224	224	224	224	224	224	224	—	224	224
Ward	—	—	—	—	—	—	—	—	—	—	—	—	—	—	—	—
Washington	471	471	471	471	471	4 71	471	471	471	471	471	471	471	—	471	471
Webb	61	—	—	—	—	—	—	—	—	—	—	—	—	—	—	—
Wharton	124	124	124	124	124	124	124	124	124	124	124	124	124	—	124	124
Wheeler	1	1	1	1	1	1	1	1	1	1	1	1	1	—	1	1
Wichita	—	—	—	—	—	—	—	—	—	—	—	—	—	—	—	—
Wilbarger	1	1	1	1	1	1	1	1	1	1	1	1	1	—	1	1
Willacy	—	—	—	—	—	—	—	—	—	—	—	—	—	—	—	—
Williamson	84	84	84	84	84	84	84	84	84	84	84	84	84	—	84	84
Wilson	6	6	4	4	4	4	4	4	4	4	4	4	4	—	5	5
Winkler	—	—	—	—	—	—	—	—	—	—	—	—	—	—	—	—
Wise	—	—	—	—	—	—	—	—	—	—	—	—	—	—	—	—
Wood	141	141	141	141	141	141	141	141	141	141	141	141	141	—	141	141
Yoakum	—	—	—	—	—	—	—	—	—	—	—	—	—	—	—	—
Young	1	1	1	1	1	1	1	1	1	1	1	1	1	—	1	1
Zapata	—	—	—	—	—	—	—	—	—	—	—	—	—	—	—	—
Zavalla	—	—	—	—	—	—	—	—	—	—	—	—	—	—	—	—
TOTAL	27,201	26,691	26,856	26,879	26,873	26,871	26,871	26,863	26,901	27,247	26,847	26,873	26,909	—	26,858	26,927

233

Table 1   Black Voting in Mississippi, 1867–1966

Year	Negro Voting Age Population	Negro Registration	Percent of Negroes of Voting Age Registered	White Voting Age Population	White Registration	Percent of Whites of Voting Age Registered
1867	98,926	60,167	66.9	84,784	46,636	55.0
1892	150,409	8,615	5.7	120,611	68,127	56.5
1896	198,647	16,234	8.2	150,530	108,998	72.4
1899	198,647	18,170	9.1	150,530	122,724	81.5
1955	495,138	21,502	4.3	710,639	423,456	59.6
1966	422,256	139,099	32.9	748,266	470,920	82.4

SOURCE: Report of the United States Commission on Civil Rights, *Voting in Mississippi* (Washington, D.C.: U.S. Government Printing Office, 1965), p. 8.

Table 2   Mississippi Primary Election, 1962

Positions	Black Candidates	Votes	White Candidates	Votes
Representative 2d Congressional District	Rev. Merrill Lindsey	1,318	Frank Smith Jamie Whitten	21,321 35,381
Representative 3d Congressional District	Rev. Robert L. T. Smith	NA	John Bell Williams	NA

The defeated black candidates were not permitted to participate in the general elections.

NA: Not available.

Table 3   Mississippi Primary Election, 1964

Positions	Black Candidates	Votes	White Candidates	Votes
Representative 2d Congressional District	Mrs. Fannie Lou Hamer	389	Jamie L. Whitten	27,222
Representative 3d Congressional District	James M. Huston	1,190	John Bell Williams	32,151
Representative 4th Congressional District	Mrs. Annie Devine	NA	William A. Winstead	NA
Representative 5th Congressional District	Rev. John E. Cameron	1,071	William Colmer	30,749
Senator	Mrs. Victoria J. Gray*	4,314	John Stennis	151,330

* Candidate of the Congress of Racial Equality.
NA: Not available.

Table 4   MFDP (Mock Freedom Election), 1964

Positions	Black Candidates	Votes	White Candidates	Votes
Representative 2d Congressional District	Mrs. Fannie Lou Hamer	33,009	Jamie L. Whitten	59
Representative 3d Congressional District	James M. Huston	16,003	John Bell Williams	8
Representative 4th Congressional District	Mrs. Annie Devine	6,001	William A. Winstead	4

Table 4   (Cont.)

Positions	Black Candidates	Votes	White Candidates	Votes
Representative 5th Congressional District	Mrs. Victoria J. Gray	10,138	William Colmer	7
Senator	Aaron Henry	61,044	John Stennis	139
	MFDP Election Vote		*Official Election Vote*	
President Vice-President	L. B. Johnson H. H. Humphrey }	63,839	52,618	

Since all the MFDP candidates were defeated in the primary election and could not get on the ballot in the general election, they held their own election and supervised it.

Table 5   Mississippi Democratic Primary Election, 1966

Positions	MFDP Candidates	Votes	White Candidates	Votes
Representative 1st Congressional District	Dock Drummond	NA	Thomas G. Abernathy	NA
Representative 3d Congressional District	Rev. Edwin King	11,000	John Bell Williams	44,000
Representative 4th Congressional District	Rev. Clint Collier	6,000	Prentiss A. Walker	NA
Representative 5th Congressional District	Lawrence Guyot	NA	William Colmer	NA
Senator	Rev. Clifton Whitley	26,000	James O. Eastland	187,000

NA: Not available.

Table 6   Mississippi General Election, 1966

Positions	MFDP Candidates	Votes	White Candidates	Votes
Representative 1st Congressional District	Dock Drummond	5,734	W. B. Alexander Thomas G. Abernathy	10,085 30,441
Representative 3d Congressional District	Mrs. Erma Sanders	7,161	John Bell Williams	30,332
Representative 4th Congressional District	Sterling Davis (Ind.)	1,054	L. L. McAllister C. V. Montgomery	15,252 32,563
Senator	Rev. Clifton Whitley	27,863	Prentiss Walker James Eastland	91,175 223,797

Table 7   Mississippi General Election, 1967

County	Positions	MFDP Candidates	Votes	White Candidates	Votes
Holmes and Yazoo	U.S. Representative	Robert G. Clark	NA	James P. Lowe	NA
Issaquena	Constable	Melvin Smith	156	Susie Edge	150
Issaquena	Justice of the Peace	Matthew Walker	197	Red Spruce	162
Madison	Justice of the Peace	U. S. Rimmer		No opposition	
Bolivar	Supervisor	Kermit Stanton		NA	
Holmes	Constable	Griffin McLaurin, Jr.		NA	

NOTE: One MFDP candidate, Alfred Rhodes, was defeated by a white candidate, Robert Ferguson. All other MFDP candidates won this election.

Table 8 Mississippi Municipal Election, 1968

County	Positions	MFDP Candidates
Holmes	Board of Education	Mrs. Arenia C. Mallory
Holmes	Election Commission	H. T. Bailey
Holmes	Election Commission	Elra Johnson
Holmes	Election Commission	Burrell Tate
Madison	Election Commission	Mrs. Florzie B. Goodloe
Madison	Election Commission	W. E. Garrett

NOTE: All MFDP candidates listed won the election.

Table 9 Mississippi Municipal Election, 1969

County	Position	MFDP Candidates
Bolton	Alderman	Bennie Thompson
Bolton	Alderman	Dudley Davis
Bolton	Alderman	L. C. Leach
Moorhead	Alderman	Sylvester Ingram
Lexington	Alderman	Robert Smith
Holly Springs	Alderman	Eddie Lee Smith
Edwards	Alderman	Judge Price, Sr.
Edwards	Alderman	Thomas Walker

NOTE: All MFDP candidates won the election with the exception of Eddie Lee Smith and Robert Smith, who were to participate in runoff elections.

Table 10   Black Voting in Alabama, 1867–1966

Year	Negro Registration	Percent of Negro Voting Age Population Registered
1867	61,295	
1906	3,654	2.0
1940	2,000	0.5
1947	6,000	1.2
1952	25,224	6.5
1956	53,366	10.3
1962	68,317	13.4
1966	246,396	51.2

SOURCES: Luther P. Jackson, "Race and Suffrage in the South Since 1940," *New South* (June–July, 1948).

Margaret Price, *The Negro and the Ballot in the South* (Atlanta: Southern Regional Council, 1959).

Sheldon Hackney, *Populism to Progressivism in Alabama* (Princeton, N.J.: Princeton University Press, 1969).

NOTE: Neither Mississippi nor Alabama keep voting statistics; consequently, the data had to be collected from numerous sources.

Table 11   Lowndes County General Election, 1966

Positions	LCFO Candidates	Votes	White Candidates	Votes
Sheriff	Sidney Logan	1,532	Frank Ryals	2,344
Coroner	Emory Ross	1,702	Jack Golson	2,301
Tax Assessor	Alice Moore	1,666	Charlie Sullivan	2,116
Tax Collector	Frank Miles	1,556	Iva Sullivan	2,075
Board of Education	Robert Logan	1,700	David Lyons	1,950
Board of Education	John Hinson	1,678	Tommie Coleman	1,951
Board of Education	Willie Strickland	1,600	C. B. Haigler	2,132

Table 12   NDPA Results in the Alabama General Election, 1968

				HOUSE SEATS		
Dis-trict	NDPA Candidates	Votes	Per-cent	White Candidates	Votes	Per-cent
1	Noble Beasley	4,806	4.9	Arnold Debron	36,946	38.0
				Jack Edwards	55,520	57.1
2	Richard Boone	12,029	11.0	Robert F. Whaley	37,506	34.3
				William Dickinson	59,716	54.7
3	Wilbur D. Johnston	6,521	7.6	George W. Andrews	79,559	92.4
4	T. J. Clemons	7,751	8.4	Bill Nichols	74,565	81.0
				Robert Kerr	9,769	10.6
5	Rev. William Branch	20,357	24.4	Walter Flowers	51,538	61.6
				Frank Donaldson	11,701	14.0
6	Thomas Wrenn	11,011	10.9	Quinton R. Bowers	30,331	30.2
				John Buchanan, Jr.	59,254	58.9
7	*James Bains	1,858	2.0	Tom Bevill	71,185	76.0
				Jodie Connell	20,557	22.0
8	*Charlie Burgess	6,855	7.7	Robert E.Jones	81,998	92.3
			U.S. SENATE			
	*Robert P. Schwenn	72,669	22.0	James B. Allen	638,774	70.0
		PRESIDENTIAL ELECTORS				
	NDPA		51,342			
	AIDP		133,837			
	Regular Democrats		438,157			

SOURCE: *Congressional Quarterly Weekly Report* (November 15, 1968), pp. 3162, 3175.

* White candidates on the NDPA ticket.

Table 13   1964 Michigan Election Results Involving Freedom
Now Party Candidates

Position	Candidates	Votes	Percentage of Votes
Governor	George Romney(R)	1,764,335	55.9
	Neil Staebler (D)	1,381,442	43.7
	Frank Lovell (SW)	5,649	0.2
	Albert B. Cleage (FN)	4,767	0.2
	James Horwath (SL)	1,777	0.1
Senator	Elly M. Peterson (R)	1,096,272	35.3
	P. Hart (D)	1,996,912	64.4
	Ernest C. Smith (FN)	4,125	0.1
	E. Sell (SW)	2,754	0.1
	S. Sims (SL)	1,598	0.1
Representative, 1st District	Robert B. Blackwell (R)	25,735	15.5
	John Conyers (D)	138,589	83.6
	Milton R. Henry (FN)	1,504	0.9
Representative, 18th District	William S. Broomfield (R)	109,777	59.5
	Frank L. Sierauski (D)	74,576	40.4
	Richard Kelly (FN)	145	0.1

NOTE: Party designations are as follows: R = Republican, D = Democratic,
FN = Freedom Now, SW = Socialist Workers, SL = Socialist Labor.

SOURCE: "1964 Election Results," *Congressional Quarterly Almanac* (Volume
xx, 1964), pp. 1041–1043.

Table 14 NDPA Candidates—1970 General Election

Position		Candidate	Votes	%
Governor		John Cashin (L)	106,700	15.5
Representative:	1st District	Noble Beasley (L)	5,679	8
Representative:	2nd District	Percy Smith, Jr. (L)	12,094	15
Representative:	3rd District	Detroit Lee (L)	5,991	10
Representative:	5th District	T. Y. Rogers (L)	14,226	21
Representative:	8th District	Thornton Stanley (L)	Other	

L: lost
SOURCE: "State-By-State Senate, Governor, House Returns," *Congressional Quarterly* (November 6, 1970), p. 2771.

Table 15 UCP Candidates—1970 General Election

County	Position	UCP Candidates
	Governor	Thomas D. Broadwater (L)
	Lieutenant-governor	Julius C. McTeer (L)
Charleston	House of Representatives	James Clyburn (L)
Charleston	House of Representatives	Herbert U. Fielding (w)
Richland	House of Representatives	James L. Felder (w)
Richland	House of Representatives	I. S. Levy Johnson (w)
Beaufort	House of Representatives	Hyman L. Davis (L)
Beaufort	County Council	Leory E. Browne (w)
Beaufort	County Council	Booker T. Washington (w)
Dorchester	Superintendent of Education	Mrs. J. W. Robinson (L)
Fairfield	School Board	Sam Smalls (L)
Georgetown	County Board of Education	Huston Parson (w)

w: won   L: lost
SOURCE: Mrs. Frieda Mitchell, United Citizens' Party member.

Table 16 Special Election—1st Congressional District in South Carolina

Counties	Davis	DeLee	Edwards
Allendale	764	334	NA
Beaufort	1,897	1,245	2,062
Berkley	5,024	709	NA
Charleston	19,065	3,647	20,719
Clarendon	1,741	228	NA
Collerton	2,987	273	NA
Dorchester	4,138	774	NA
Hampton	1,584	311	NA
Jasper	621	508	NA
TOTAL VOTES RECEIVED	44,720	8,029	32,227

NA: Not available
SOURCE: South Carolina Election Commission, Telephone Interview, August 27, 1971, Time: 2:30.

Table 17   MFDP Candidates—1971 General Election

County	Position	MFDP Candidate
Bolivar	Supervisor	Kermit Stanton
Bolivar	Constable, District 3	Shelton Woodley
Marshall	Supervisor, Beat 3	Charles Anthony
Marshall	Circuit Clerk	Oscar Lee Fant
Marshall	Tax Collector	Quitell Gibson
Marshall	Justice of Peace	C. K. Brittenum
Marshall	Supt. of Education	Eddie Lee Smith, Jr.
Quitman	Constable, Beat 2	Jimmy Edwards
Quitman	Supervisor, Beat 2	William Franklin
Hinds	Constable, Beat 2	John Jones
Yazoo	Justice of Peace	Arthur Shafer
Yazoo	Constable, Beat 2	Bristol Bunch

Map 1 Mississippi Counties with Black Political Parties and Organizations (1964–1968)

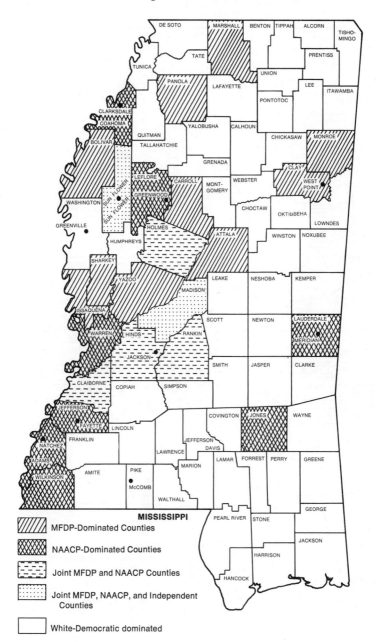

MISSISSIPPI

- ▨ MFDP-Dominated Counties
- ▩ NAACP-Dominated Counties
- ⊡ Joint MFDP and NAACP Counties
- ⊡ Joint MFDP, NAACP, and Independent Counties
- ☐ White-Democratic dominated

Note: Independents are active in almost all the counties.

Map 2 Counties with Black Political Parties and Organizations in Alabama (1965–1968)

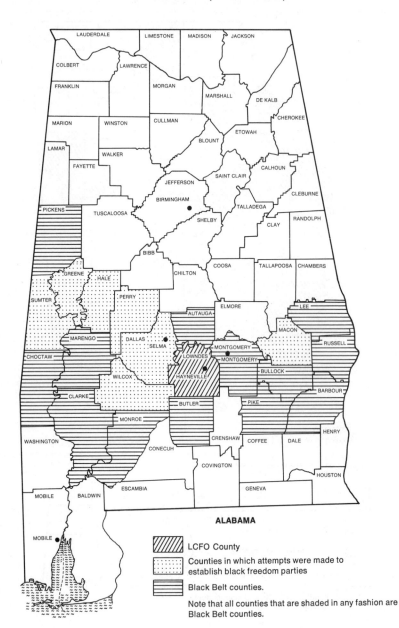

ALABAMA

///// LCFO County

.... Counties in which attempts were made to establish black freedom parties

≡≡≡ Black Belt counties.

Note that all counties that are shaded in any fashion are Black Belt counties.

Map 3 Alabama Counties in Which NDPA Candidates Have Been Elected to Office

ALABAMA

Figure 1 Votes Received by Black State Parties

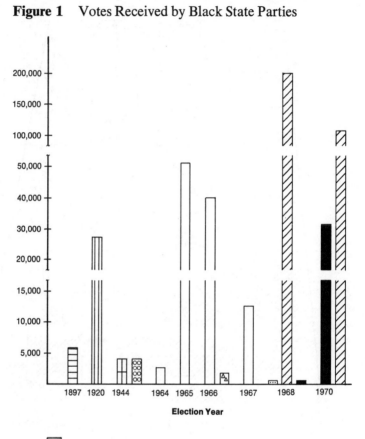

Negro Progressive party

Black and Tan Republican party (Texas)

South Carolina Progressive Democratic party

Black and Tan Republican party (South Carolina)

Mississippi Freedom Democratic party

Lowndes County Freedom Organization

Party of Christian Democracy (No Votes)

National Democratic party of Alabama

United Citizens party

Figure 2   Votes Received by Black National Parties, General Election (1968)

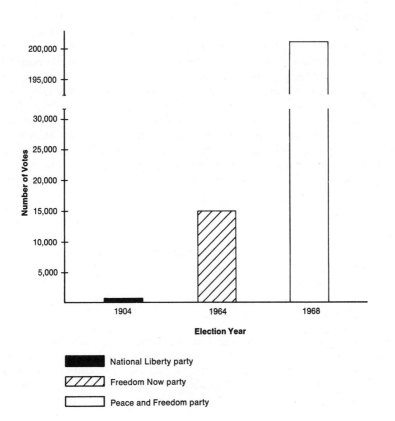

Document 1   The Constitution and By Laws of The National Democratic Party of Alabama

Preamble

As citizens of Alabama who demand the right to support only candidates for local, State and National office in general elections who desire to affiliate, associate, align themselves with and fully support The National Democratic Party and, as citizens who resent the fact that twice in less than a quarter of a century Electors supporting the Nominees of The National Democratic Party for President and Vice President of The United States were excluded from the ballot of our State, notwithstanding the fact that on each occasion the Nominee of The National Democratic Party for President was the then serving President of the United States, we do ordain and establish the following Constitution for The National Democratic Party of Alabama, thereby assuring all the people of this State that never again will Electors supporting the Nominees of The National Democratic Party be excluded from the ballot of Alabama. Based upon this guarantee, and by our actions here, a further resentment we intend to absolve is the attendance of Delegates from Alabama to The Democratic National Convention who fail, refuse or even pledge themselves not to support the Nominees of that Convention. In establishing this Party and adopting this Constitution we shall further guarantee that no person shall serve as a Delegate to The Democratic National Convention from Alabama who does not fully support the Nominees of that Convention at its conclusion, and no Delegate from this State will ever again vacate or be denied his seat at said Convention because of his or her failure to support the Nominees of said Convention in past elections or in future campaigns.

Article I

The name of the party shall be "The National Democratic Party of Alabama."

Article II

The official emblem of The National Democratic Party of Alabama shall be the picture or facsimile of an eagle, his head wings raised, standing inside a circular band with the following wordage inscribed on said band in lettering running counter-clockwise: "The National Democratic Party of Alabama."

Article III

Section I All powers and authority to conduct any and all affairs of the party shall be vested in a Central Executive Committee. Said Committee shall have the power to set its membership, elect its officers and shall be the final authority on any question involving the party, its officers, nominees, and/or district and county committees. The Central Committee, except as otherwise provided by law, shall have sovereign, original, appellate, and supervisory power and jurisdiction of all party matters throughout the state, and each county thereof. It is empowered and authorized to prescribe and enforce rules, regulations and penalties against the violation of party fealty including removing or debarring from the party office or party privilege anyone within its jurisdiction, including a member of this committee, who violates such fealty or its rules or its other lawful mandate.

This committee shall be known as The Executive Committee of the National Democratic Party of Alabama and may be called The Democratic Central Committee.

Section II The Democratic Central Committee shall be composed of not less than thirty-two (32) members, four (4) from each Congressional District, nor more than two hundred (200) members, twenty-five from each Congressional District, chosen by majority vote by the plan in force at the time of election. Each member must be a qualified voter, and shall have and retain his citizenship and the right to vote in the District from which he is chosen, and should he lose his citizenship by permanently removing his vote from said District, then this shall constitute a vacancy in such membership. Vacancy shall be filled by appointment or election of the person who is recommended to the Committee by a majority of the members then remaining in the Congressional District concerned; and further provided, that should there be no one person named or recommended to fill a vacancy by a majority vote of the Congressional District concerned, then in such event the said vacancy or vacancies shall be filled by a majority vote of the entire Committee.

Section III The term of membership begins immediately after all members elected have been certified as provided by law and said term is for four years from the time of certification and until their successors are elected and certified. Within thirty days after all members are certified, a meeting of the Committee shall be held on call of the Chairman of the preceding Committee for the purpose of organization and to consider any business which may properly come before the Committee, to which a notice in writing shall be given to the members at least ten days prior to

Document 1   (Cont.)

such meeting. Such organizational meeting shall continue in session until the elective officers of this Committee are chosen.

Section IV   The Central Committee shall meet at such time and place as the Committee may determine, or a majority thereof, or upon the call of the Chairman.

The Central Committee shall review, on appeal, the decision of the County Committees in all cases concerning the nomination of County officers and all matters relating to rules and policies. The Central Committee has supervisory power over County Committees and is authorized of its own motion to set aside any action of a County Committee when it may deem proper and legal to do so.

Section V   All officers of this Committee shall serve until their successors are elected or appointed and said officers shall be: (a) Chairman, (b) Vice Chairman, (c) Vice Chairman of Women's Division, (d) Secretary, (e) Treasurer; and a Chairman Pro tem may be chosen for a full meeting or any part thereof. A Secretary Pro tem may be appointed by the Chairman as occasion may require. The Treasurer shall be appointed by the Chairman. The offices of Secretary and Treasurer, when deemed advisable, may be filled by the same person, but the Treasurer may be a banking institution. The Secretary and Treasurer shall at all times be under the direction of the Chairman, and shall report and serve as required by him, and all appointees of the Chairman hold at his pleasure. All officers of the Committee, except Vice Chairman of the Women's Division and Treasurer, shall be selected from bonafide members of said Committee.

The Chairman is authorized to appoint a stenographer or reporter to take the minutes of the meetings; also, any other agents or assistants as may be necessary for that purpose. The minutes of each meeting shall be transcribed and printed or otherwise duplicated and a copy thereof furnished each member within sixty days after each meeting. The Chairman of this committee is authorized and empowered to reject declarations of candidacy, with or without a trial before the committee, notwithstanding the affidavit, if he believes the affidavit to be untrue, with a right of appeal on the part of the candidate to the Central Committee for review. Unless otherwise provided for in these rules, the rules as to parliamentary procedure governing the House of Representatives of this State shall be in force and govern all meetings of this Committee or any sub-committee or committees thereof.

The order of business shall be as follows: 1. Assembly and roll-call. 2. Vacancies in membership filled. 3. Minutes, unless dispensed with. 4. New business, in the call or otherwise. 5. Unfinished business, old or new. 6. Adjournment. The order of business may be changed at any time by the Chairman, in the absence of objection.

The State Chairman votes, and if a tie occurs, the proposition is lost. In emergencies the Chairman, at his discretion, may take a vote of membership by mail or referendum on any matter, except as otherwise provided by law or the rules of this Committee, he fixing the time to vote, but a vote so taken shall not be opened or cast at a meeting.

Proxies are never allowed in The Central Committee, nor in a County Committee.

Suspension of rules may be had by two-thirds concurring vote of those voting, provided at least a quorum votes, but shall not be had by mail or referendum.

Order or procedure of motions and the like shall be as follows: 1. Adjourn. 2. Adjourn to fixed time. 3. Referring to Committees. 4. Postpone indefinitely. 5. Previous question. 6. Lay on the table. 7. Postpone to fixed time. 8. Amend.

At all meetings of the Committee a majority vote shall prevail except upon motion to change or suspend the rules established for the government of this Committee. Thirty percent of said membership plus the chairman, or such number of members as may be required by law of the Committee, shall constitute a quorum. The Chairman of this Committee is hereby authorized and empowered to create any special or standing committee, including a finance committee and vest in them any powers he deems necessary to conduct affairs of the Central Committee and all members shall serve at his pleasure.

The term of office of members of the Central Committee shall begin immediately after all members elected have been certified as provided by law and said term shall continue for four years from the time of certification and until their successors are elected and certified. Within thirty days after all members are certified a meeting of the Committee shall be called by the Chairman for the purpose of organization and to consider any business which may properly come before said Committee. The Chairman of the Central Committee shall serve until his successor is elected. All officers of the Central Committee hereafter elected shall be elected from bonafide members of said Committee. The Chairman of the Central Committee must be elected for a four year term. This rule to become effective after January 1968. Funds of the Committee shall be kept on deposit in a bank in the Committee's name, or the name of the sub-committee, as

Document 1   (Cont.)

the case may be. The Central Chairman may place funds to the bank credit of the sub-committee from time to time as convenience may suggest. Funds shall be disbursed by bank draft or check drawn by the Treasurer and counter-signed by the Chairman, or, when more convenient, drawn by the Chairman of a sub-committee against funds to its credit. Assessment payments by candidates shall be required as per statutes, and, if statutes should not expressly permit, then only by way of request.

Assessments are fixed by the Central Committee, or its sub-committee duly authorized, as to all offices filled by the vote of a territory greater than a single county, and by County Executive Committees as to all offices filled by the vote of a single county, except members of the Legislature and Congress, Circuit Judges and Circuit Solicitors from a district or circuit consisting of only one county or less, for which the Central Committee shall fix the assessments.

Obligations of this Committee or its sub-committees may be paid by the State Chairman or sub-chairman as the case may be, out of committee funds, without waiting for a meeting of the Central Committee.

Sub-committees may incur the reasonable and necessary expenses of carrying out their purposes and shall report the receipts, disbursements and expenses. The actual and necessary expense of a member of a sub-committee incurred by him for traveling within the State, or in the necessary discharge of his duty as such committeeman, may be paid out of the Central Committee's general funds, but shall not be taxed as any part of the costs of a contest or appeal on contest.

The Central Chairman's expenses, whether for postage, stationery, long or short distance telephone or telegraph messages, freight, express, parcel post, railroad or other transportation, office help, or other expense incurred in attending meetings of any of the sub-committees of the Central Committee as requisite, or otherwise incurred in the discharge of the duties of his office, shall be paid or reimbursed from the Committee's general fund. Accounts of officers, sub-committees, and agents should be audited from time to time, especially at the end of campaigns, and the Chairman may appoint a committee therefor at any time, of not more than three members, at his discretion.

State office includes any that is state-wide or filled by the vote of the whole State, and any office of which the whole or greater part of the emolument is paid by the State. Central Executive Committeemen and Committeewomen are Central Party officers. A district, circuit or division office is one filled by the vote of a district, circuit or division. A county office includes any other office than the above stated, that may be filled by the vote of a single county or less territory.

Whenever a special election is called to fill a State office, or the office of a representative in Congress, except the offices of State Senator and Representative, the Central Committee may, at its discretion, nominate a candidate of the Party therefor, or provide for a nomination by primary election, or convention, or other method in vogue in the Party at the time. Where there is ample time for using the customary method of primary or convention, etc., then that should be used. But the Committee determines as to the emergency or circumstances.

When the special election is for the office of State Senator in a district embracing more than one county, the State Chairman, in conjunction with the members of the Central Committee residing in the district affected, or a majority of them, present at a meeting called by the State Chairman for that purpose may nominate a candidate of the Party therefor. The Chairman shall vote only in case of a tie, unless he is a member of the delegation from the Congressional District where said vacancy may occur.

When the special election is for any county office, or for representative or state senator in a district of only one county, the county executive committee may act in the same way and with like power and duty, regarding such office, as first above provided for the Central Committee.

Certificates of nomination shall be promptly made by the same presiding officer or other officers as in cases of nominations at primary elections or conventions.

When a nomination has been made and becomes vacant before the election, the vacancy may be filled by use of any of the above stated plans for making nominations for special elections and may be applicable or adaptable to use, in the judgment of the State Chairman who shall advise or direct action as occasion may suggest or require. But a vacant nomination for a circuit judgeship filled by the vote of a single county shall be filled by the Central Committee under provision above. The nomination filled shall be certified as requisite for the original nomination. These rules may be amended, altered or repealed after written notice, showing what change is proposed, is furnished the members of the Committee ten days before any regular or called meeting of the Central Committee. If the change be proposed at a meeting, it shall lie over at least twelve hours.

Such amendment or alteration or repeal shall be adopted or carried by a vote of a majority of the members voting, if a quorum votes, and if taken on referendum or by mail, it shall require a concurring majority of all members of the Central Committee to effect the change or amendment.

Document 1   (Cont.)

The Central Committee may make any rules or regulations for the purpose of enforcing this Constitution which are not inconsistent therewith.

STATE OF ALABAMA
County of Madison

I, _____, Chairman of The National Democratic Party of Alabama, do hereby certify that I am the custodian of the records of the said Central Committee of The National Democratic Party of Alabama, and that the foregoing is a full, true and correct copy of the rules ordained and established by The National Democratic Party of Alabama as shown by the records of my office, with all amendments thereto.

_____

Chairman of The National Democratic
Party of Alabama

Document 2 Objectives and Principles of The National Democratic Party of Alabama

The National Democratic Party of Alabama was founded with the following objectives and principles.

We Resolve:

1. To support the platform and programs of the National Democratic Party of the United States and to provide a vehicle in Alabama for their expression and implementation.

2. That all voters in the State of Alabama have the right to vote for any and all major candidates for the highest offices in our land; and that any breach or abrogation of this right is an INEXCUSABLE VIOLATION OF THE PUBLIC TRUST, regardless of the financial, political or social station of those persons who have allowed such a situation to exist in fact.

3. That the hostile racial atmosphere in our state is an artificial situation which has been deliberately cultivated by our traditional political leaders; they have a vested interest in setting the races against each other, specifically for the exploitation and deprivation of the vast majority of Alabama's people, both black and white. We are determined to put an end to this vicious, unconscionable conspiracy against the people of Alabama.

4. To re-establish meaningful and effective communication and co-operation with the national administration in Washington.

5. To provide an opposition voice to the political Lilliputianism of the conservative right.

6. To facilitate progressive educational and economic programs designed to upgrade the standard of living of ALL Alabama citizens.

7. To establish a vigorous political party that will develop and supervise effective campaigns for national, state and local candidates.

8. To support the delegate for President of the National Democratic Party, to place electors on the ballot in the General election in November 1968 pledged to support that nominee, and to send delegates to the National Convention pledged to support the nominee of that convention.

9. To establish two Commissions, each of which shall report by January 15, 1970. The first a *Commission on Political Structure* to: a. study the political structures of Alabama for the purpose of determining how politics and political power in Alabama actually operate and to mend specific changes needed in Alabama to insure that every person is directly involved in the decisions that directly affect his own life. The second, a *Commission on Economic Justice* to: a. study the Alabama financial situa-

Document 2 (Cont.)

tion to determine the true repositories of wealth, the way in which that wealth is attained and retained, and how that money is used or not used for the influencing of politics and the oppression of others and to b. recommend ways in which the poor and others now without sufficient or significant wealth can attain access to the repository of wealth, and ways to establish in Alabama economic justice and freedom from want for all and ways to free politics from economic influences.

10. To challenge the Garrett Act and all laws that inhibit the freedom of a legal political party to nominate the candidates it wishes for all open offices on state and local levels.

Document 3 Platform of The National Democratic Party of Alabama

The following is a condensation of the NDPA platform which was adopted at the party's first annual convention in Birmingham, Alabama; July 20, 1968.

1. Restructure the state's tax system to remove the heavy tax burden from the shoulders of the workers and the poor and insure that the wealthy pay their share.

2. Abolish the Wallace-Cater act and all other special privileges which the state presently grants to big business.

3. Begin using state money to aid the workers and poor people of Alabama instead of helping the rich grow richer.

4. Establish small industries in rural areas. These must be industries which will serve the needs of the local people and not industries which exploit the workers and natural resources of the area to make profits which the local people have no share in.

5. Establish stricter controls over industry to prevent the pollution of our water and air.

6. Guarantee all citizens equal protection under the law, including equal opportunity for employment, education and housing. An end to all discrimination based on race and economic position.

7. Guarantee every citizen the right to peacefully protest the actions (or inaction) of any person, group or political unit, including the state itself.

8. Demand that the U.S. Government eliminate existing racial discrimination within its own programs in Alabama, paraticularly the department of agriculture and U.S. Employment Service.

9. End the Draft.

10. Abolish capital punishment.

11. Establish programs to provide free legal services for the poor.

12. Revise the present bail bond laws to provide for the release of minor offenders and some felons on their recognizance.

13. Abolish the position of Justice of the Peace and restructure the whole lower court system to insure all defendants a fair trial.

14. Effect a racial balance in all juries reflecting population of the court's Jurisdiction.

15. Reorganize the prison system to provide humane treatment of inmates in order to rehabilitate them to become useful members of society.

16. Guarantee students their full rights as citizens and all members of the academic community the opportunity to participate fully in all levels of social and political life.

17. Guarantee every Alabamian the right to a free education.

18. Provide for the truthful teaching of history in our schools. Spe-

Document 3   (Cont.)

cifically providing for a truthful history of Black People and other minority groups to be taught.

19. Establish co-operatives of small farmers to collectively buy feed, seed, and farm equipment, and to sell their products.

20. Design farm programs to favor the small farmer over the giant landowners.

21. Guarantee rights of collective bargaining for farm workers.

22. Restructure welfare programs to consolidate state, federal and local programs into a single comprehensive program which provides medical care, adult education and job training, food subsidies and decent employment.

23. Remove welfare programs from the control of bureaucrats and put them into the hands of the people they are designed to help.

24. Guarantee rights of collective bargaining to all workers.

25. Enlarge the minimum wage to cover all wage earners and guarantee them a decent standard of living.

26. Demand that the U.S. Government end its attempt to stop history by trying to militarily maintain the status quo throughout the world. The resources of this wealthy nation should be used to end poverty and oppression in this country and around the world, not to prop up dictatorships and protect the profits of big business.

27. Demand an immediate withdrawal of all American troops from Vietnam and a call to begin international conferences to dismantle all weapons of mass destruction.

28. Abolish the State Sovereignty Commission and in its place establish a State Commission on Human Relations.

29. Liquidate the state liquor monopoly and return it to free enterprise.

Selected Bibliography

Books

American Political Science Association, Committee on Political Parties, *Toward a More Responsible Two-Party System* (New York: Holt, Rinehart and Winston, Inc., 1950).

Anderson, Jack, *Washington Exposé* (Washington, D.C.: Public Affairs Press, 1967).

Aptheker, Herbert (ed.), *A Documentary History of the Negro People in the United States* (New York: Citadel Press, Inc., 1951).

———— (ed.), *One Continual Cry* (New York: The Humanities Press, Inc., 1965).

Bailey, Harry A., Jr. (ed.), *Negro Politics in America* (Columbus, Ohio: Charles E. Merrill Books, Inc., 1967).

Bailey, Stephen K., *The Condition of Our National Political Parties* (Santa Barbara, Calif.: Center for the Study of Democratic Institutions, 1959).

Banfield, Edward, *The Moral Basis of a Backward Society* (New York: The Free Press, 1958).

Barbour, Floyd (ed.), *The Black Power Revolt* (Boston: Horizon Books, 1968).

Belfrage, Sally, *Freedom Summer* (New York: Viking Press, 1965).

Bennett, Lerone, Jr., *Black Power* (Chicago: Johnson Publishing Company, 1968).

————, *Confrontation: Black and White* (Chicago: Johnson Publishing Company, 1965).

————, *The Negro Mood* (Chicago: Johnson Publishing Company, 1964).

Bentley, A. E., *The Process of Government,* ed. Peter Odegard (Cambridge, Mass.: Harvard University Press, 1967).

261

Binkley, W. E., *American Political Parties* (New York: Alfred A. Knopf, Inc., 1944).

Carmichael, Stokely, and Charles Hamilton, *Black Power: The Politics of Liberation in America* (New York: Random House, 1967).

Carter, Hodding, *So the Heffners Left McComb* (Garden City, N.Y.: Doubleday & Co., Inc., 1965).

Casodorph, Paul, *The Republican Party in Texas* (Austin: The Pemberton Press, 1965).

Clarke, Jacquelyne Johnson, *These Rights They Seek: A Comparison of the Goals and Techniques of Local Civil Rights Organizations* (Washington, D.C.: Public Affairs Press, 1962.

Cloward, Richard, and Lloyd Ohlin, *Delinquency and Opportunity* (New York: The Free Press, 1960).

Cole, A. C., *The Whig Party in the South* (Gloucester, Mass.: Peter Smith, 1962).

Cunningham, Noble E., Jr., *The Jeffersonian Republicans in Power* (Chapel Hill: University of North Carolina Press, 1960).

DuBois, W. E. B., *Black Reconstruction* (New York: Harcourt Brace Jovanovich, 1935).

Eldersveld, Samuel J., *Political Parties* (Chicago: Rand McNally & Co., Inc., 1965).

Foner, Philip S. (ed.), *The Life and Writings of Frederick Douglass*, 4 vols. (New York: International Publishers, 1950).

Franklin, John Hope, *The Free Negro in North Carolina, 1790–1860* (Chapel Hill: University of North Carolina Press, 1943).

———, *From Slavery to Freedom* (New York: Alfred A. Knopf, Inc., 1967).

Frazier, E. Franklin, *The Black Bourgeoisie* (New York: The Free Press, 1957).

Gosnell, Harold, *Negro Politicians* (Chicago: University of Chicago Press, 1966).

Grant, Joanne (ed.), *Black Protest* (New York: Fawcett Books, 1968).

Gross, Bella, *Clarion Call: The History and Development of the Negro Convention Movement in the United States from 1817 to 1840* (New York: N.P., 1947).

Hackney, Sheldon, *Populism to Progressivism in Alabama* (Princeton, N.J.: Princeton University Press, 1969).

Hare, Nathan, *The Black Anglo-Saxons* (New York: Marzani and Munsell, 1965).

Harper, Ida, *The History of Woman's Suffrage* (New York: National American Woman Suffrage Association, 1922).

Heard, A., *A Two-Party South* (Chapel Hill: University of North Carolina Press, 1952).

Herring, Pendleton, *The Politics of Democracy* (New York: Holt, Rinehart and Winston, Inc., 1940).

Hesseltine, W. B., *The Rise and Fall of Third Parties* (Washington, D.C.: Pu'·lic Affairs Press, 1948).

————, *Third Party Movements in the United States* (Princeton, N.J.: D. Van Nostrand Co., Inc., 1962).

Hoffman, Nicholas von, *Mississippi Notebook* (New York: David White, 1964).

Holt, Len, *The Summer That Didn't End* (New York: William Morrow Co., 1965).

Hughes, Langston, *Fight for Freedom: The Story of the NAACP* (New York: W. W. Norton & Co., Inc., 1962).

Huie, W. B., *Three Lives for Mississippi* (New York: WCC Books, 1965).

Hulett, John, Stokely Carmichael, and J. Benson, *The Black Panther Party* (New York: Merit Publishers, 1966).

Jack, Robert L., *History of the National Association for the Advancement of Colored People* (Boston: Meador Publishing Co., 1943).

Keech, William, *The Impact of Negro Voting: The Role of the Vote in the Quest for Equality* (Chicago: Rand McNally & Co., Inc., 1968).

Kellogg, Charles Flint, *NAACP: A History of the National Association for the Advancement of Colored People* (Baltimore: Johns Hopkins Press, 1967).

Key, V. O., Jr., *Politics, Parties, and Pressure Groups* (New York: Thomas Y. Crowell Company, 1962).

————, *Southern Politics in State and Nation* (New York: Alfred A. Knopf, Inc., 1949).

King, Martin Luther, Jr., *Why We Can't Wait* (New York: Signet Books, 1964).

Knout, James, *The Origins of Prohibition* (New York: Alfred A. Knopf, Inc., 1925).

Ladd, Everett C., Jr., *Negro Political Leadership in the South* (Ithaca, N.Y.: Cornell University Press, 1966).

Lawson, Kay, *Political Parties and Democracy in the United States* (New York: Charles Scribner's Sons, 1968).

Leiserson, Avery (ed.), *The American South in the 1960's* (New York: Frederick Praeger, 1964).

Lipset, Seymour M., *Political Man* (Garden City, N.Y.: Doubleday & Co., Inc., 1960).

Litwack, Leon, *North of Slavery: The Negro in the Free States, 1790–1860* (Chicago: University of Chicago Press, 1961).

Logan, Rayford W., *The Betrayal of the Negro* (New York: Collier Books, 1965).

Lubell, Samuel, *The Future of American Politics* (New York: Anchor Books, 1956).

———, *White and Black: Test of a Nation* (New York: Harper & Row, Publishers, Inc., 1964).

Martin, Rosco C., *The People's Party in Texas: A Study in Third Party Politics* (Austin: The University of Texas Press, 1933).

Matthews, Donald R., and James Prothro, *Negroes and the New Southern Politics* (New York: Harcourt Brace Jovanovich, 1966).

McCord, William, *Mississippi: The Long, Hot Summer* (New York: W. W. Norton & Co., Inc., 1965).

McCormick, Richard P., *The Second American Party System* (Chapel Hill: University of North Carolina Press, 1966).

Merton, Robert K., *Social Theory and Social Structure* (New York: The Free Press, 1957).

Moon, Henry Lee, *Balance of Power: The Negro Vote* (Garden City, N.Y.: Doubleday & Co., Inc., 1948).

Myrdal, Gunnar, *An American Dilemma,* rev. ed. (New York: Harper & Row, Publishers, Inc., 1962).

Nash, Howard P., Jr., *Third Parties in American Politics* (Washington, D.C.: Public Affairs Press, 1959).

Neumann, Sigmund (ed.), *Modern Political Parties* (Chicago: University of Chicago Press, 1956).

Odegard, Peter H., *American Politics* (New York: Harper & Row, Publishers, Inc., 1947).

Owens, James R., and P. J. Staudenraus (eds.), *The American Party System* (New York: The Macmillan Company, 1965).

Price, Margaret, *The Negro and the Ballot in the South* (Atlanta: Southern Regional Council, 1959).

Quarles, Benjamin, and Leslie Fishel, *The Negro American: A Documented History* (Atlanta: Scott, Foresman & Company, 1967).

Rossiter, Clinton, *Parties and Politics in America* (Ithaca, N.Y.: Cornell University Press, 1960).

———, *1787: The Grand Convention* (New York: The Macmillan Company, 1966).

St. James, W. D., *National Association for the Advancement of Colored People: A Case Study in Pressure Groups* (New York: Exposition Press, 1957).

Schattschneider, E. E., *Party Government* (New York: Holt, Rinehart and Winston, Inc., 1942).

Schlesinger, Arthur, Jr., *A Thousand Days* (Boston: Houghton Mifflin Company, 1965).

Smith, Samuel D., *The Negro in Congress* (Chapel Hill: University of North Carolina Press, 1940).

Smith, T. C., *The Liberty and Free Soil Parties in the Northwest* (Cambridge, Mass.: Harvard University Press, 1897).

Sorauf, Frank T., *Party Politics in America* (Boston: Little, Brown & Company, 1968).

Spero, Sterling D., and Abram L. Harris, *The Black Worker* (New York: Columbia University Press, 1931).

Spindler, Allan, *Political Parties in the United States* (New York: St. Martin's Press, Inc., 1966).

Stone, Chuck, *Black Political Power in America* (Indianapolis: Bobbs-Merrill Co., 1968).

Sutherland, Elizabeth (ed.), *Letters from Mississippi* (New York: McGraw-Hill Book Company, 1965).

Theaphane, Sister M., *A History of Third Parties in Pennsylvania* (Washington, D.C.: Catholic University Press, 1938).

Truman, David, *The Governmental Process* (New York: Alfred A. Knopf, Inc., 1951).

U.S. Civil Rights Commission, *Political Participation* (Washington, D.C.: U.S. Government Printing Office, 1968).

————, *Voting in Mississippi* (Washington, D.C.: U.S. Government Printing Office, 1965).

Walton, Hanes, Jr., *The Negro in Third Party Politics* (Philadelphia: Dorrance & Co., Inc., 1969).

Warner, W., and Paul Lund, *The Social Life of a Modern Community* (New Haven: Yale University Press, 1941).

Watters, Pat, and Reese Cleghorn, *Climbing Jacob's Ladder: The Arrival of Negroes in Southern Politics* (New York: Harcourt Brace Jovanovich, 1967).

Wesley, Charles, *Neglected History: Essays in Negro–American History* (Wilberforce, Ohio: Central State College Press, 1965).

Wharton, Vernon L., *The Negro in Mississippi, 1865–1913* (New York: Harper Torchbooks, 1965).

Wilson, James Q., *Negro Politics: The Search for Leadership* (New York: The Free Press, 1965).

Woodson, C. G., *A Century of Negro Migration* (Washington, D.C.: Association Publishers, 1918).

Woodward, C. Vann, *Origins of the New South, 1877–1913* (Baton Rouge: Louisiana State University Press, 1951).
Ziegler, Harmon, *Interest Groups in America* (Englewood Cliffs, N.J.: Prentice-Hall, Inc., 1965).

Journal and Magazine Articles

Abbott, W. C., "The Origin of English Political Parties," *The American Historical Review*, Vol. 24, No. 3 (July 1919), 578–602.
Abramowitz, Jack, "The Negro in the Populist Movement," *Journal of Negro History* (July 1953), 257–289.
"Ala. Demos Fake Reform," *The Eagle Eye* (February 1970), 1.
Ames, William Lloyd, "The Legal Status of Free Negroes and Slaves in Tennessee," *Journal of Negro History* (July 1919), 254–272.
Analavage, R., "A Victory in Defeat in Lowndes," *National Guardian* (November 19, 1966), 1.
Barnes, E., "Independent Politics: The Significance of the Black Panther Party," *Young Socialist* (October–November 1966), 1.
Bell, H., "National Negro Convention of the Middle 1840's: Moral Suasion vs. Political Action," *Journal of Negro History* (October 1957), 247–260.
————, "The Negro Convention Movement, 1830–60: New Perspectives," *Negro History Bulletin* (February 1951), 103–105, 114.
Booker, Simeon, "50,000 March on Montgomery," *Ebony* (May 1965), 53.
Brisbane, R. H., "The Negro Vote as a Balance of Power Factor in the National Elections," *Quarterly Review of Higher Education Among Negroes* (July 1952), 97–100.
Brittain, Joseph M., "Some Reflections on Negro Suffrage and Politics in Alabama—Past and Present," *Journal of Negro History* (April 1962), 127–138.
Brown, Charles, "Reconstruction Legislators in Alabama," *Negro History Bulletin* (March 1963), 198–199.
Carmichael, Stokely, "What We Want," *New York Review of Books* (September 22, 1966), 5–7.
Cashin, John, "Black Judases' Handicraft," *The Eagle Eye* (May 1970), 4.
"Challenge Is Real, The," *The Nation* (June 21, 1965), 659.
"Chicago: NDPA at the Democratic Convention," *The Eagle Eye* (July 1969), 4.

Cleghorn, Reese, "Who Speaks for Mississippi," *The Reporter* (August 13, 1964), 32.

Cook, Samuel Dubois, "Political Movements and Organizations," *Journal of Politics* (February 1964), 130–153.

———, "The Tragic Myth of Black Power," *The New South* (Summer 1966), 61.

Cruse, Harold, "The Fire This Time," *New York Review of Books* (May 8, 1969), 13.

Daniel, Johnnie, "Changes in Negro Political Mobilization and Its Relationship to Community Socioeconomic Structure," *Journal of Social and Behavioral Sciences* (Fall 1968), 41–46.

Eisenberg, Bernard, "Kelly Miller: The Negro Leader as a Marginal Man," *Journal of Negro History* (July 1960), 186–193.

Fleming, Walter, " 'Pap' Singleton, The Moses of the Colored Exodus," *American Journal of Sociology* (July 1937), 61–71.

Foner, Eric, "Politics and Prejudices: The Free Soil Party and the Negro, 1849–1852," *Journal of Negro History* (October 1965), 239–256.

"Forming a New Political Party," *The Herald* (November 1, 1968), 1.

Fox, Dixon Ryan, "The Negro Vote in Old New York," *Political Science Quarterly,* Vol. 32 (June 1917), 252–275.

Garvin, R., "Benjamin or 'Pap' Singleton and His Followers," *Journal of Negro History* (January 1948), 7–23.

Granger, Lester B., "The National Negro Congress: An Interpretation," *Opportunity* (May 1936), 151–153.

———, "The National Negro Congress . . . Its Future," *Opportunity* (June 1940), 164–166.

Gross, Bella, "The First National Negro Convention," *Journal of Negro History* (October 1946), 435–443.

———, *"Freedom's Journal* and the Rights of All," *Journal of Negro History* (July 1932), 241–286.

Guyot, Lawrence, and Mike Thelwell, "The Politics of Necessity and Survival in Mississippi," *Freedomways* (Spring 1966), 120–132.

———, and ———, "Toward Independent Political Power," *Freedomways* (Summer 1966), 246–254.

Hadnott, Sallie M., v. *Mabel S. Amos, The United States Law Week* (March 3, 1969), pp. 4257–4258.

Haugh, Joseph C., "Reapportionment and Present Negro Politicians," *The Christian Century* (February 9, 1964), 30.

Hoffman, E., "The Genesis of the Modern Movement for Equal Rights in South Carolina, 1930–1939," *Journal of Negro History* (October 1959), 363–369.

Jackson, Luther P., "Race and Suffrage in the South Since 1940," *New South* (June–July 1948), 4–5.

Kopkind, Andrew, "Lair of the Black Panther," *The New Republic* (August 13, 1966), 10.

———, "Seat Belts for Mississippi Five," *The New Republic* (July 24, 1965), 16.

Link, A. E., "The Negro as a Factor in the Campaign of 1912," *Journal of Negro History* (January 1947), 81–99.

Mabry, William Alexander, "Disfranchisement of the Negro in Mississippi," *Journal of Southern History,* Vol. 4 (August 1938), 318–333.

Minnis, Jack, "The Mississippi Freedom Democratic Party," *Freedomways* (Spring 1965), 264–278.

"Mississippi and the NAACP," *Crisis* (June–July 1966), 31.

"Mississippi Challengers," *The New Republic* (October 2, 1965), 8.

"Mississippi: What's in a Name?" *Newsweek* (September 21, 1964), 34.

"Mrs. Cashin Calls Party Reform 'Farce,' " *The Eagle Eye* (February 1970), 1.

"Over 50,000 Registered in Mississippi," *Crisis* (January 1966), 39.

Patton, James W., "The Progress of Emancipation in Tennessee," *Journal of Negro History* (January 1932), 71–73.

"Presidential Candidates from 1788 to 1960," *Congressional Quarterly* (special report, 1961), 23–24.

Quarles, Benjamin, "Frederick Douglass and the Woman's Rights Movement," *Journal of Negro History* (January 1940), 35–44.

Robinson, W. P., Sr., "Democratic Frontiers," *Journal of Human Relations,* Vol. 2 (Spring 1954), 63–71.

Rogers, W., "The Negro Alliance in Alabama," *Journal of Negro History* (January 1960), 38–44.

Rose, Harold M., "The All-Negro Town: Its Evaluation and Function," *The Geographical Review* (July 1965), 362–381.

Rovere, Richard, "Letter from Washington," *The New Yorker* (October 16, 1965), 233–246.

Rudwick, Elliot M., "The Niagara Movement," *Journal of Negro History* (July 1957), 177–200.

Scheiner, S. M., "President Theodore Roosevelt and the Negro," *Journal of Negro History* (July 1962), 169–182.

Shuggs, Roger, "Negro Voting in the Ante-Bellum South," *Journal of Negro History* (October 1936), 351–364.

Simmons, Althea, "50,000 New Voters," *Crisis* (October 1965), 498.

Slaff, George, "Five Seats in Congress: The Mississippi Challenge," *The Nation* (May 17, 1965), 527.

Spindler, Allan P., "Protest Against the Political Status of the Negro," *The Annals of the American Academy of Political and Social Science* (January 1965), 49–51.

Taylor, Alrutheus, "Negro Congressmen a Generation After," *Journal of Negro History* (April 1922), 127–171.

Taylor, Joseph H., "Populism and Disfranchisement in Alabama," *Journal of Negro History* (October 1949), 410–427.

Thornbrough, Emma Lou, "The National Afro-American League, 1887–1908," *Journal of Southern History* (November 1961), 494–512.

Vose, Clement E., "Litigation as a Form of Pressure Group Activity," *Annals of the American Academy of Social and Political Science* (September 1958), 20–31.

Walton, Hanes, Jr., "Blacks and the 1968 Third Parties," *Negro Educational Review* (January 1970), 19–23.

————, "The Negro in Early Third Party Movements," *Negro Educational Review* (April–July 1968), 73–82.

————, "The Negro in the Progressive Party Movements," *Quarterly Review of Higher Education Among Negroes* (January 1968), 17–26.

————, and J. Taylor, "Blacks, the Prohibitionists, and Disfranchisement," *Quarterly Review of Higher Education Among Negroes* (April 1969), 66–69.

Ware, Gilbert, "Lobbying as a Means of Protest: The NAACP as an Agent of Equality," *Journal of Negro Education* (Spring 1964), 103–110.

Watters, Pat, "The Negroes Enter Southern Politics," *Dissent* (July–August 1966), 365–367.

Wesley, Charles, "Negro Suffrage in the Period of Constitution Making, 1787–1865," *Journal of Negro History* (April 1947), 153–167.

————, "The Participation of Negroes in Anti-Slavery Political Parties," *Journal of Negro History* (January 1941), 39–41.

Wieck, Paul R., "Southern Democrats: Not What They Used to Be," *The New Republic* (August 3, 1968), 13–15.

Wilson, James Q., "Two Negro Politicians: An Interpretation," *Midwest Journal of Political Science* (November 1960), 346–369.

Work, Monroe, "Some Negro Members of Reconstruction Conventions and Legislatures and Congress," *Journal of Negro History* (January 1920), 63–125.

Unpublished Material

Clepper, Lawrence Dixon, Jr., "A History of the Republican Party in Louisiana 1900–1952" (Baton Rouge: Louisiana State University, M.A. thesis, 1963).

Dumas, Frederick Joseph, "The Black and Tan Faction of the Republican Party in Louisiana 1908–1936" (New Orleans: Xavier University, M.A. thesis, 1943).

Howze, Elizabeth, "Minor Parties as Catalysts of Social Change: Their Influence on the Policies of the Major Parties in the United States" (Atlanta: Atlanta University, M.A. thesis, 1964).

McCain, W. D., "The Populist Party in Mississippi" (University, Miss.: University of Mississippi, Master's thesis, 1931).

McLemore, Leslie Burl, "The Freedom Democratic Party and the Changing Political Status of the Negro in Mississippi" (Atlanta: Atlanta University, M.A. thesis, 1965).

McMillan, Malcolm C., "A History of the Alabama Constitution of 1901" (University, Ala.: University of Alabama, M.A. thesis, 1940).

Unjer, Samuel, "A History of the National Woman's Christian Temperance Union" (Columbus: Ohio State University, Ph.D. thesis, 1933).

Uzee, Phillip D., "Republican Party in Louisiana 1877–1900" (Baton Rouge: Louisiana State University, Ph.D. thesis, 1950).

Walton, Hanes, Jr., *The Politics of the Black and Tan Republicans* [Forthcoming].

Index